Routledge Revivals

The Rhythms of Life

Originally published in 1929, this title is a series of essays on science at the beginning of the twentieth century. Including biology, chemistry, physics and psychology it covers a range of topics, from heating the house to suspended animation. This title can now be read and enjoyed in its historical context.

The Rhythms of Life

and Other Essays in Science

D. F. Fraser-Harris

ROUTLEDGE REVIVALS
Routledge
Taylor & Francis Group

First published in 1929
by George Routledge & Sons Ltd.

This edition first published in 2021 by Routledge
2 Park Square, Milton Park, Abingdon, Oxon OX14 4RN

and by Routledge
605 Third Avenue, New York, NY 10017

Routledge is an imprint of the Taylor & Francis Group, an informa business

Publisher's Note
The publisher has gone to great lengths to ensure the quality of this reprint but points out that some imperfections in the original copies may be apparent.

Disclaimer
The publisher has made every effort to trace copyright holders and welcomes correspondence from those they have been unable to contact.

ISBN: 978-1-032-01179-0 (hbk)
ISBN: 978-1-003-17763-0 (ebk)
ISBN: 978-1-032-01191-2 (pbk)

THE RHYTHMS OF LIFE

AND OTHER ESSAYS IN SCIENCE

By
D. F. FRASER-HARRIS
M.D., D.Sc., F.R.S.E.

LONDON
GEORGE ROUTLEDGE & SONS LTD.
BROADWAY HOUSE: 68-74 CARTER LANE, E.C.
1929

PRINTED IN GREAT BRITAIN BY
M. F. ROBINSON & CO. LTD., AT THE LIBRARY PRESS, LOWESTOFT

PREFACE

Some of the essays included in this volume have already appeared either on this or the other side of the Atlantic.

It is a pleasure to thank the Editor of *The Cornhill Magazine* for permission to republish the article dealing with Plague and the Litany; and the Editor of *Chambers' Journal* for his kindness in allowing me to print again the articles on "Suspended Animation" and on "Blaming the Air". I have also to express my indebtedness to the Editor of *Nature* for granting me permission to use the article on "Physiology and Vital Force" which was published in that journal in April, 1925; and to the Editor of *Discovery* for allowing me to reprint the articles on "Animal Electricity" and "Animal Heat" which appeared in *Discovery*.

Through the kindness of the Editor of *The Birmingham Mail*, I am enabled to reprint the article on " What the microscope has achieved for mankind ", which was originally published in the *Mail* in November, 1927. The essay on " Lost Arts " first appeared in 1925 in the July number of the *Dalhousie Review*, and I have to thank my former colleague, Professor H. L. Stewart, the Editor, for his courtesy in enabling it to reappear as a chapter of this book.

D. F. F.-H.

CHISWICK.
January, 1929.

CONTENTS

THE RHYTHMS OF LIFE

CHAPTER I

A PHENOMENON is called rhythmic when it recurs at equal intervals of time, or, at any rate, not at cognisably unequal ones. The dripping of water from a leaky tap is rhythmic, but the noise of a tray falling downstairs is not. The universe is full of rhythms. The succession of the seasons, the alternation of day and night, the phases of the moon, the ebb and flow of the tide, the recurrence of spring and neap tides, the November flight of meteors, the yearly rise of the Nile, and so forth are all examples of cosmic rhythms. The precise magnitude of the time-interval is of no consequence, for in the case of waves of light the interval may be only some millionths of a second, whereas the return of a comet, such as Halley's, to our solar system, may be a matter of seventy years or so. The vibrations of the ether and the behaviour of the comet are both rhythmical or periodic.

Music is essentially rhythmic; in fact, it is the periodic character of the vibrations of the air that constitutes music as distinguished from noise. The vibrations of the air objectively constituting noise are highly irregular or arhythmic.

A clap of thunder is not rhythmical. In a rhythm something occurs at equal intervals of time; if this something recurs at unequal intervals, the rhythm sometimes is spoken of as "irregular." The ordinary usage is to make the word "rhythm" synonymous with "regular rhythm", the only sense in which the term will be employed in what follows. It is owing to the regularity of recurrence of eclipses, the equinox, meteors, comets, etc., that these phenomena can be predicted with an accuracy that makes astronomy as an exact science so justly admired. The periodicities of rhythms in the non-living world may be matters of years, months, weeks, days, hours, minutes, seconds or fractions of a second.

Coming now to the realm of life, we find rhythms pervading everything. The plants, with striking regularity, have their own times each year for putting forth the buds, unfolding the leaves, bursting into flower, and finally, allowing all the perfumed beauty of the corollas to fade in order that the fruit shall be formed as a life in death. Thus the poetess sang—

> " Leaves have their times to fall,
> And flowers to wither at the north wind's breath ;
> Thou hast all seasons for thine own, O Death."

In plain prose, there is no rhythm about death.

" Chestnut Sunday " is approximately the same Sunday, and " Apple Blossom " week is as near as may be the same week, each year.

If one lives in the country one is able to watch the unerring precision with which each kind of tree puts forth its blossom. The wild plum or sloe is one of the earliest, then comes the pear, then the cherry, then the apple, and so on. Each has its own week for the annual exhibition of virginal loveliness.

The opening and closing of flowers is rhythmic, the rhythm depending on the waxing and waning of the intensity of daylight.

Doubtless the most familiar rhythms are met with in the world of animal life. Here we have the striking rhythmic actions of animals as in flocks and herds, of animals as individuals, and of the organs, tissues and cells of the animal body. The migration of birds is annual in rhythm. It is only part of the truth to say that the waning light and diminished heat and food are what constrain the birds to leave us; they *know* when to leave us. Migratory birds which have spent all their lives well-fed in the captivity of Regent's Park, nevertheless become restless at the approach of autumn. Again, those animals which hibernate during the winter know when to betake themselves to their hiding places, whence they come not forth until the spring. The cuckoo returns almost on the same day every year.

The rhythm of the sexual activities of birds is one of the most characteristic things about their behaviour. It is only in the spring that the "livelier iris changes on the burnish'd dove", but it is *every* spring. Even a decerebrated male pigeon will "coo" energetically at the breeding season, although if the hen bird be placed near him he will take no notice of her. The sexual rhythm is inherent in the nervous system, but in the absence of the brain it is a meaningless and mechanical rhythm.

Only those who have lived much in the country have any adequate notion of the reality of these biological rhythms.

Practically all the activities of one's daily life are rhythmic; the most obvious perhaps being the regular alternation of waking and sleeping. There is a well-marked rhythm in our digestive organs, in the organs of excretion, and most pronouncedly in the beating heart.

Rhythm pervades the world of animal life; just watch that transparent jelly-fish in the limpid summer sea, and you will notice how the edges of the umbrella contract or pulsate with that slow and regular rhythm of about thirty in the minute. Equally obvious rhythms are those of the wings of birds and other flying things, of fins in swimming, of the legs in walking and dancing. Large birds fly with slow, leisurely rhythm, small birds with a fast one; just as tall men have a slow stride, short men have a more rapid step. Regular rhythms are everywhere; if Nature abhors a vacuum, she also abhors "fits and starts"; living Nature does everything "decently and in order".

The periodicity of the heart's action is an

excellent example of a rhythm of animal origin. Seventy-two times in the minute this wonderful hollow muscle contracts in systole on the contained blood forcing it out into all the arteries of the body; and seventy-two times in the minute does it dilate in diastole and suck blood in from the veins leading to it. The duration of its cycle is therefore eight-tenths of a second ($\frac{60}{72}$); and in health during the many years of a long life it practically does not vary from this value. If for more than a few minutes the heart's rhythm remains distinctly irregular, then we conclude that something is amiss with this wonderful organ within the breast.

Sometimes we come across a heart with a congenitally fast rhythm, a condition called tachycardia; and sometimes one with an abnormally slow rhythm, a condition called bradycardia. Whereas the rhythm of the heart-beat is for each individual one of a certain average rate, it varies in different individuals according to height and age. Thus, tall persons have slower hearts than short people; and infants have a heart-rate about twice as fast as adults. The whale and the elephant have very much slower heart-beats than the mouse or the sparrow. The heart-beat in these small animals is so fast that the pulse cannot be counted in the usual way. Until recently we had no reliable information about it, but by an electrical method it has been ascertained with great accuracy. For instance, the rabbit's heart beats at four a second.

The pulse-rate, which in health is the same thing as the heart-rate, is very much slower in the cold-blooded than in the warm-blooded animals. Thus, in a fish or frog the heart contracts only about forty times in the minute, or about half the human rate. This relatively slow rate can be quickened by making the heart beat in warm salt water. A study of the warm-blooded heart proves to be full of interest. The heart can be accelerated by warmth and slowed by cold, but it is its affectability by nerve impulses that is so remarkable. It is a matter of common knowledge that the heart can be made to beat much faster at one time and slower at another through nerve impulses alone. Everybody knows that emotions can influence the heart very markedly. Thus, of course, it has come about that "the heart" and certain emotions are taken as synonymous. Certain emotions disturb it in that they cause it to beat more rapidly, while others slow it and enfeeble it.

Now physiologists have discovered two distinct sets of nerves which influence the heart-rate; the one set on being stimulated makes the heart faster and stronger (accelerator and augmentor nerves), the other set on being stimulated makes the heart beat more slowly and may stop it altogether (inhibitory nerves). Evidently the former set arouses the heart to greater activity, the latter induces in it less activity, than the normal.

The rhythmicality of the heart is not conferred on it by the action of nerves, by the presence of blood, by the temperature of the blood, or by any other "external" condition; its rhythmicality is inherent, it is spontaneous or autogenic. The rhythm of the heart is of the essence of its life; the microscopic cells of the embryo heart beat with a definite rhythm as soon as they are perceptible at all, and before nerves have reached them or the blood has been formed.

The heart is not the only rhythmic portion of the circulatory system. In all animals, portions of the large veins have the power of rhythmic contraction: in the bat they contract sixteen times per minute. In some animals (frogs, for instance) there are pulsatile sacs or lymph-hearts, dilatations of the lymphatic vessels, beating visibly under the skin of the back.

Many other organs exhibit rhythms. The activity of the stomach is rhythmic, and that of the intestines over which waves of contraction pass at short intervals; the activities also of the gall-bladder, the urinary bladder and the uterus are all rhythmic.

An interesting thing about rhythmic organs is their inability to have the rate of their rhythm forced beyond a certain limit. No amount of stimulation of the accelerator nerves can increase the rate of the heart-beat beyond a certain limit. Similarly, heating the heart will raise the rate of the rhythm, but only up to a particular figure which cannot be exceeded. Working with the pigeon, the author found that the greatest number of beats per minute which the heart (auricle) could give was 300, or five a second, and beyond that it was not possible to force it. Not only, then, is rhythmicality inherent in the living substance of the heart, but also a power of resisting all influences to accelerate it beyond a certain limit, an expression of what has been called " functional " or " physiological inertia ".

Let us take another example of rhythmic activity as seen in the cilium. A cilium is a minute, whip-like outgrowth of living protoplasm projecting from the surface of a cell. There are millions of these cilia covering the mucous membranes of the nose, throat and bronchial tubes, which lash mucus, dust and germs towards the nostrils and mouth. Now, these cilia lash backwards and forwards at a characteristic rate of ten to twelve in the second. Just as the heart makes seventy-two systoles and seventy-two diastoles in a minute, so the cilium bends forwards ten times and backwards ten times in a second, or 600 times a minute, about eight times as fast as the heart. Otherwise put, the period of ciliary oscillation is one-tenth of a second instead of eight-tenths.

But the rhythmicality of the cilium is as inherent as that of the heart. The cilia receive no nerves ; therefore, not being innervated, they cannot possess any rhythm conferred on them from outside by nerves, the neurogenic rhythm. The cilia are, however, easily influenced in their rate of vibration by changes of temperature and by drugs and poisons. By warming the cilia they lash faster and faster until they attain a speed of about twenty a second, beyond which they cannot go, one more example of a limit set. Conversely, cold and narcotics like chloroform slow and finally stop their action just as they do that of the heart.

Let us take the case of breathing. Normally, an adult breathes about sixteen to eighteen times a minute, that is to say, in a wholly unconscious fashion his diaphragm—the great, curved muscle between the chest and the abdomen—descends eighteen times and rises eighteen times in the minute. There is, therefore, a respiratory rhythm just as there is a cardiac and a ciliary. Now the diaphragm would not make any descents were it not that it was receiving nerve-impulses through its nerves (phrenics). After these nerves have been cut, the diaphragm is absolutely still. Clearly, then, the rhythm of the activity of the diaphragm is not inherent, but, on the contrary, is conferred by nerves or is neurogenic. The rhythm of eighteen to twenty a second must be the rhythm of discharge of nerve impulses from the nerve cells or " centres " from which the phrenic nerves come. It is the nerve cells that have this rhythm, not the nerves as conductors and not the diaphragm as a muscle.

The actual cells from which the phrenic nerves proceed are, however, not the breathing centre, which, situated higher up in the central nervous system, constrains the phrenic centres to issue their periodic discharges of nerve-impulses. The chief respiratory centre possesses the real respiratory rhythm, which, like the heart's, varies with age and other circumstances. We know very well that the rate of breathing can be profoundly altered by emotional states : some conditions —for instance, states of excitement—greatly increase the rate ; others slow it or stop it for a time, as in the phrase, " it fairly took my breath away ".

Experiments have shown that heated blood accelerates the breathing and that cold slows it, and there are drugs which have analogous actions. Further, the will can for a time abolish the rhythm altogether. Divers are able intentionally to " hold their breath " : on the other hand, the will, if we so wish it, can hurry up the rhythm beyond the rate of the normal. This property of having a rhythm which can be altered by the will is quite a rare one amongst the centres of the nervous system.

The normal respiratory rhythm is, then, an additional example of a rhythm inherent in something—in this case in the cells of a nerve centre—but capable of responding to outside influences. And again, there are limits set, for neither by the will, nor by emotion, nor by heated blood, nor by drugs, can the rate of the breathing centre be forced beyond a certain maximum value.

Breathing is to all intents and purposes an involuntary, unconscious activity; the diaphragm rises and falls throughout life, whether we wake or whether we sleep, with a regularity that is as constant and with efforts that are as untiring as those of the heart itself. In a word, the rhythm of breathing is not voluntary, although we can interfere with it voluntarily.

But, of course, the nervous system can give us many examples of rhythms of voluntary origin. Take the very simple case of tapping one's finger on the table or on an electric key. I can tap my forefinger once a second, twice a second, three times a second, and so on, until I am tapping it so fast I can barely count it. When this rate is reached, an instrument of simple construction can prove that the finger is being flexed and extended at from ten to twelve times a second. We may note in passing that this is exactly the same as the ciliary rate. Now the instrument will show that beyond ten to twelve a second the ordinary person cannot go, although it is possible to train musical technicians to "trill" at a considerably greater rate than that of ordinary people. Still, even for experts a limit is soon reached. The rhythm of the cells of the centres giving rise to the nerves to the fingers is evidently of such a kind, that, whereas the cells can be made by the will to assume any slow rhythm from one to twelve a second, they cannot ordinarily be forced beyond their limit.

What, then, is the rate of inherent rhythm of these centres? Probably ten to twelve a second. It is reasonable to suppose that these cells have a normal, natural, inherent rate of discharge which may be the same as their maximal rate. Neither by the will nor by artificial stimulation can this maximum be exceeded, not even when the rhythm of the artificial stimulation is much higher than twelve a second. The nerve cells have physiological inertia towards rates of stimulation greater than that of their own maximal rhythm. The respiratory centre, on the contrary, we saw, had a normal rate which was *not* also its maximal.

Rhythm or intermittency pervades the nervous system. It has been ascertained that we cannot utter syllables (articulate) at a greater rate than ten to twelve a second. What we may call the articulation centre has its upper limit set at this figure which we have so frequently encountered already. The numerical identity of the rhythms of cilium, musculo-motor nerve centre and articulation centre is probably not accidental.

The frequencies of insects' muscles are of the following orders: The wings of the dragon-fly vibrate at twenty-eight a second, those of the wasp at 110, of the bee at 190, and of the house-fly at 330 per second. The late Professor Mosso asserted that the pitch of the note of a bee setting out on its day's rounds was perceptibly higher than that of the note heard at the close of the day.

Finally, it is probable that the receiving or sensory portions of the brain are constructed in such a manner that they, too, have limits in dealing with rhythmic or intermittent presentations.

The spokes of a slowly rotating bicycle wheel can be perceived as separate bright lines, but when the wheel is revolving rapidly the individual spokes fuse into one bright metallic surface, just as the separate slats of a paling viewed from an express train fuse into one continuous surface. The grooves of the milling on the edge of a metal disc spun rapidly under the finger are perceived as constituting a rough but continuous surface. The fusion of the members of a series of instantaneous photographs of moving objects presented in very rapid succession to the eye, as in the kinematograph, is due to this incapacity of the brain to resolve as distinct in consciousness the separate components of the physical series.

If the interval between the successive impressions is longer than about one-fortieth to one-fiftieth of a second we do not get fusion, but the well-known and disagreeable state of "flicker". This was common in the early moving-picture houses, called incorrectly "cinemas". These and many other cases prove that there are strict limits to the perception of rhythms by our brains.

The causes of vital rhythms and periodicities are virtually unknown. Physiologists can describe vital rhythmic actions in their own precise language, but that is all. To say that the cardiac cycle is constituted by the two alternating and opposite phases of katabolic systole and anabolic diastole does not bring us much nearer an understanding of the cardiac rhythm. Protoplasm, in general, tends to act intermittently. Just as a single tap given to a jelly or to a spring will make these oscillate or vibrate for some considerable time thereafter, so a single or continued stimulus given to living matter will cause it to discharge energy in a vibratory or intermittent manner.

Nor do we comprehend any better the significance of the particular time-duration of the interval between the recurring events which are being studied. Why, for instance, should the human heart beat seventy-two times a minute and not seven or 700? Why should we breathe eighteen times and not eight or eighty times a minute? Why should the cilium bend ten times a second as its normal rate and just twice as fast, but no more than that, when urged to do its utmost? These things are mysteries. The rhythms of functional activity in the female reproductive organs are familiar facts of physiology, but what induces the rhythm and why the periodicity should be as it is are problems at present entirely unsolved.

Probably the necessity of rest to prevent fatigue or exhaustion is one of the purposes of vital rhythms. The heart, for instance, can continue to beat so indefatigably just because the duration of its time of rest (diastole) in the cycle is longer than that of its activity (systole). We sleep by night in order to be active by day. All work and no rest is a physiological outrage; rhythm is an expression of that physiological normality in which work alternating with rest is most economically performed.

Spontaneous rhythmicality is the great mystery of life, the central puzzle in biology; if we knew what rhythm really was, understood it "all in all", we should perhaps "know what God and man is".

CHAPTER II

ANIMAL ELECTRICITY

MANIFESTATIONS of electricity seem to be associated with almost every kind of activity in the universe. In the non-living world, such things as friction, the evaporation of water, the transference of heat, the passage of liquids through membranes, chemical activity and magnetism are all accompanied by the production of electricity. It would be difficult to name any physical process in which electricity does not participate directly or indirectly.

The living body and its tissues are no exception to this universal happening.

Let us first consider a muscle in the living body as regards its relations to energy. Since muscles are warm, they must be continually producing heat.

In fact, by far the greatest amount of heat set free in the body has had its origin in the muscles. Even when the muscles are what we call "at rest" they are still producing heat, though, of course, far less of it than when they are in action.

When muscles go into activity they evolve in addition to heat a certain amount of electric current. As may be imagined, it is much more difficult to prove that muscles produce electricity than to show that they give rise to heat, for to demonstrate their electric currents we have to use a very delicate instrument, far more complicated than the thermometer, called the galvanometer.

Tested by the galvanometer it is found that muscles give rise to no electric disturbance so long as they are at rest, but the moment they go into activity or contract they are responsible for a current which at once makes itself evident in the galvanometer. These currents are of very low voltage, but they continue to run as long as the muscle is in activity.

Now the heart is a muscle—a hollow, complicated muscle—and each time it beats or contracts it gives rise to a feeble electric current which is well demonstrated by means of a mirror galvanometer in a dark room. The mirror galvanometer was invented by Lord Kelvin to indicate the presence of electric currents in submarine cables, but it has been found well adapted to display currents of animal electricity. In this instrument a spot of light reflected from the mirror moves to the right hand or to the left on a white wall every time a current passes round the galvanometer.

Now since the heart is an automatically beating organ, and can continue to beat for many hours after it has been removed from a cold-blooded animal, the electric currents to which it gives rise will continue to swing the mirror so long as the heart itself survives. Indeed, the mirror continues to swing for some hours after all visible signs of life have left the heart. It is an impressive sight: in the stillness of the dark room the spot of light maintains its silent oscillations at the exact rhythm of the beating of the tiny living heart of the long-dead frog.

The beating heart of the embryo chick in the egg, when only just formed, can actually produce sufficient electric disturbance to influence the galvanometer.

If we bring the heart to a standstill, without killing it, by the application of some appropriate drug, then no electricity is manifested until the beating is resumed.

The latest development in the study of animal electricity is to photograph the currents of the beating human heart. This is done to-day by means of a very delicate and costly apparatus called the "string" galvanometer, because in it a fine filament oscillates.

In the original method the oscillations of mercury in the capillary electrometer were photographed. The record is called an electrocardiogram.

Clinical medicine has thus been provided with a new method of diagnosis in heart disease, for the form of the record becomes noticeably altered in abnormal conditions of that organ.

One of the most interesting demonstrations of electricity of animal origin can be made with the retina of the living eye. Having killed a frog, we remove an eye and place it in connexion with the galvanometer in the dark room. The excised eye will live quite long enough to show a current when a lighted taper is held for an instant opposite the pupil. The retina in the depths of the eye responds to the stimulus of light by producing an electric current, and curiously enough yields an increase of current when the light is withdrawn.

All living tissues respond to stimulation by evolving electricity. For instance, when a nerve conducts its impulses, the only easily observable phenomenon is a series of electric currents in it. When a gland secretes, when a muscle twitches, when the heart beats, when the eye sees, electricity is always produced. As might be supposed, the absolute intensity of these currents is very small, of the order only of 0.01 volt. The late Dr Waller showed that so relatively inactive a tissue as the crystalline lens of the eye could nevertheless produce an electric current if the stimulus (an electric one) was sufficiently energetic.

There *is*, then, such a thing as animal electricity; but this electricity of animal origin is a physiological fact that has been overlaid by more nonsense than almost any other. The fantastic absurdity called "electro biology" was much heard of sixty or seventy years ago.

Animal tissues produce no "magnetism", as the physicists understand that term. The supposed power of magnets to induce the hypnotic state was long ago shown to be possessed by all sorts of agents that have nothing whatever magnetic about them.

All living things, vegetable as well as animal, can produce electricity; leaves, flowers, fruits if stimulated, can give rise to a current. It has actually been proved that a young unripe apple gives a better response than an old ripe one.

The man who discovered animal electricity was an Italian, Luigi Galvani, Professor of Anatomy in the University of Bologna. He discovered it accidentally. Galvani noticed that when the living hind legs of a dead frog, which were hanging over a copper hook laid on an iron railing, came in contact with the iron, the leg-muscles twitched. Galvani at once concluded that these convulsions of the legs were somehow an expression of animal electricity, but Alessandro Volta, his brother Professor in the University of Pavia, proved that, in the experiment just quoted, there is indeed electricity developed—not, however, by the living tissues, but at the contact of the two dissimilar metals, the copper hook and the iron railing. When the toes, blown against one of the uprights of the railing, completed the circuit through the legs, their muscles twitched.

Galvani nevertheless persevered in his efforts to demonstrate the reality of electricity of animal origin, and succeeded in devising a number of convincing experiments known as "contractions without metals". Quite the most striking of these is to allow the nerve supplying a muscle to lie over the isolated beating heart. At each beat of the heart, the current produced by the heart stimulates the nerve which in its turn causes the muscle to twitch: it is a very curious sight to see the living leg of a dead frog jerking at the exact rhythm of the frog's excised heart.

Curiously enough, it is in the group of the fishes that we find the most spectacular production of electricity. One of these, an eel-like creature, a native of certain warm South American rivers, can give a shock whose intensity is at least 400 volts. A specimen of one of these fishes was placed in the new aquarium at the Zoological Gardens, London. These electric eels are a family (Torpedo) which has developed this curious power as a means of protection from their enemies, or for the purpose of killing their prey.

The microscope makes it quite clear that in the electric fishes certain muscles have been profoundly altered so that, instead of producing movement and heat as ordinary muscles do, they manufacture electricity but at an intensity vastly greater than does any other living tissue.

Now just as ordinary muscle depends for its activity on impulses reaching it by means of motor nerves from nerve-centres, so too the electric organ is under the command of the cells of a nerve-centre. In fact, the nerve-cell in the spinal cord which " fires off " the electric battery of one side is by far the largest nerve-cell known. Each of these cells has one huge outgrowth of fibre which, proceeding down towards the battery, breaks up into a large number of small fibres for the various plates or discs of the electric organ.

The fish can discharge its salvos very much after the manner of a battleship discharging hers. It always discharges the shocks when it is handled or frightened, but it can also produce them by voluntary effort. The discharge is not of the nature of a constant current, it is rather that of a series of recurring impulses. They are quite powerful enough to give a man a most disagreeable shock. By means of suitable apparatus the currents can be made to ring a bell or cause a lamp to glow.

We are forced to admire the fertility of

Nature, how in one instance she can derive a maximum of heat and a minimum of electricity from a muscle, and in another, having meanwhile altered that muscle, can now obtain a minimum of heat and a maximum of electricity. Truly her ways are worth finding out !

CHAPTER III

ANIMAL HEAT

ONE of the most noticeable features of an animal is that it can produce heat. Biologists long ago came to the conclusion that it was by the oxidation, chiefly of the carbon and hydrogen in or by the living substance, that animal heat was generated. By " long ago " we mean the time of the great chemist Lavoisier (1780), who, though he made some mistakes in animal chemistry, certainly understood that animal heat and the heat of combustion were alike in this, that they were both due to oxidations. Before the discovery of oxygen by Priestley and Lavoisier, (1774), this position could not have been attained, although both Lower and Mayow of Oxford by 1669 had arrived at the conclusion that there was something in the atmosphere (Mayow called it " nitro-aerial particles ") which was essential for the maintenance of animal life, and for all sorts of combustions. This was the dawn ; Priestley and Lavoisier were morning stars ; we live to-day in the high noon of the understanding of animal heat.

The chemical view of the origin of animal heat was, however, lost sight of by two such eminent thinkers of the eighteenth century as Boerhaave and Hales, who held that the heat of the body was due to the friction between the blood-corpuscles and the blood, and between them and the walls of the vessels. This is known as the iatro-physical theory of animal heat. One can do no more than mention the famous view of Stahl (1687), that the principle of fire was " phlogiston ", a Teutonic will-o'-the-wisp that retarded the advance of thermo- and bio-chemistry for quite a hundred years.

But if by " long ago " we mean the centuries before the Christian era, we shall find that Aristotle, for instance, taught that animal heat was something absolutely unique. Aristotle believed that animal heat was something *sui generis*, something of an essentially different order from heat of non-vital origin—the heat of a fire for instance, or of a gas compressed, or of friction. He thought that the ultimate source of bodily heat was an eternal essence, the source of being of heaven and the stars, which latter were imagined as intelligent existences. This was, of course, the foundation of astrology, the notion that these celestial intelligences could interfere in human affairs, and were capable, through the harmony of their movements, of creating music, the " music of the spheres ".

The idea that prevailed for a very long time was that the blood, recuperated by the food in the intestines, was kept fluid in the heart by the heat there, but that the heart, becoming too hot, had to have cold air sucked in by the lungs to cool it. This teaching actually lingered until the time of Harvey, the discoverer of the circulation of the blood, who died in 1657.

Animal heat, as distinguished from every other kind, was thought to have quite special curative powers. Thus we are told in the Book of Kings that when King David " was old and stricken in years . . . they covered him with clothes but he gat no heat ". His servants recommended that a young girl should be brought to impart heat to him; " let her lie in thy bosom that my Lord the King may get heat ".

Our present view is that one of the abilities of living matter is to oxidize carbon and hydrogen to form carbon dioxide and water, which process cannot be effected without the evolution of a certain amount of heat. One of Lavoisier's ideas was that all the animal heat was produced in the blood of the lungs, that the lungs were the furnace of the body, and that the heat was carried thence by the circulating blood. We now know that the blood itself is responsible for the production of very little heat, and are quite certain that it is in the muscles that by far the greatest amount of bodily heat is manufactured. That a bloodless muscle can produce heat even after it is cut out of the body was proved by Helmholtz for the first time in 1848.

Everyone is familiar with the distinction between cold-blooded and warm-blooded animals; but this classification has lost its meaning. We now speak of animals which are able to maintain a constant temperature, and of those which are unable to do so, and these correspond to the old warm- and cold-blooded animals respectively. Those animals whose body temperature rises and falls as the temperature of their environment rises and falls are now known as poikilothermic, and those which are able to maintain a constant temperature, however much (within limits) the temperature of the environment rises or falls, are known as homoiothermic animals.

This classification has been found necessary because of facts such as the following: the temperature inside a hive of bees, insects classed as "cold-blooded", may even in winter rise to 21° C. above that of the outer air; a mammal, a "warm-blooded" animal, when hibernating, has a temperature almost the same as that of its cold environment; the temperature of a newly born mouse goes up and down with that of its surroundings; a frog or fish placed in warm water becomes as warm as the water. In other words a cold-blooded animal can, in certain circumstances, become warm-blooded, and a warm-blooded animal can become cold-blooded; so that all seems confusion.

The important point, of course, is not whether the animal's body feels hot or cold to human touch at any given moment of observation, but whether the animal can or cannot maintain a constant temperature while the temperature of its environment varies.

Healthy birds and mammals are able to keep their body temperature the same, no matter how high or low (within limits) the temperature of the environment goes. The temperature of all other creatures rises with a rise and falls with a fall of the outside temperature. In this latter class we must include the human infant, hibernating mammals, and newly hatched birds.

The power possessed by all living things, plants included, to produce heat as one of the manifestations of their vitality is referred to as thermogenesis. No doubt the actual amounts of heat produced by different animals are very different: a fish in unit time per unit of its weight is producing vastly less heat than a man, and a man less than a bird; but they are all producing heat.

The chief thermogenic sources are muscles (including the heart), the liver and the other glands; these, and not the blood, are the chief seats of heat-production. A frog whose blood has been replaced by a weak solution of common salt still continues to excrete carbon dioxide for some days, showing that oxidations are still going on in it although it has no blood at all. It is just as certain that an animal producing carbon dioxide is producing heat by the oxidation of carbon somewhere within its body as that a candle which is liberating carbon dioxide is producing its heat through the oxidation of the carbon of its fat.

Measurement of the quantity of heat is effected by means of the calorimeter, the principle being that the heat produced by any particular substance is absorbed by a known weight of water, which is, in consequence, raised a certain number of degrees in temperature.[1] A water-calorimeter is, then, essentially a metal box surrounded by a known quantity of water. To ascertain how much heat an animal gives out in a certain time, it is only necessary to place it in the inner box, which is, of course, properly ventilated. The heat that radiates from its skin is conducted through the box to the water; the heat of its expired air is absorbed by the water, the temperature of which, we shall say, has risen through n degrees. We shall suppose that the animal has done no "external work" while it has been in the calorimeter. If the weight of water is w units, then w multiplied by n is equal to the number of calories of heat lost by the resting animal in a given time.

[1] The large calorie, or unit of heat, is defined as the quantity of heat transferred to one kilogramme of water (2.2 lb.) in order to raise it one degree Centigrade in temperature.

The problem might now be faced, From what materials does the body manufacture heat? Since the body only very exceptionally absorbs any heat from outside sources—heat of the Tropics or a Turkish bath—it is quite clear that it must constantly be taking in the wherewithal to manufacture heat so continuously. Except in starving animals the source of heat is the oxidation of the food.

Just as a steam-engine transforms the potential chemical energy of the coal into the kinetic forms of energy—heat and external work (movement)—so the animal body transforms the potential energy of the food into the active forms of heat and muscular movement. Both are machines for transforming energy; the one is of iron, the other of protoplasm, but in both equally is the great law of the Conservation of Energy obeyed. This may be said to have been one of the mathematico-physical intuitions of that great mathematico-physical physiologist Helmholtz. For a long time it was thought that the animal organism was outside the scope of this great generalization; but it is known that an animal in a calorimeter will produce as many calories of heat in a given time as would have been generated by the burning of a weight of food equal to that of the food utilized during the period of observation. It is only a question of difference of rate in the setting free of the heat; in burning the food we get all the heat out at once, in digesting it we get out just as much heat, but it is liberated much more slowly. The inhabitants of cold countries are pre-eminently fat-eaters; the notion that fats give heat and sugars other forms of energy is probably not altogether fallacious.

The actual amount of heat that each adult loses per twenty-four hours is, in round numbers, about three thousand calories, the ultimate source of which is the oxidation of the various oxidizable chemical elements in the food of twenty-four hours. Knowing that one gramme of protein (flesh) yields us 4 calories, one gramme of sugar 4, and one gramme of fat 9, it is not difficult to construct a dietary containing, potentially, the necessary heat.

The portions of the total heat-loss borne by each system have been determined as follows—

Heat radiated and conducted from the skin, 2190 calories, or 73 per cent. of the total.

Heat lost in evaporating water from the skin, 435 calories, or 14.5 per cent.

Heat lost in evaporating water from the lungs, 216 calories, or 7.2 per cent.
Heat lost in warming the expired air to body-temperature, 105 calories, or 3.5 per cent.
Heat lost in warming the dejecta, 54 calories, or 1.8 per cent.

Of recent years a great many experimental studies have been made on the precise quantity of heat liberated by a healthy person completely at rest in bed (but not asleep) and taking no food. This amount of heat is usually stated in calories per square metre of the skin per hour. The method gives us the true heat-production of the tissues uncomplicated by the changing conditions, such as the taking of meals, the variations of temperature, muscular work and other factors. It is called the "basal metabolism"—a better name would be, the resting minimal heat production. Already it has provided data valuable in scientific medical diagnosis. In round numbers it is about 100 calories per hour.

In human beings the skin is *the* system of heat-loss, being responsible for the loss of 87.5 per cent. of all the heat lost. This is not so in some animals, in the dog, for instance, whose hairy coat does not permit its skin to perspire. The dog loses heat largely by its expired air, and by the radiation and evaporation of water from its tongue ; thus on a hot day it pants and puts out its tongue.

Obviously our clothes prevent the loss of heat, and the more effectually the worse they are as conductors of heat. For this reason flannel, wool and furs are so much "warmer" than linen or cotton, which are materials from the vegetable kingdom, and therefore not the natural clothing of animals.

An animal is not only a transformer of energy, it is the most economical transformer known ; for whereas in the very best steam-engines we obtain about 12 per cent. of the original potential energy as motion (external work), in the animal we get as much as 25 per cent. in the form of useful work. And whereas in the engine a great deal of the heat set free is lost or wasted from the engineer's point of view, the animal heat, so far from being wasted, is essential to the protoplasm to provide it with the optimum temperature for the performance of its vital activities.

The muscles as energy transformers differ from an engine in possessing two distinct powers, heat-producing and work-producing, or the thermogenic and dynamogenic powers respectively. Now the interesting thing is that, although a muscle cannot do work without producing heat, it can continue to produce heat without actively contracting, without doing work. In this latter state it is said to be in a condition of tonus or tone. No doubt when sufficiently analyzed, tonus is discovered to be a state of imperceptible or incipient contraction. Again, when a muscle having shortened continues to support a weight, but shortens no more, it continues to produce heat although in the sense of the physicists it is not doing any external work: thus dynamogenesis and thermogenesis are separate capabilities. But further, the two related capacities of muscle for heat-production and work-production only vary *pari passu* within certain limits.

As a muscle lifts heavier and heavier weights, it sets free more and more heat each time; and also if it raises the same weight each time, but under the influence of increasingly strong stimuli, it will evolve more and more heat each time. In this latter case the dynamogenic effects are the same throughout the series, while the thermogenic effects are greater and greater. As fatigue supervenes, the heat-producing faculty becomes impaired long before the work-producing. Thus very tired muscles may be able to lift the load to the height to which they raised it when fresh, but they now do so with the greatest possible economy as regards their store of potential energy, for they evolve the minimal quantity of heat. They oxidize material to as slight a degree as possible. Muscular work and heat are thus not quantitatively parallel products: there is nothing comparable with this in a machine of human construction.

As regards the kinds of food from which we derive heat, our ideas have undergone changes since the time when the German chemist Liebig divided foods into flesh-formers and heat-givers; the "meaty" stuffs and cheese he placed in the former group, the starches, sugars and fats in the latter. After having been much criticized, this classification by Liebig is admitted to be substantially correct. While sugars and fats do not build up tissue, but are found to be normally oxidized more or less directly for heat-giving or work-producing purposes, the proteins (flesh-formers) both repair tissue waste (by their nitrogen-containing moiety), and also contribute to heat-production by the non-nitrogen-containing substances into which in digestion they are split up. Liebig told the truth, but not the whole truth.

If during a certain time a person's temperature remains constant, that person is losing as much heat as he is producing. In technical language, thermogenesis, or heat-production, is just balanced by thermolysis, or heat-loss. Obviously, since we are constantly producing heat, unless we were as constantly to lose it, we should get hotter and hotter, and would damage our tissues by fatal fever. If no heat were lost at all, our temperature would rise 1° C. in half an hour ; in thirty-six hours our body fluids would be boiling ; in another thirty-six, autocremation would be far advanced. Now it is very well known that the temperature of a healthy man (98.4° F., 37° C.) hardly differs by a degree from one year's end to the other, or from the Poles to the Equator.

We may now ask ourselves the question, how it comes about that some animals have, and others have not, the power to keep their body temperature constant. Does not a fall of temperature necessarily depress vitality, and a rise, within limits, exalt it ? The answer is that protoplasm as protoplasm is certainly depressed by a fall and stimulated by a rise of temperature, which can be well seen by the slowing effect of chilling an isolated frog-heart and the accelerating effect of warming it. It would seem, then, there ought to be no such things as animals of constant temperature (warm-blooded). The solution to the puzzle is the high development of the nervous system in animals known as homoiothermic. In a mammal, when the temperature falls, the first result is loss of heat from the skin and an incipient depression of the temperature, but, through the nerves of the skin, impulses are sent into the nervous system which emerge as reflex stimuli to cause contraction of the skin vessels and increased heat-production in the muscles. The constriction of the skin vessels shuts some blood out of the skin and so diminishes heat loss, while the increased tone of the muscles increases heat-production, and thus the loss of heat due to the fall of temperature is so rapidly compensated that the temperature does not finally fall. Shivering is the familiar reflex effort on the part of the muscles to increase their heat as a result of the heat loss.

This power of balancing thermogenesis against thermolysis we call " thermotaxis " ; the homoiothermic animals have, while the poikilothermic animals have not, the power of thermotaxis. Now, fever (pyrexia) is the upsetting of thermotaxis, the disturbance of this beautiful thermic balance. Theoretically, fever, or a rise of temperature, may occur if the heat production is too rapid for the heat loss, or, on the other hand, the heat production being unaltered, if the heat loss is diminished in rate. Both these states of the upset thermal balance occur. Sir William Hale-White has shown that whereas in pneumonia and erysipelas the fever is due to increased heat-production, in typhoid fever and in suppuration the rise of temperature is due to a diminution in the heat loss.

Fever is to-day regarded by physicians in a totally different light from what it was even a few years ago—in itself a wholly bad thing, to be reduced at any cost. The increased heat production is looked on as a reaction on the part of the living cells to the noxious stimulus of the micro-organisms or their soluble poisons, a response of a protective nature. Hence the indiscriminate lowering of the temperature by drugs (antipyretics) is not now nearly so common as it used to be. It is recognized as possible that the increase of heat (fever) may be evidence of sufficient vitality on the part of the living protoplasm to withstand the assaults of the infective agents, the increased heat being the biophysical response to the micro-organic insults. The drugs which benefit fever most are now regarded as doing so, not because they lower the temperature, but because they attack the specific cause of the malady; quinine, for instance, in malaria destroying the parasitic *Plasmodium malariæ*, the salicylates antagonizing the poison of rheumatic fever, and so forth. Those versed in vegetable physiology have been able to show that even in the case of parasites attacking trees there is a rise of temperature as a reaction to these assaults, and therefore botanists actually speak of "fever" in plants.

Of course, it is not to be imagined that in no circumstances is fever, or very hot blood, injurious to the body. Within the last few years definite experiments have been made showing that blood hotter than a certain temperature does permanently damage the cells of the central nervous system.

A short exposure to 47° C. or a longer one to 42° C. kills the cells of an animal's brain by coagulating one of the essential constituents of their living substance. "Sunstroke", as it is called, is the result of the too hot blood injuring the cells of the brain, especially those related to consciousness. When the cells are only slightly injured the person may recover, and be "a little queer in the head" for the rest of his life; if, however, the cells are decidedly overheated, as in "heat-stroke" or "heat-apoplexy", death in collapse supervenes, the person never regaining consciousness. Heat-stroke of this kind may occur in places to which the sun never gains access, as, for instance, in front of the furnaces of a steamer in the Red Sea.

On the other hand, depression of the temperature of the blood below its normal is as fatal, although not so rapidly, and for quite other reasons. Great loss of heat depresses the tissues so that death results. What is known to coroners' juries as, "death from exposure" is really due to heat-loss. An underfed, poorly clothed, and perhaps also alcohol-intoxicated person falls asleep out of doors on a frosty night; so much heat is lost that the heart and nervous system never recover; the person never wakes. The lowest (subnormal) temperature in man—namely, 80° F.—that has been reached, has been recorded under these conditions.

CHAPTER IV

PRECONCEIVED PERFECTION

ATTEMPTS have been made to hinder the progress of science by many things but by none more than by preconceptions. These ideas were very often assertions purporting to embody some religious opinion or doctrine to which everything new must conform or forthwith be rejected.

For instance, it was assumed by the early Greek philosophers that, since the circle was a "perfect" figure and the heavenly bodies were also perfect—as seemed then self-evident—these heavenly bodies must revolve in circles. The Ptolemaic system in astronomy was based on this assumption. There was thus considerable opposition to the demonstration that the planets revolved in ellipses. These perfect bodies moving in perfect circles were supposed to make perfect harmonies—"the music of the spheres". No one had heard it; but that did not matter; it must be perfect music since it was produced in heavenly places.

Galileo was greatly worried over these preconceived notions about perfection. The sun was perfect—that was self-evident; yet Galileo had been rash and irreverent enough to discover " spots " on the luminary. These spots were physical appearances discernible by the telescope; but Galileo's critics, choosing to take the term in the sense of moral blemishes, condemned the astronomer as a thoroughly impious person.

This ascription of moral worth to inert objects has been the cause of a good deal of trouble from time to time in the history of progress.

In the case of Galileo, it was not simply that he asserted the earth moved round the sun, but that he had declared the heavenly bodies, like this terrestrial globe, "corruptible ".

He might have been warned by the fate of Copernicus, whose work, disproving that this small planet was the centre of the universe, was placed on *The Index*. The theologians seem to have been very sensitive about astronomical heresy. Bruno was burnt because he had speculated, amongst other things, on the " plurality of worlds ".

The orthodox view was geocentric and anthropocentric: this planet was the most important in creation, and man the most important being in it.

This sort of thing we find also in Aristotle's view of animal heat. Aristotle regarded the heat of the animal, and particularly the heat of the human body, as of a far finer essence than heat of non-vital origin. The heat in the human body was supposed to be something allied in its essence to the energy displayed by the stars, which, regarded as sentient beings, were held to preside over human destiny. The expressions, "ill-starred" and "my stars!" refer to this belief.

The view lingered for a long time, although the acute mind of Shakespeare evidently doubted it, for he makes Cassius say—

> The fault, dear Brutus, is not in our stars
> But in ourselves that we are underlings.

Notions of preconceived perfection troubled the great William Harvey, the discoverer of the circulation of the blood. It is, of course, of the essence of the Harveian doctrine that the blood, the same blood, which leaves the left side of the heart by the arteries for distribution to the body, returns by the veins to the right side of the heart. It is like the procession of stage-warriors: there may be only a dozen of them; but as they go out at one door and come in by another they create the impression of a never-ending procession; yet it is always the same twelve men.

One of Harvey's correspondents, Dr Caspar Hoffmann of Nüremberg, had objected to the idea of the circulation, because he considered that Harvey had

> impeached Nature of folly and error, had imputed to her the character of a most clumsy and inefficient artificer in suffering the blood to become recrudescent and making it return again and again to the heart in order to be reconcocted, to grow effete, as often, in the general system, thus uselessly spoiling the perfectly made blood merely to find her something to do.

Hoffmann's amazing criticism amounts to this: The blood cannot keep on returning to the heart because that indicates an imperfect arrangement; now the arrangements of the heart are perfect; therefore there is no circulation. The results of experimental research could not be correct because, forsooth, Hoffmann believed that the heart works "perfectly" in some manner other than that involving a circulation of blood through it. This is the *à priori* argument *in excelsis*. It is extremely typical of the sort of reasoning that proceeds from preconceived ideas. It was employed to quite within our own day.

Another excellent example is the criticism which Stensen had to endure for saying that the heart was a muscle. Nicholas Stensen, the Dane, was a doctor of medicine and an eminent man of science who studied anatomy and biology experimentally with great success. His dissections showed him that the heart was a complicated arrangement of muscular fibres; that it was, in fact, a hollow muscle. His critics, however, held that as the soul was in the heart, it was impossible that the heart could be a "common muscle"; the mere suggestion was rank impiety. Stensen was duly censured for such irreverence. To us to-day it seems ludicrous that such puerile criticism should have stood in the way of physiological discovery; but the strangling power of preconceived ideas is vast.

The progress of anatomy in the Middle Ages was very much impeded by the ban placed upon dissection by the Mohammedan injunction against it. The Koran decreed that to touch a dead body made a person ceremonially unclean; dissection, especially of the human body, was consequently impossible. The Jews had no greater liberty in this respect than the Arabs. The result was that the Jewish and Arabian doctors of the Middle Ages kept on repeating the statements of the Greek and Roman writers on anatomy. They verified nothing and they discovered nothing.

It was one of the minor results of the Renaissance that the study of *practical* anatomy was revived and introduced first into the medical schools of the Continent and then after a due interval into England.

The case of Tagliacozzi is typical of opposition to science through preconceived notions about theoretical perfection. Gasparo Tagliacozzi was an Italian surgeon who flourished in the middle of the sixteenth century, and who had specialized in those operations known as "plastic", whereby he repaired noses, ears and lips by grafting skin from the arm. The operation for a new nose (rhinoplasty) was his most famous achievement. He had plenty of opportunity to perform such operations, for both in duelling and in the perpetual wars of that period, the most prominent feature of the face was apt to be mutilated.

By his scientific brethren his work was thought very highly of, and he is commemorated by a life-sized statue in the anatomical theatre of the University of Bologna. But in other circles it aroused the fiercest opposition: he was denounced for his impiety in daring to alter the human countenance "made in the image of God"! The excitement even outlasted his life; for after many years in the grave, his bones were dug up and scattered by order of the ecclesiastical authorities. The gravamen of the charge against Tagliacozzi was his irreverence in interfering with the human face; it would seem to have been quite allowable to mutilate this sacred part of the body in war, but thoroughly immoral to try to remedy the damage.

Benjamin Franklin demonstrated the identity of lightning and electricity, and recommended the use of lightning-conductors; but he had the greatest possible difficulty in overcoming resistance to his recommendations on the ground that he was interfering with the divinely sent thunder and lightning.

Yet another case of the same sort of thing

is the opposition to Jenner's discovery of the efficacy of vaccination against small-pox. Jenner had many trials to bear; in some quarters it was not thanks he got for his trouble in showing mankind how they might avoid one of the most dreadful scourges that have ever afflicted it.

A Rev. Dr Rowley, who otherwise would have remained unheard of, evidently imagining himself honoured by special participation in the divine counsels, declared—

> Small-pox is a visitation from God, but cow-pox is produced by presumptuous man. The former is what Heaven has ordained, the latter is a daring violation of our holy religion.

Such nonsense is intolerable. How could Jenner possibly be responsible for cow-pox, which, as a disease of cattle, was in existence æons before he was born?

To concoct theoretical, *à priori* statements about the supposed divine or other origin of disease was nothing short of an outrage on an investigator who was endeavouring to discover a remedy for a world-wide scourge that had preyed upon mankind from the very dawn of history.

But before the time of Jenner there was similar trouble over inoculation of small-pox itself. This practice was based on the fact, familiar enough to everyone in the reign of George I, that anyone who had had small-pox was extremely unlikely to get it a second time. The Turks, Circassians and Chinese had for long inoculated small-pox in the hope that by having it mildly they would be immune from it when an epidemic came.

Lady Mary Wortley Montague, wife of the British Ambassador at Constantinople, had been so impressed with the immunity from serious small-pox conferred by the previous inoculation of it, that she caused her infant, born in Constantinople, to be inoculated there.

But, as Voltaire, in his "Letters on England," says—

> The chaplain represented to this lady, but to no purpose, that this was an unchristian operation, and therefore that it could succeed only with none but infidels.

Truly a discriminating specificity of action—a new test for believers! As is well known, Lady Mary introduced inoculation into England and thereby undoubtedly saved thousands of lives.

The story of the opposition to the views of Franz Joseph Gall, the founder of the pseudo-science of phrenology, is another case in point. Gall was not objected to because he taught an absurd system of cerebral physiology, but because he had outraged religion in Vienna by teaching that mental and moral qualities had their physical basis in the brain. He was "materialistic" because he asserted that mental and moral states were conditioned by (brain) matter; and to be "materialistic" in 1800 was the next thing to being an atheist. It was well for Oliver Wendell Holmes, when he published his *Mechanism in Thought and Morals*, that he did not live in Vienna in 1800.

Gall was groping after what we now call the localization of functions in the brain; and he was the first to hint that there was a centre for speech in the grey matter, a region of the organ of the mind devoted to the expression of ideas by appropriate words. All subsequent work has confirmed his contention. The title of his objectionable work was: "The Anatomy and Physiology of the Nervous System in General and of the Brain in Particular, with Observations on the Possibility of Recognizing Various Intellectual and Moral Dispositions of Man and of Animals by the Configuration of their Heads".

To attribute man's moral qualities to any physical organ was reprehensible in a high degree; and so Gall was driven from righteously scandalized Austria and took refuge in Paris, where he practised as a physician and lectured on the brain until his death in 1828.

Had the experimental physiology of the brain and nervous system been in a more advanced state when Gall was studying cerebral localization, the chances are he would not have lost his way as he did in the intellectual morass of phrenology.

One of the best examples of attempts to obstruct the beneficent progess of medical science, by alleging it contrary to nature and to religion, is that of the introduction of chloroform.

It was assumed that pain must not be removed by any "artificial" means, that to abolish pain even of childbirth was "con trary to Nature". Just as Tagliacozzi had been denounced as sacrilegious for tampering remedially with the human countenance, so Simspon was villified for endeavouring to mitigate human pain. When a lady told him that it was contrary to Nature for him to remove the pains of childbirth, he replied—

It was 'contrary to Nature' for you to come over the water in a steamer to see me.

When the Scottish clergy quoted from Genesis the curse on Eve—" in sorrow shalt thou bring forth ",—Simpson quoted against them: " And the Lord God caused a deep sleep to fall upon Adam, and he took one of his ribs and closed up the flesh instead thereof ". From this Simpson argued that prior to this very early case of resection of a rib there was due preparation made for it by general anæsthesia.

If we did nothing except what is conformable to a state of Nature, we should still be wrapped in sheepskins and be living in the dens and caves of the earth.

CHAPTER V

CIRCULATIONS

A CIRCULATION is the return of a moving object to the place where it started.

When in the theatre they wish to represent the marching of an army, and they have only four-and-twenty stage warriors (who cannot be expected to be "terrible as an army with banners") the stage-manager makes these four-and-twenty men enter the stage by one door and leave it by another. If they do this sufficiently often, it gives a spectator the impression of the marching of a large body of men: the illusion of quantity was created by a circulation.

Bank-notes circulate, because after no matter how many transferences from one person to another, the notes return to the bank which issued them.

The circulation of water is one of the most obvious of Nature's great cosmic circulations.

We know that the water of the sea, lakes,

rivers and of the damp earth is being constantly evaporated into the atmosphere where it may remain unseen for a long time.

Sooner or later it is condensed into some visible form, dew, mist, fog or cloud.

The particles of the clouds run together, and, becoming too heavy to float, fall to the earth as rain, snow, sleet or hail.

It is certain that the *same* particles of water have been doing this for millions of years.

It is quite possible that a particle of the water of a cloud may be one of many million particles drunk by an animal on some occasion; it then passed into the animal's blood and was carried through that long circuit of the arteries, capillaries and veins of the body; finally it reached the kidney whence it was thrown out of the body, or reached the lung, whence it was exhaled as a particle of vapour such as is seen on a cold or very damp day.

The biblical description of " the rain that cometh down and the snow from heaven, and returneth not thither " is true only of one aspect of the circulation of water.

The circulation of the blood is, of course, the most familiar example of matter returning to the place whence it started. A particle of blood leaves the heart, passes by the arteries to the capillaries, thence to the veins and so back to the heart again—and this ceaselessly.

It is the *same* blood.

Harvey insisted that if it is *not* the same blood which keeps on going round and round, we are landed in the absurdity of having to admit that in (say) an hour, the heart will pump out into the body very much more blood than the body of the animal is known to possess. This consideration he gave as one of the proofs of the circulation.

The body of a man has about three and a half litres of blood, let us say five at the most; the heart throws out at each beat about 60 cubic centimetres; now there are about 70 beats per minute, so that the heart per hour deals with 60 by 70 by 60 or 252,000 cubic centimetres, or 2,520 litres. But the whole body contains certainly not more than five litres; so that unless the same blood returns to the heart, the heart in an hour would eject about 500 times as much blood as the body possesses, "which is absurd!"

Take now the case of an atom of carbon in a piece of cane-sugar which we have just eaten. It is digested, and passing into the blood goes to the liver, where it may be stored for days in the form of a kind of starch. *Finally it leaves the liver* as sugar again, and once more entering the blood-stream is carried to the muscles and other tissues, where it is oxidized to carbon dioxide. This gas enters the blood, and being carried to the lungs is there exhaled into the atmosphere as an invisible molecule of gas. The same carbon atom therefore which began its journey in a solid piece of sugar is now floating in the air as part of a molecule of gas. How long it may float about no one can tell; but at last it will be taken in by some green plant, and under the influence of sunlight on the living substance in the leaves will be united to hydrogen and oxygen and so condensed to form starch. This starch the plant finally turns into sugar, and so we are where we began.

This sort of thing has been going on ever since plants and animals lived together on the earth. A rather longer cycle is gone through by an atom of nitrogen which is one of the elements in the protein of the grass. The grass is eaten by a cow, and, we shall suppose, the beef becomes part of a human being. Some of the nitrogen of the human being is thrown out of the body as urea, a substance which in the soil is decomposed into ammonia and water. The roots of the grass absorb the ammonia; and its nitrogen is built up into the protein with which we started. This circulation of nitrogen can go on for ever.

But it is clear there is a circulation of matter all the time between plant and soil and soil and plant. This autumn's dead leaves decomposing at the foot of the oak and being absorbed by its roots, will become next summer's leaves and acorns. The body we bury to-day will sooner or later be broken up into its component salts, which, absorbed from " mother earth ", will be reincorporated into future living beings. And what happens once can go on happening endlessly.

" Dust to dust and ashes to ashes " is the poetical form in which this is expressed in the Prayer-book. If translated into the language of modern science it expresses one of the most important truths concerning the intimate relations between three things, the soil, the living, and the dead.

" Imperial Caesar dead " might in time have become a constituent of the body of a slave!

CHAPTER VI

THE EYE AS A CAMERA

THERE are several very close resemblances between the mammalian eye and a photographic camera.

The essential parts of a camera are, a sensitive plate to receive the image of some object being photographed, and a lens to form that image. The camera, like all other optical instruments, is blackened inside.

If for the sensitive plate we substitute one of ground glass, then on that plate we can observe from behind the camera the small, inverted image of the person about to be photographed.

This is what the photographer sees when he throws a black cloth over his head and seems for a little while to be lost to the world at the back of the camera. He is looking at the minute image of the " sitter " shining through the translucent glass plate.

The double convex lens which is responsible for the image is possessed of such properties that if it be placed in front of a large, distant object, it will produce on a screen close to it a small, inverted image of that object: like Luther, "it cannot do otherwise".

Now the human eye is exactly such a camera: it has a double convex lens in front, and a sensitive plate (the retina) behind, and it is blackened inside. The "black eye" of popular acception refers not to this internal pigmentation but to an accidental, external disfigurement. The objects of the outer world are relatively far from the lens compared with the retina which is quite close to the lens.

It follows from this state of matters that the image of the external world cast by the lens upon the retina must be very small, and also completely upside down. This fact can be proved if one does not grudge a rather troublesome dissection as follows.

If we fix the eye of a sheep or ox a few feet away from a bright lamp, and then take a razor and shave away carefully the tough coat at the back of the eye (sclerotic) until the delicate retina comes into view, we can just make out the tiny image of the lamp upside down. We are looking at the retinal image shining through the dead retina just as the photographer sees the sitter's image shining through the dull glass plate which he uses before he inserts the sensitive plate itself. Though difficult to carry out, this observation is very instructive since it gives us ocular demonstration that there is in the eye a real image of the outside world and that it is, as regards that world, upside down. Yet we do not see the world upside down; it is only our accomplished writers of paradox who can turn the world upside down.

This is scarcely the place to discuss the problem why we do not see the outer world inverted. Both the psychologists and the metaphysicians have something to say about it, the gist of their remarks being that, as we have no direct knowledge of the existence of the retinal image at all, we cannot consciously be dealing with it. Unless it were for anatomists and physiologists, we should never know that there was such a thing as a retina or that it had an inverted image focused upon it.

The extreme minuteness of the image in

the eye is a fact which very few people realize. The entire surface of the retina is only about one square inch, and not by any means all of this surface receives the image of the outer world. The image is received on a specialized, slightly hollowed spot which is about 1/12th of an inch in diameter (the macula lutea). This really means that the image, say, of St Paul's Cathedral, viewed a few hundred yards away, is all condensed upon a tiny spot at the back of the eye about 0.0045 of a square inch, and that in this image the dome is down below and the steps and the pavement are up above.

It is well known that no lens can give a clear image of a near object and of a distant object at one and the same time. When a photographer wishes to focus a near object, he pushes the lens farther in, and when he wishes to focus a far object, he pulls the lens out. In the mammalian eye this bodily movement of the lens cannot take place on account of the way in which the lens is suspended in the eye.

But a very remarkable thing happens; the lens itself becomes thicker in the centre, that is a stronger lens when a near object has to be focused, and flatter in the centre, that is weaker, when a distant object has to be focused. All this, which happens quite outside our consciousness, has nothing analagous in the case of the camera ; in a certain sense it shows the very great superiority of the eye to the camera.

There is one more resemblance between the eye and the camera with which we may close this study. The camera has a number of metal discs called " stops " with circular holes in them. These diaphragms the photographer uses to sharpen the image. It is another property of a double convex lens that the rays passing through the margins of it tend to blur the image. When the photographer, therefore, wants to cut off these rays, he slips one of the stops in front of the lens so that the central rays pass through the aperture and form the image while the marginal rays are cut out and so prevented from taking part in the formation of the image.

Now the eye has an exactly similar apparatus in the circular iris with its central circular aperture the pupil. The opaque iris cuts off the marginal rays which are not wanted, while the pupil allows the image-forming rays to pass through the centre of the lens. In this way the iris sharpens the image exactly as does the photographer's "stop".

The size of the pupil is altered by the activity of certain microscopically small muscles in the iris; when the light is very bright the pupil becomes small, when the light is feeble it becomes dilated. This action goes on entirely outside our knowledge. The mechanism of the symmetrical closing in of the circular aperture in the iris is very perfect and has been imitated in the "iris-diaphragm" of the modern microscope.

Finally, why is the inside of the eye blackened? For the same reason that all optical instruments are blackened inside—to prevent internal reflexions, and the general glare that would result from having the interior of the eye incapable of absorbing stray light, that is, light not employed in forming the image.

CHAPTER VII

PREDICTION IN BIOLOGY

PROBABLY nothing impresses us with the dignity and soundness of science so much as the accurate fulfilling of some one of its definite predictions. In a mathematical science, such as astronomy, prediction may be said to be an inevitable part of the investigator's duties, since the phenomena he deals with are necessarily of a recurring order, but in any science it is a valuable method of putting a theory to the test or of estimating the value of a working hypothesis. For instance, the Russian chemist, Mendelieff, having arranged the elements known to chemists in certain natural series, which nevertheless contained gaps, predicted that before long these gaps would be filled up by elements yet to be discovered. Those of us who have followed the development of chemistry know that these chemical prophecies have come true. The objective reality of those properties on the possession of which Mendelieff's series was constructed, was thus established.

In the non-mathematical sciences, prediction may be said to be supplanted by prescience or prophecy. Thus, when the great William Harvey wrote to his friend Horst (1654), " Many things still lie hidden . . . destined to be drawn up into the light by the indefatigable diligence of coming ages ", he had some, but no adequate, idea of how truly he spoke as a prophet. In a vastly fuller way than he could possibly have imagined, this prescient utterance has been fulfilled. By the " indefatigable diligence " of the great Italian biologist, Marcello Malpighi, Harvey's own generalization as to the circulation of the blood was verified to ocular demonstration by means of the microscope (1660). In a thousand ways have Harvey's words been justified; has not " diligence " triumphed over all the technical difficulties in the way of preserving and analyzing the living tissues? Do we not by histo-chemical diligence preserve for ever from decay those very invisible blood-vessels which Harvey's eyes never saw, but which he was so certain existed? How transported with joy would he have been to know that we can fill them with a substance which, solidifying in them, demonstrates their presence with the utmost clearness. Diligence has literally brought them to light; the master's prophetic vision saw that which was invisible.

Those engaged in studying the intricacies of the nervous system seem at all times to have indulged in prediction. Thus, the Father of Anatomy, Vesalius himself, ventured to assert (1543) that by mere dissection of the brain no further discoveries as to its functions would be made. Three hundred years of anatomy have justified his belief in the comparative sterility of the study of the gross anatomy of the nervous system, at least as regards the discovery of function. Not by dissection, as Vesalius knew it, but by microscopical investigation, by inference from careful experiment and by injuries accidentally produced, have the activities of the brain been made clear to us. Vesalius has been justified in his prophecy that dissection is a barren art, but not justified if he meant to predict that the cerebral functions would be for ever beyond the ken of the students of living things.

A most prescient physiologist, the Dane, Nicholas Stensen, prophesied that, as regards the central nervous system, no further advances in understanding it would be made "without a special manner of preparing it". This was uttered in 1668, and has been completely justified. The preparation of the substance of the brain and spinal cord to fit them for microscopical examination was surrounded by so many difficulties that not for nearly two hundred years was it possible to make these structures sufficiently transparent. The difficulties in dealing with the cerebral substance were such that they overcame that Alexander of Biology, Malpighi, who declared that the brain was a gland which secreted spirits. So far astray is it possible to be led when the time has not yet come for the fulfilment of a prophecy!

Yet another seventeenth century prophet, but this time a false one! The great Sydenham, the English Hippocrates, though a contemporary of Harvey, was not a disciple of Harvey. He saw no use in Harvey's discovery, and consequently ignored it: in particular, he despised the study of the minute structure of tissues, or "histology" as it is called to-day.

Again, according to his scholarly biographer, the late Dr Payne, Sydenham prophesied " that the human intellect will never be able to understand the use of the different parts of the brain ". Supremely difficult as we know this study to be, surprising advances have been made in it, but just by the experimental method of Harvey rather than by the mere observational method of Sydenham. By that very method of research, the microscopical, which Sydenham trusted least, a very great deal of excellent physiological work has been achieved.

A contemporary of William Harvey and of Thomas Sydenham was a certain Gideon Harvey, " Physician to the Tower ", chiefly remembered for his coarse but amusing attacks on the College of Physicians. In what follows he describes the type of doctor of the school of his great namesake, a description which we can imagine Sydenham fully endorsing—

" They flay dogs and cats ; take livers, lungs, calves' brains, or other entrails, dry, roast, parboil them, steep them in vinegar, etc., and afterwards gaze on little particles of them through a microscope ; then obtrude to the world in print whatever false appearances gleamed into their eyes ; and all this to no other end than to beget a belief in people that they who have so profoundly dived into the bottomless pores of the parts must undeniably be skilled in curing their distempers."—("The Conclave of Physicians." Second edition, 1686.)

In the same strain of unbelief as to the possibility of histological demonstration wrote no less a man than the philosopher, John Locke, a close friend of Sydenham. He committed himself to this: "That Nature performs all her operations in the body by parts so minute and insensible that I think nobody will ever hope or pretend, even by the assistance of glasses or other inventions, to come to a sight of them".

Professor Osler, in his delightful essay on Locke, tells us a significant fact apropos of this remark: that on the top of the page on which it occurs there is a sentence in Sydenham's handwriting fully confirming his friend's scepticism. In modern language, Locke said there was no future for histology or bio-chemistry, which were futile attempts to unravel the intricacies of texture and of function wholly inaccessible to man. Now it is precisely in these two realms that the greatest conquests in medicine have been made, for the microscope and the test-tube have been two of the most powerful weapons in her peaceful armamentarium.

Sydenham was a great physician, a great observer in the realm of disease, but he was no prophet either in his own or any other country. He fell into an error, not uncommon in robust but not broad minds, of imagining that there cannot be anything of much value outside that which these minds readily understand.

Prophecy has always occupied an important place in scientific discovery.

Jenner prophesied that the patient whom he had previously vaccinated against small-pox on being inoculated with small-pox would fail to take it. This was the boy Phipps who had been inoculated by Jenner with the virus of cowpox (vaccinia) on 14th May, 1796, and on the following 1st of July had been inoculated with fluid from a vesicle of a case of genuine well-developed human small-pox: the boy did not take the disease at all. Jenner waited until the 19th of July, and, finding that the boy was still quite well, could no longer delay, but wrote to his friend Gardner as follows: "Listen to the most delightful part of my story. The boy has been inoculated for the small-pox which, as I *ventured to predict,*[1] produced no effect.

[1] The italics are mine.—D. F. F.-H.

I shall now pursue my experiments with redoubled ardour ".

One of the most interesting writers on the mind and its organs—the brain and the nerves—Prochaska, of Vienna, makes a remark of great interest with regard to those workers who were to come after him. It concerns the two roots of the spinal nerves. The structural differences between the two roots of a spinal nerve, the upper with its swelling or ganglion, the lower without any ganglion, had long been familiar to anatomists. Prochaska knew that one of the chief nerves of the head, the fifth or trifacial, had also two roots, one large and ganglionated, the other small and non-ganglionated. He was thus led to speak prophetically in the following words—

> " He who shall unravel the uses of the ganglia will also give a reason why the fifth pair of cerebral nerves pass through the semi-lunar ganglion (with the exception of the fasciculus which joins the third division) without touching the ganglia, and why only the posterior roots of the spinal nerves enter the ganglia, whilst the anterior roots pass by without any communication with them." (1784.)

Now this was precisely what Sir Charles Bell did twenty-seven years after the above was written. Bell in the first place showed that the upper or posterior roots of the spinal nerves were functionally exactly the opposite of what Prochaska supposed them to be, namely, nothing less than nerves whose ganglia prevented them conducting impulses into the nervous system. By conclusive experiments Bell proved that these posterior roots were, in point of fact, the only avenues *into* the spinal cord, and that their ganglia in no way interrupted impulses passing through them.

Of the nature of the nerve-impulse or *vis nervosa* as he called it, Prochaska wrote in these words: "Possibly the diligence of the very sagacious observers of Nature may discover whether that principle be electricity or phlogiston or some species of air or the matter of light or something compounded of these" (1784). Many "sagacious observers" since 1784 have done their best to discover the nature of the nervous impulse; and while physiologists would agree that it was not phlogiston or a species of air or the matter of light, not all would so readily put the first possibility out of court. With the formulation of the doctrines of electro-chemistry has risen an attempt to explain nervous activity, not indeed in terms of electricity as we know it flowing in wires, but in terms of electrically-charged particles—ions—constrained to set themselves in certain positions at certain moments in such a manner that electrical phenomena can be manifested.

A particularly interesting example of unfulfilled prophecy in biology occurs in the writings of no less a man than Johannes Müller, probably the most encyclopædic of Germany's scientific encyclopædists. He has been treating the nature of nervous action, and then he utters the following prediction as regards the velocity of propagation of the nerve-impulse: "We shall probably never attain the power of measuring the velocity of nervous action, for we have not the opportunity of comparing its propagation through immense spaces as we have in the case of light" (1835).

Müller believed, as did other leading biologists as late as 1835, that the velocity of the nervous impulse was something prodigiously great, of the same order of magnitude as that of light; indeed, that the act of thinking was performed with "the speed of light". We still speak of a thought "flashing into the mind", and of things occurring with "the speed of thought". Exactly fifteen years after this prophecy was made, Hermann Helmholtz, in 1850, measured the rapidity of the nerve-impulse in the motor nerves of the frog, and showed it to be perfectly calculable, not much more than about 90 feet a second. He subsequently measured it in human nerves, and found it to be about 360 feet a second. Once again we see the danger of venturing to predict any limitations to the possibilities of experimental science.

The last case of prophecy regarding the functions of the nervous system which we shall notice is one by the amateur physiologist George Henry Lewes, well known as the biographer of Goethe and the first husband of " George Eliot ". He ventured to predict that when the posterior roots of the spinal nerves were cut, the erection of the hairs on an animal's back would be no longer possible, in other words, he committed himself to the belief on *à priori* ground that the posterior roots would be found to carry impulses *out* of the spinal cord.

The passages relating to this prophecy are so interesting in more than one respect, that it will be well to have them before us—

" The posterior nerves being distributed to the skin can, it is obvious, only exercise a motor function in as far as they are related to moving organs or muscles. Now in the skin there are such organs, insignificant enough and only discovered within the last few years; these are muscular fibres surrounding the hair-follicles, and it is these which the posterior nerves cause to contract. If there were no muscular fibres in the skin, the posterior nerves would have no motor function; but they would have the possibility of exercising such a function—the same in kind as that of the anterior nerves. Thus does anatomy assure us that both nerves are sensory and both nerves motor. With this torch in our hands let us enter the otherwise obscure path of experimental inquiry. . . . The conclusion seems irresistible that the muscular sensibility is derived through the anterior or muscle-nerves. . . . There has been no collection of facts to throw light on the movements of the muscular fibres in the skin, but it is worth inquiring what share they have in the erection of 'quills upon the fretful porcupine' or the hairs on the back of an irritated dog. Division of the posterior roots would, I should anticipate, prevent the quills of the porcupine from rising up. But there is no experimental evidence on this subject present. . . . There is no fundamental distinction between the two nerves, both are sensory and both are motor; but they are so in different degrees."

When the late Professor Langley and Sir Charles Sherrington in 1891 came to examine these roots experimentally, they found the exact opposite of this prophecy of Lewes to be the true state of matters. The "pilo-motor" fibres, as they called them, did *not* pass through the posterior roots, but left the spinal cord by the anterior, so that section of the posterior roots does *not* paralyze the hair-muscles. In fact, there is no real exception to the Bell-Magendie law that all impulses entering the cord do so by the posterior roots, and that impulses leaving it do so by the anterior roots.

The passages just quoted are an excellent example of library or *à priori* physiology. Anterior to all investigation by experiment, the author gets hold of a principle of functional symmetry which he thinks ought to hold good in the case of the two nerve-roots. It is a torch to light up the otherwise obscure path of experimental inquiry! Experimental inquiry, on being made, discovers the exact opposite of what the anatomical light indicated. Therefore, anatomical torches by themselves are not to be trusted; and further, however respectfully *à priori* philosophy should be treated, *à priori* physiology most emphatically is not to be encouraged.

Another definite prediction was Pasteur's regarding the prophylactic inoculations for anthrax in sheep and cattle in 1882. The incident is so well known that it need not be repeated in all its detail. Pasteur had just perfected his method of protecting animals from a virulent disease by repeated injections of the attenuated poison of the same disease. The experimental conditions, prescribed for him by an agricultural society, were that twenty-five sheep were to be inoculated against anthrax, and, after an interval, to receive a virulent culture of the germs of that disease; at the same time twenty-five normal (uninoculated) sheep were to receive some of the same virulent culture. Pasteur accepted the challenge with equanimity. "The twenty-five unvaccinated sheep will all perish", he predicted, "the twenty-five vaccinated ones will survive"—and lo, it was so. The crowds who came to Pouilly-le-Fort to see the crucial experiment fail and to jeer at the man of science were converted then and on that very spot; and "the whole of France", wrote Pasteur's son-in-law and biographer, Valery-Radot, "burst out in an explosion of enthusiasm".

CHAPTER VIII

THE SIGNIFICANCE OF "PLAGUE, PESTILENCE, FAMINE, AND SUDDEN DEATH" IN THE LITANY

CERTAIN parts of the Litany must often have struck us in church as peculiarly inapplicable to our present conditions.

This would apply with especial emphasis to the prayer, " From lightning and tempest; from plague, pestilence, and famine; from battle and murder, and from sudden death, Good Lord deliver us ". But when we remember that these words were put together for the first Prayer Book of King Edward the Sixth, published in March, 1549, our opinion about their inapplicability should be considerably altered.

The Plague, or Black Death, had never really left this country since it had been introduced from the Continent in 1348. It entered England at a port in Dorsetshire and spread over the whole country during the next year.

So conspicuously was 1349 a "Plague year" that in a certain official document of the 23rd year of the reign of Edward III it is alluded to as "in tempore pestilentiae".

The Plague kept on breaking out from time to time until, after its last explosion in London in 1665, the Great Fire cleared it from the Metropolis for ever.

It can easily be shown that the Plague was a feature of the reign of Henry VIII. For we find constant references to that epidemic disease we call "Bubonic Plague", and now know to be due to infection with a specific bacillus, the *Bacillus Pestis*. It came originally *via* Southern Europe from the East, where it still exists. In Florence it was the occasion of Boccaccio's "Decameron".

It was to escape the Plague of 1665 that Milton left London and went to live in a cottage still standing at Chalfont St Giles in Buckinghamshire, where he wrote much of "Paradise Regained". It was, too, on account of Plague that Newton left Cambridge and, returning to his native Woolsthorpe, saw the apple fall that led to such momentous calculations.

Of course efforts were made to combat the pestilence, but with very little success.

The burning even of various kinds of aromatic wood in the streets had no effect. Attention was early directed to the decomposing garbage and to the filthy state of the streets and their open sewers.

Not for about two hundred years after this date (1525) were the scientific principles of ventilation understood, so that the houses, even of the wealthy, where there was no overcrowding, were lamentably deficient in fresh air. There was a most unfortunate impression abroad that smells were in themselves disease-bringing, and that the air was in itself " pestilential " and ought, therefore, at times to be carefully excluded. Thus Erasmus in one of his letters (undated but written between 1512 and 1515) recommends that the windows of the English houses " be made to fit much more tightly than they do, and that there be no access of noxious winds through gaping seams ". In 1543 the first serious order to have the streets of London cleaned was promulgated. It commanded the killing of dogs, where to-day we should kill the rats.

It is quite interesting to learn that Erasmus highly disapproved of the English houses, as built with too little regard to the aspect of their doors and windows towards the sun. But until well within our own memory this factor was often not reckoned with by architects.

Of course far more important than all these things was the disposal of the bodies of persons dead of the Plague itself. The burial of the dead had for many years before the time of Henry VIII been a serious problem even in the "no-plague" years. The churchyards attached to the London City churches, never large, were constantly being built over as the need for new houses became urgent. New spaces were from time to time acquired, but these had to be attached to the consecrated houses, the monasteries, and the monks came to regard the fees for the burials as an important part of their income. It is therefore evident that the suppression of the monasteries did not tend to improve the public health, however much it may have improved ecclesiastical morality.

During the whole reign of Henry VIII and as late as 1549 the Black Death was a very real and serious happening. Now it was in Henry's reign that the first version of the English Prayer Book made its appearance. It was confessedly to be in harmony with the new views of the Reformers, that is, it was anti-Papal, but the specific mention of Plague is so interesting to us, seeing that this cannot but be an allusion to the Black Death. The Plague had been a scourge from the year of Henry's accession, when it was in Calais as well as in England. In 1511 the mother of Edward V died of it. In 1513 the Venetian ambassador writes home that in London 200 deaths a day are taking place from the Plague, and that it had reached the fleet. In 1515 twenty-seven nuns died of the Plague within a few days in a convent at the Minories. In 1517 the state of matters was worse, for the Plague was now accompanied by the Sweating Sickness or *Sudor Anglicus,* the third visitation of that pestilence since its introduction by the army of King Henry VII in 1485. In October 1517 the Court was still away from London at Windsor, and by November 16 things had become so bad that the Venetian envoy implored the Senate of Venice to allow him to return, as he thought it was time to "escape from sedition, sweat and plague". By "sedition", an Italian writing in 1513 could only have meant the doctrines of the Reformers. On July 22, 1518, the ambassador again asked to be recalled, as two of his servants had died of the Plague, and he himself had had the sweating sickness twice in one week.

In 1529 Campeggio, the papal legate, wrote that the Plague had begun to rage very vigorously. In 1531 the Venetian Ambassador reported 300 to 400 deaths from Plague a week. The summer of 1540 was a sickly one, and a new type of disease, the "hot ague", came to be mentioned; this may have been "the new ague" to which we find a reference in 1537. In 1543 there was a great death (*magna mortalitas*) which lasted so long that the Michaelmas term had to be kept at St Albans.

It is, therefore, perfectly certain that those scholars who composed the first English version of the Litany (1543) had the best of reasons for wishing to be delivered from Plague and pestilence—namely, the presence of the horrors of these all around them.

Now sudden death is one of the characteristics of the Plague. Defoe and all those who have described it have laid stress on this feature. The Plague was sudden in its onset and sudden in its ending. It was the extremely swift course it ran that so terrified all classes alike. In these circumstances it is not at all remarkable that we should find the prayer to be delivered from "sudden death" associated with the prayer to be saved from Plague and pestilence.

In the first Prayer Book of King Edward VI, printed in March, 1549, we can thus perfectly understand why "lightning and tempest" are mentioned in the same prayer as "sudden death", just because they are such preeminently sudden occurrences.

In this connexion it is interesting to read in a document, dated July 18, 1551, preserved in the Calendar of State Papers, the phrase, "the extreme plague of sudden death". It is an order from the King (Edward VI) and his Council to the Bishops commanding them to exhort the people to a diligent attendance at Common Prayer so as to avert the displeasure of Almighty God who has visited the realm "with the extreme plague of sudden death"—the very words of the Prayer Book published only two years before. But these measures do not seem to have produced much result, for Queen Elizabeth, on August 1, 1563, had to appeal directly to the Archbishops of Canterbury and York to give orders for a day of general prayer "on account of the Plague" (Calendar of State papers, Elizabeth, Vol. XXIX, 1563, Aug. 1).

The reference to famine in the Litany is equally interesting. The famines of mediæval England were notorious for severity and frequency. Dr Creighton, in his scholarly "History of Epidemics in Britain", records the occurrence of no fewer than twenty-two great famines in England between A.D. 679 and 1322, or one in about every thirty years. Creighton quotes a well-known proverbial saying of the Middle Ages, "Anglorum fames, Gallorum ignis, Normannorum lepra" (Famine for the English, St Anthony's Fire for the French, and leprosy [or syphilis] for the Normans).

But more than this; besides famines by themselves and pestilences by themselves, there were "famine-pestilences", or pestilences accompanying or immediately following upon famines. The pictures of the "rude plenty" of the tables in the castles of England in the Middle Ages may be true pictures—but of what was in the Baron's Hall, not of the inside of the cottages. The memories of the famines were quite vivid enough to cause those who composed the Litany to mention them when they were thinking of the pestilences to which they were so closely related. Thus " famine " comes to be specifically referred to.

Finally, it is interesting to recall that in its long-forgotten origin, the Litany was closely related to pestilence. So far back as A.D. 590, Pope Gregory I, stirred by pestilence that followed on an inundation of the Tiber, ordered the singing of a special Litany, " litania septiformis ". This form of invocation was a hymn-like prayer in which all the following took part—clergy, laity, monks, virgins, matrons, widows, children, and representatives of the poor. The three days before Ascension, Rogation Days, were to be devoted to the chanting of this Litany. Thus, when in church we hearing the priest asking to be delivered from lightning, plague, pestilence, and sudden death, instead of fixing our attention on the inapplicability of it to our modern life, we might remember that that prayer was composed some two hundred years before lightning-conductors had been devised, and while as yet the soil of England was soaked with the poison of Plague, and its churchyards were overflowing with the bodies of Plague victims.

The Black Death was a sudden *death*; it was in terms of no metaphor that in 1549 people craved to be delivered from it. Only sixty years before, the most deadly Sweating Sickness had been a dreadful epidemic in England, so that most of the divines who drew up the Prayer Book of Edward VI could have remembered the first visitation of one of the worst pestilences that ever visited our shores. They had all lived through a reign, that of Henry the Eighth, scarcely a year of which had been free from the Black Death.

It must therefore have been with a peculiar sense of the nearness and the terrible reality of these things that those good men prayed with poignant and personal supplication to be spared a visitation of " Plague, pestilence, famine, and sudden death ".

CHAPTER IX

ARE WOMEN MORE SENSITIVE THAN MEN?

At one time it was the common belief that women as compared with men were more "sensitive".

It was supposed that they had more delicate sensations, a finer "ear for music", a more perfect appreciation of colour, a more discriminating sense of touch, a more delicate sense of smell than had the coarser creature, man.

When these beliefs came to be tested by the rigorous methods of modern physiological psychology, some of them were found to be far from the truth. At the outset we must distinguish acuteness of sensory perception from emotional affectability. The two things have nothing to do with each other. A person may have the acutest hearing and be as cruel as Nero, or he may be colour-blind and yet exceedingly kind-hearted.

Sensations and emotions are quite distinct

aspects of the mind or consciousness, but, popularly, they have been a good deal confused.

Because women were " delicate ", in that they had smaller bones, weaker muscles, and (it was thought) more easily aroused emotions, they were called more "sensitive" ; but if this means having acuter sensory perceptions, the statement requires to be examined critically. If by sensitive, " fastidious " is meant, it would perhaps be a more correct pronouncement.

Let us in the first place consider the senses of smell and taste so closely associated and yet psychologically quite distinct.

We have only five true tastes : sweet, bitter, acid, alkaline (soapy) and salt ; and these never leave us even when we have a bad cold-in-the-head.

For a cold-in-the-head blocks up our nose, where are found the end-organs for smelling, and so what really vanish are our perceptions of odours and flavours, *smells* in fact, and not tastes at all.

Now women perceive the five true tastes just as perfectly as men do ; but the odours they do not.

The enjoyment of food and cooking is

very largely a matter of the appreciation of these odours and flavours; so that a gourmet is a person who enjoys his food, fruit, wines, etc., because his sense of smell is acute, not because his five true tastes are in any way different from those of other people.

It was long ago pointed out that there is no feminine form of "gourmet", the French apparently assuming that the person who especially appreciates good cooking is a male. Of the word "gourmand" there is a feminine form, a gourmand is merely a person who eats largely.

It is owing, therefore, to a deficient sense of smell that women are not so critical about flavours, odours, "bouquets" of wines, etc., as men are. Thus, too, it comes about that it is always men who are tea-tasters or professional connoisseurs of wines.

It used to be true that the flavour of the tea was better in men's clubs than in women's.

This general impression of the inferior delicacy of the female sense of smell was fully confirmed in an elaborate research done some years ago by two American professors who examined the olfactory sense in a large number of men and women. In this connection we may recall the fact that it is women who are apt to overdo the use of scent, nor does this seem to be a recent failing, for Saint Clement of Alexandria wrote: "Let a few unguents be selected by women such as will not be overpowering to a husband."

The next sense in which women are deficient is the muscular sense or sense of movement and of resistance to muscular effort; it is sometimes called "the sixth sense".

The muscular sense tells us, for instance, just how hard to strike a nail, how much effort is required to twist round various sizes of screws, how heavily we may press on a spring, how powerfully turn a key, and so on.

In particular, as a teacher of practical physiology, I used to note that in those exercises where a long, delicate, easily broken lever of straw with a paper writer on it had to be pressed against a recording surface with just the right amount of pressure, it was always the men who first acquired dexterity in this manipulation. The women broke more of these straw levers during the session, for they pressed the lever either too tightly against the smoked surface or not tightly enough.

For the third and last sense in which women are deficient, let us take the sense of the perception of cold.

It is men who first perceive or complain of a draught. It is a matter of common observation how many fewer clothes women can wear with apparent comfort than can men. At one time this was attributed to the larger amount of fat under the skin, which most women have as compared with men; and while in some cases this may be part of the explanation, it will not account for the thin, spare girls of to-day in their flimsy dresses being quite as comfortable as their plumper sisters of a generation ago.

Cold does not seem to produce such impressions of discomfort in women as it does in men.

And this agrees with that other well-attested fact that women endure pain better, in some cases much better, than men, for the perception of cold and of pain are closely allied.

Thus summing up we may say: women have a less acute sense of smell, of cold, and of muscular sensation.

CHAPTER X

BLAMING THE AIR

"When in doubt" blame the air seems to have been the precept followed by such of mankind as tried to get at the origins of certain things.

Not once or twice in the course of the history of discovery the air has been blamed for ill effects when the source of the trouble was something quite different. There are at least four outstanding examples of this curious mistake: the first when the idea got abroad that malaria was caused by the air or vapours from marshes; the second when night air was thought to be injurious; the third when the oxygen of the air was believed to be the source of the origin of living "germs"; and the last when the air was blamed for the "going bad" of wounds.

The belief that malaria was, as the name indicates, due to "bad air" (Italian, *mal aria*) is a very old one. But we can easily see how it arose, for the source of the scourge seemed to be in the neighbourhood of marshes and damp places. The invariable association of damp air and malaria seemed too obvious to be weakened by the question: How can air, damp or dry, be in itself the source of any disease, seeing that air is the very breath of life?

So firmly was the malign influence of marshes believed in that the term "paludism" (from the Latin *palus*, a marsh) was given to it. We now know that all that marshes have to do with malaria (ague) is to be the places where the mosquitoes breed that carry the parasites of that disease.

Before the discovery of the microscopic causes of a vast number of diseases—most of them made within living memory—it was so very easy to mistake one thing for another as the source of some particular kind of mischief. The search for causes, which is science, is notoriously difficult, and before one has got a clue, it is very easy to be misled. Damp air seemed always associated with ague, therefore as vapours and nothing else could be *seen*, the damp air was credited with the mischief. It was entirely false; damp air may predispose to illness, but neither vapour nor air of itself is the specific origin of any disease.

The next example is the notion that night air is bad. Until quite recently this was firmly believed. As in most errors, there is a germ of truth in it. During the night, living vegetation exhales carbonic acid gas, and this same substance is one of the waste-products of animal breathing. Carbonic acid gas has long been regarded as poisonous to animals. It is the old story of calling a thing a poison, and then regarding it as such in all dilutions.

Alcohol is a "poison"; above a certain concentration it is thoroughly injurious; below a certain dilution it is anything from a stimulant to a negligible quantity. The idea that night air is bad arose from an injudicious and, indeed, erroneous remark of the Dutchman, Ingenhouz, who in 1779 discovered the fact that during the hours of darkness plants exhale carbonic acid gas. So they do, but not in such a concentration so as to harm either men or animals.

The third example of supposing that the air was the source of some particular thing when that was something totally different is in connection with the origin of life itself.

It is not so very long ago that the great controversy whether life can arise from the non-living was closed. The dispute in its final stages became narrowed down to the problem whence arose the living things that undoubtedly were found growing in carefully sealed-up flasks of organic material put aside for a day or two in a warm place. Before the microscope was applied to the problem, it could not be known that " the life " in these flasks consisted in myriads of extremely minute organisms—the micro-organisms of putrefaction—having gained access to the putrescible material and continued to live in it.

It all looked as though the air was to blame, for if the flask of broth was left open to the air, life appeared in the broth ; and even if the air in the flask was corked up there were still evidences of vitality in the organic contents. The air seemed to have been the cause of the living things.

But in reality it was not so ; after a long and bitter controversy it was shown that air from which everything had been filtered off through cotton-wool, or which had been passed through a red-hot tube, would not give rise to life in the flask.

It was the mistaking of one thing for another—mistaking the carrier of the living things for the things themselves. The oxygen of the air does indeed support life, but it can no more give rise to life than can any other gas or mixture of gases.

The fourth attempt to blame the air was in connection with the introduction of antiseptic surgery. It had for long been a familiar observation that wounds exposed to the air—and more particularly to indoor air—"went bad". This exposure to the air—especially hospital air—as we now know, meant exposure to dust and the invisible microbes; but before Lister applied the microscope to this problem, the true cause of wounds "going bad" was not suspected. The air as usual was blamed for the frequently disastrous condition of open sores.

With infinite patience Lister showed that it was not the air but what it held that was to be blamed, not what it was but what it carried that was objectionable. Under the microscope Lister beheld the minute cellular forms which were causing the pus to putrefy, and so once again the air was exonerated.

We now know that pure air is very beneficial to wounds; like all living things, wounds are the better of fresh air. On high mountains and in the germ-free air of the ocean surgeons know well that wounds heal rapidly.

Lastly, fresh outside air was at one time actually supposed to be detrimental to people suffering from consumption of the lungs; so these unfortunate ones were shut up in hot rooms from which fresh air was excluded. To leave phthisical people sitting out-of-doors, as is done to-day, was not so very many years ago regarded as a species of murder.

As far back as 1840, Dr George Bodington, of Sutton Coldfield, published his "Essay on the Treatment of Pulmonary Consumption", in which he pointed out the advantages of dry, cool air for closing and healing cavities and ulcers of the lung. But like all new things it was resisted: Dr Garrison, in his "History of Medicine", tells us that "Bodington's theory was so roughly handled by the medical critics of his day that he was discouraged from carrying it into practice to any extent".

The pioneer painfully smooths a path which others who follow him tread in comparative comfort.

CHAPTER XI

HEATING AND VENTILATING THE HOUSE

Two Age-long Problems

It would be safe to say that most people confuse ventilation with heating. They assume that because a hall, room, or railway carriage is cold it must be well ventilated, and, conversely, that because any of these is warm it must be badly ventilated.

But a room may be warm and well ventilated, or it may be cold and badly ventilated. From the standpoint of physics the two problems—how to heat and how to ventilate—are quite distinct.

To heat a room is to bring the temperature of the air in it to such a degree that it is not "chilly" (unpleasantly cool) to a person in indoor clothing at rest in that room.

To ventilate a room is to provide for the ingress of pure out-of-door air, and the egress of used air *without* a *draught.*

A draught is air in motion taking heat from the skin so rapidly that it is unpleasant, and may be dangerous to health. Any one can ventilate a room by creating a draught; all he has to do is to open the door and the window, when the air is more or less rapidly blown out of the room (perflation). But, except for a short time, no one could endure that draught; only the most fanatical fresh air "fiend" would enjoy it.

We are not contemplating the pleasant draughts so desired in the tropics, and occasionally during an English summer, but the ordinary, every-day rush of low temperature air chilling the skin and often predisposing to definite illness. It would seem that women are much less sensitive than men to draughts and cold generally. Their cold-perceiving nerves seem less acute. Thinly clad, they can endure without apparent discomfort degrees of cold that to the mere man would be quite intolerable. Many of them, as we know, enjoy sitting in a railway carriage facing the engine with the full blast of the cold air rushing on to them.

The pleasantest room is that where the incoming air is fresh, directly derived from out of doors and somehow heated to a temperature of about 65° F. This will not disagreeably cool the skin of a healthy person inactive in that room.

Now in the vast majority of cases, the ordinary open coal fire does not fulfil these conditions, for although it does change the air efficiently, it heats it very poorly. It is estimated that from 60 to 90 per cent. of the heat of the domestic fire rushes up the chimney, the remainder being radiated into the room. This radiated portion warms any solid objects it may encounter, and after a long time the air is warmed by contact with these. But all the time the air so slowly warmed is tending to flow up the chimney.

Thus it is that a person facing a fire may have his face and hands scorched, while his back is kept quite cold by the draught. In other words, the old-fashioned English open fire ventilates well from the first, but heats poorly later on.

Its other drawbacks—the cost of coal, dust, cinders, smoking chimneys, the cleaning of grates and flues, and the occurrence of fogs in cities—are, in the well-known phrase, " too familiar to mention".

Now it is supposed that the Americans and Canadians have solved the problem of heating a building by the method of having hot water or steam circulating continuously through metal pipes called "radiators" which yield their heat directly to the air of the room. It is quite true that the air can be heated in this way to temperatures far above 65° F., to 70°, 75°, or 80° F., as may be desired.

But most people from Great Britain find these higher temperatures distinctly disagreeable, largely because the air so heated is not also being removed. Naturally the coils provide neither for the incoming of fresh air nor the outgoing of used air.

A great many bedrooms on the American continent are not provided with fireplaces, flues, or other apertures to afford escape of the tainted air, which, so long stagnant, acquires a "stuffy", disagreeable odour.

On many winter days the windows, which are often "double", cannot be opened, because the very cold air rushing in would freeze the water in the coils.

It is true that in some of the better-constructed houses the two systems—open fires and hot water pipes—are employed, and little fault can be found with such an arrangement.

But in a very large number of Canadian

houses the bedrooms are not provided with open grates, and hence the anomaly of the prevalence of tuberculosis in a country of vast unoccupied spaces, for tuberculosis is pre-eminently a bedroom disease.

The system of central heating as usually installed does not provide for the changing of the air. Architects know well that if we provide for the exit of the used air, the incoming air will look after itself; if, now, we warm this latter, then we have solved the age-long problem of heating and ventilating.

However well warmed the ordinary brick house may be, it is rather wasteful of heat, for brick allows heat to escape faster than stone does. Wet bricks are particularly bad in this respect.

One of the latest devices for keeping houses warm is to use hollow bricks; the air inside them, being a bad conductor of heat, conserves the heat of the house to a very considerable extent. Air-filled spaces are also used in the latest type of house, where the walls are constructed of hollow concrete blocks.

The utilization of this principle does not seem to be any discovery of our own time, for the Romans certainly used hollow bricks in their buildings.

We may see some of these hollow bricks amongst the ruins of the Roman baths at Bath, and amongst the *débris* of camps and villas erected during the Roman occupation of Britain.

The Romans seem to have understood the economical use of heat, and also to have known how to heat their houses by a method much superior to that of the open fire. They heated *the floor first.* They built the floor over a space, the hypocaust, so that hot air from a fire or furnace could be made to traverse this space below the floor. Thus the room was heated from the floor upwards; and it is well known that if our feet are warm we do not feel cold, but if our feet are cold, then no matter how warm the rest of us may be, we cannot feel comfortable. Fine examples of hypocaust have recently been unearthed at Folkestone.

This warming of the floor from below is obviously quite different from the sending up of hot air through gratings in the floor, as we often see done in cathedrals and other large buildings. This is called heating by convection. It is a wasteful method, for the heated air rushes up past the people towards the roof, so that the atmosphere far above their heads gets heated first.

In the new cathedral at Liverpool the Roman method of heating the *floor* by hot air has been adopted.

A system of heating has been devised which has overcome most of the objections to all other systems. It consists in embedding the hot water pipes in the floors, walls or ceilings, so that these large surfaces, soon becoming warm, radiate their heat into the rooms.

In this—the so-called "panel" system—the air itself is not used as a medium of heat transmission, so that it is possible to ventilate the building without an undue loss of heat.

These coils can be placed below floors of every kind of material—wood, marble, slate, tiles or mosaic work.

The stuffy smell of warm rooms is due to the volatilizing of organic dust; in the panel system this dust does not become disintegrated to anything like the extent that it undergoes over exposed hot water coils. Thus it is that buildings heated on the panel system have so little of the stuffy smell characteristic of most hot rooms.

Heating by gas is, of course, much cleaner than by coal, but the gas-fire comes under the same condemnation as the coal-fire, in that it is better as a ventilator than as a heater of a room, and this only when it is connected with a properly constructed flue. The idea that gas-fires are unhealthy is quite a mistaken one: provided that the products of combustion are removed, the gas-fire is as "healthy" as the coal fire.

One reason why the British find the air of rooms heated by hot pipes disagreeable is that such air tends to become much too dry. In too few instances do we find the "harmless necessary" vessel of water provided. The water evaporating into the air makes it comfortable for breathing. Air that is too dry irritates the throat and lungs, inducing the catarrh from which, as is well known, so many of our American friends suffer.

The latest source of heat is electricity; in that it does not consume the oxygen of the air, it is an excellent one, and it may be quite inexpensive if it be produced by water power instead of the combustion of coal. Electric heaters can be employed to heat the incoming air in a much more convenient fashion than can coal or gas. Better still, electrically-heated wires, etc., can be buried under the floors, in the walls, or in the ceilings, thus allowing these large surfaces to become true radiators of heat.

To conclude, then, a perfect system of heating and ventilating in winter is one which provides for the inflow of pure, out-of-doors air warmed to at least 65° F., and subsequently, if necessary, moistened, but not saturated with vapour, the used air being finally discharged into the ocean of the atmosphere.

CHAPTER XII

PHYSIOLOGY AND "VITAL FORCE"

EFFORTS in the past to account for the mysterious powers and properties of living beings have in the main consisted of bringing in some supra-sensible, immaterial, ultra-cognizable "principle" or "entity". This has been known under different names as time went on, but they have all referred to the same thing—psyche, pneuma, the anima sensitiva of Van Helmont, the life principle of Stahl, the Bildungstrieb of Blumenbach, the vita propria of Bordeu, the vitalis agens of Barthez, the Lebenskraft of Reil, the entelechy of Driesch, the elan vital of Bergson, and the biotic energy of Moore. It is of the essence of "vitalism" to explain life in terms of the less known, to account for the properties of a living being by the indwelling activity of an entity, agent, or force which, by its very metaphysical nature, is inaccessible to human investigation.

To assert that each organ, tissue, and cell is as truly alive as is the whole organism is not "vitalism", but a correct physiological observation, for the isolated organ—heart or liver—can perform its vital functions long after separation from the body to which it belonged; and as Ross Harrison and Carrel have proved, the cell taken from its tissue can live for years in its morphological isolation. To say these organs have an independent life (whether it is said in English or in Latin, *vita propria*), is to report an observation; to say that life is due to a "life force" or "entelechy" is to state a theory.

If the vitalists had always been careful to admit that their view was only a theory of life, much acrimonious discussion would have been avoided; but when they declared that theirs was the only right view, their virtual claim to omniscience failed to arouse in many minds the enthusiasm expected. These unconvinced people tried to explain life in terms of what they knew at least a little about—the non-living world around them; and they were in consequence called "materialists" and their theory "mechanistic". Now theirs is a theory no less than is the vitalistic. The materialistic theory is that the observed known—the properties and behaviour of living organisms—may be explained by applying to them our knowledge of the laws and properties appertaining to the non-living world. It is an explanation of the known in terms of the more known rather than the less.

The term "materialist" ought not to be used as one of reproach; the materialist is almost always a sincere searcher after truth, who, starting from his colleague the physicist's knowledge of the properties and behaviour of *non*-living matter, attempts to apply these to the behaviour of living matter. He finds that many of the laws that hold good in the world of the non-living seem to be equally applicable to that of life. In particular, he finds that vital heat, for example, is not in its essence different from heat of non-vital origin, that the great generalization of the conservation of energy holds good for the mammalian body, that "vital" processes are accelerated by a rise, and retarded by a fall, of temperature exactly like "purely" chemical reactions in a test-tube. He is able to say in the language of his chemical colleagues that living matter (protoplasm) behaves in many respects like an irreversible colloidal emulsoid hydrosol.

The materialist found, as a matter of fact, that so many vital activities seemed to be the outcome of the operation of laws already proved true for the non-living universe, that he finally made so bold as to assert—and here he made the first mistake—that the mystery had vanished, and that protoplasm, chemically speaking, was only an excessively complicated form of matter. To this view Loeb committed himself. He wished us to believe that he had proved that the dividing line between the non-living and the living had been removed, and that we might pass by a number of gradations from physico-chemical simplicity at one end of the series to great physico-chemical complexity at the other. Somewhere on the way one passed from the non-living to the living. Here the materialist went beyond what his premises allowed him; in this he was rash; but rashness inheres in the enthusiasm of youth, and biology is a very young science.

But the vitalist, too, had always been rash, for he had the boldness to go beyond experience. He had asserted, for instance, that urea and sugar could never be made without the agency of life, because he had never found these substances anywhere except in living animal or vegetable tissues. When, therefore, in 1828 Wöhler made urea in a test-tube, and in the 'eighties of last century Fischer synthesised sugars, and when indigo was produced that had never seen a plant, and when the hormone adrenalin was constructed artificially, vitalism received a set-back, and materialism a corresponding encouragement. The anti-vitalistic view was further strengthened by the discovery that many ferments, solely the products of life, dealt with their "substrates" exactly like the inorganic catalysts so well known to chemists. Finally, when Loeb, by altering either the density or composition of sea-water, caused the unfertilized eggs of the sea-urchin to begin to undergo development, the days of vitalism seemed numbered.

The materialist has, indeed, shown us how the plant is able to synthesise a carbohydrate from carbon dioxide and water through the stage of formaldehyde; but he himself is very far indeed from making a scrap of nucleated protoplasm, and until he does that, since we know no life apart from nuclei, it seems exceedingly improbable that he will be able to synthesise any kind of living substance. The materialist goes far beyond his observations when he maintains that the laws of the non-living world are the only laws which operate in the sphere of the living. It is one thing for them to operate there, it is another for them to operate *alone*.

Life and living things are *sui generis*. It is better to admit at once that, so far as our experience goes up to this hour, life is unique. Prof. J. A. Thomson gives the following features of the uniqueness of living matter thus (Gifford Lectures, St Andrew's, 1915-6)—

1. Its capacity for enregistering experience which, in the hereditary relation, is an expression of physiological inertia.

2. The self-maintaining tendency of the organism.

3. Its variability, or the capacity to give origin to the new.

Living matter can do what no non-living matter can—assimilate material wholly unlike itself; evolve from a minute and relatively homogeneous speck into an obvious and heterogeneous organism; reproduce its kind either by casting off buds or by gametes; pass through a life-cycle of irreversible stages, from infancy to youth, maturity, senescence, and death.

So far as we can judge, the higher animals possess a variety of energy, nerve-energy, which also is *sui generis*. Finally, in the realm of the living we encounter those phenomena called "subjective", the world of consciousness with all its modes—sensation, emotion, volition—a world which, so far as we know, never exists apart from living matter, and is absolutely unique.

Certain critical vitalists sometimes blame physiologists for investigating living things by the methods of chemistry and physics. The late Sir James Mackenzie wrote (*British Medical Journal*, March 1, 1924): "Physiologists place the organ in artificial conditions, employ artificial stimulation and obtain artificial results . . . such as the all-or-nothing law".

Now this criticism is rather hard to bear, because we have no methods or apparatus other than these "artificial" ones. Although the biologist is investigating phenomena that are *sui generis*, he has unfortunately no apparatus which is adapted exclusively to biological use. The physiologist uses test-tubes, retorts, induction-coils, and galvanometers because there are no two kinds of instruments, one for biologists, and one for physicists. It is rather hard that, having been forced to use these things and having by so doing obtained results valuable to medicine, he should be stigmatized as a materialist.

When we speak of " the mechanism " of gastric digestion, we merely use the expression as a conveniently short one for all those processes which are involved in the vital manufacture of pepsin and hydrochloric acid from neutral blood, their separation through and by the mucous membrane, and their solvent action upon food in the interior of the viscus. Nothing more " mechanical " is meant than this, and this is not mechanical at all. Only the last process, the solution of the protein, can go on *in vitro* ; only life can manufacture pepsin from blood, or an acid from alkaline or neutral salts, and separate these without digesting the wall of the stomach in the very act itself. It is most unfortunate that anything to do with a machine should be mentioned in this connection.

Because the stomach " works " rhythmically and predictably we may call it a machine for turning out pepsin from blood, and liken it to a machine for turning out (say) newspapers, but the secretion of pepsin is not mechanical, nor is the output of newspapers vital. Processes that closely resemble each other are not necessarily identical. In a decerebrated animal the same predictable reflex action can be obtained time after time from the same stimulus, and we may speak of the inevitableness of "the mechanism" of reflex arcs, but in no other sense is the spinal cord a machine.

Non-vitalistic physiologists are blamed not merely for speaking of organs and organisms as machines, but also for daring to study organs and systems by themselves, whereby, it is alleged, they have lost sight of the wonderfully co-ordinated activities of the animal as a whole.

It would seem that the physiologists can never do anything right; at a time when nothing was known of the heart, or of the liver, or of the retina, what else could the investigator do than confine his attention to one thing at a time? Some of us, indeed, are trying to take a comprehensive synthetic outlook over the whole field of vitality, but that could not have been done by the pioneers, who could only push their way slowly into an unknown territory.

One would infer from the obituary notice of the late Sir James Mackenzie in *The Times* (January 27, 1925) that physiology is bankrupt. Sir James is quoted as having said: "When this" [his own view of physiology] "is realized, the whole of the physiological interpretation of the functional activities of organs will have to be scrapped. This is one of the results that I anticipate".

The physiological methods by which were discovered the localization of cerebral function, reciprocal innervation, the endocrine function of the adrenals, the thyroid gland, and the pituitary, by which insulin was isolated and adrenalin synthesised, cannot be discredited.

The experimental work of Schafer, Bayliss, Starling, Sherrington, Pavlov, MacLeod, and the Hills is not only not to be scrapped, but is frankly to be recognized as the logical modern basis of practical medicine. The researches that led up to electrocardiography, with which Sir James Mackenzie himself was so conspicuously associated, are another illustration. From some of his expressions the incautious reader might suppose that current physiology was useless as an introduction to medicine, and that the secret of success in diagnosis and treatment consisted in the reinstating of a "vital force". Mackenzie, writing in the *British Medical Journal* (March 1, 1924), thus expressed himself: "The reason for the lack of progress in respect of [knowledge of] living matter has been the absence of a knowledge of a vital force!" The whole tenor of this paper is that we must distrust the results of "artificial" stimulation of tissues because the effects of these are not normal, are not the same as those produced by the "vital force". The experimenter, in fact, comes under a heavy condemnation. We are further told that because we do not better understand pain and why certain reflexes occur, this "vital force" must be postulated.

The term "impulse" plays a large part in this neophysiology. We are told: "Where a cell discharges its energy in the shape of its peculiar [? particular] function, it at the same time discharges an impulse". We must know, therefore, where in the conceptual scheme of things, which has served physiology so well for the last thirty years, we can place this all-important "impulse".

As regards protoplasm three concepts are fundamental—(*a*) its affectability (irritability), (*b*) the stimulus that may operate upon it, and (*c*) its own response. The behaviour of a living efferent nerve may best illustrate the relations between the members of this biologic trinity. The neuroplasm, in virtue of its possessing the property of responding to a stimulus (affectability), and having received a stimulus, responds by giving rise to an excited state which travels down the nerve as the impulse to the effector organ at the periphery, say a muscle, which twitches when the impulse impinges on it.

Let us suppose that the stimulus is a blow on the nerve, or a pinching of it, seeing that the electric stimulus of the induction coil was regarded so unfavourably by Mackenzie. Of course the existence of this impulse is an inference from what happens: a nerve receives a blow at one end and a muscle twitches at the other; something must have passed down the nerve, and that something we have for a long time called the impulse. It is said to travel down the nerve by reason of the nerve possessing conductivity.

The other indication that something is passing along the nerve is that if a galvanometer be substituted for the muscle, then when a blow is given to the nerve, the galvanometer records the presence, for a very short time, of an electric disturbance in the nerve. We infer that this electric current is an outward and visible sign of the existence of the invisible nerve-impulse. But just here a very important conclusion is reached, namely, that the impulse in the nerve on arriving at the muscle is for the muscle a stimulus to it to "contract"; the impulse in the living nerve can, then, an instant later, be the stimulus for the living muscle, the response of which is a state of shortening or contraction.

We infer that in the intact animal the nerves are conveying impulses normal or homologous, exactly similar to our laboratory ones, because if a nerve *in situ*, for example the phrenic, is connected to a galvanometer, electric currents in this case also are seen to pass through that instrument. These natural (normal) impulses must be the natural (normal) stimuli for the muscles *in situ*.

All this is very elementary; but it is evidently necessary to restate it because it accounts for everything that Mackenzie observed without calling in the aid of a "vital force" at all. We fail completely to see where and why this force needs to be invoked, and why physiology is bankrupt if it is not so introduced.

If this "vital force" is another name for the nerve-impulse—and it can scarcely be synonymous with either "stimulus" or "response"—then it is a superfluous term. If it is not a synonym for any of the three, then it is some fourth thing for which apparently there is no place in the scheme which has served biology so well in the past. The neo-physiologist may reply: it *is* a synonym for the nerve-impulse, but it comprehends "impulses" in all other tissues. Mackenzie's own words, in a paragraph headed "The *impulse* a *vital force*", were: "An impulse is the product of cell-activity, it can only be conveyed by living structures and acts by stimulating cells to discharge their function . . . it differs from all other forces".

If the impulse in this passage be confined to *nerve*-impulse, no fault can be found with it, for the nerve-impulse is the product of (nerve) cell activity, it can be conveyed only by the living structures of the nerve, it acts by stimulating (muscle) cells to discharge their function (of shortening), and it differs from all other forces in that, as a nerve-impulse, it is *sui generis*. But why declare that unless we call this impulse a "vital force", physiology is to be discredited ("scrapped")?

We do not need an additional name for the nerve-impulse; if we are forced to give it a new name, why give it one so redolent of obscurantist animism?

It is, however, quite clear that by "impulse" Mackenzie meant something that was active in all the tissues, for he speaks of *cells* in the widest sense. Now what are these impulses in tissues other than neural? What impulses are there in muscle, connective tissue, gland, fat, bone? In muscle we have states of contraction; and we can *call* them "impulses" if that will rescue physiology from the scrap-heap, but one fails to see what is gained thereby. As for "impulses" in connective tissue, fat, or bone, we have no evidence of them. In glands, doubtless, some states of excitation can travel (slowly) along, but again we see no benefit from calling them "impulses".

It is difficult to see, therefore, why physiology is to be declared as proceeding on a totally wrong road. It may frankly be admitted that there is in physiology more than is dreamed of by the mechanistic philosophy. The laws of matter that has never lived have failed so far to account for certain facts, for example, about absorption both from intestine and bladder, and for certain facts about urinary secretion. It has been shown that living membranes act very differently from dead ones.

The materialistic view of life has failed signally to account for certain realities of our experience of which consciousness is the group name. Huxley himself made his bow to consciousness and waived it away as an epi-phenomenon. For the materialist, consciousness cannot be a cause of neural activity ; nor can states of body affect mind, for mind is an illusion. The mechanistic theories are incapable of throwing any light on the central fact of experience, the permanence of personality amid the flux of matter.

Prof. Haldane has well said that "living" and "mind" are not reducible to simpler terms ; they are the axioms of biology ; and this thinker firmly believes that physiology is being retarded by mechanistic conceptions which deprive us of a complete view of life. As Prof. J. A. Thomson has said:[1] "We need new concepts such as that of the organism as a historic being which has traded with time". "We need these new concepts because there are new facts to describe, which we cannot analyse away into so-called simpler processes."

The most reasonable position to assume as regards vitalism is to insist that there is no compulsion for the biologist to be either a "materialist" or a "vitalist". It is quite open to him to say that as he is dealing with an order of things that is unique, with existences that are *sui generis*, and that as his science is so young, he is not yet in a position to dogmatize and declare that *qua* life there are no categories beyond those which the physicists and the chemists recognize.

Of all the many wise things Prof. Thomson said in his Gifford Lectures at St Andrews (*loc. cit.* vol. 2, p. 147), this is surely one of the wisest: "We regard the question as one of the many *false dichotomies* with which man in his search for clearness has been led astray".

[1] "System of Animate Nature" (Williams and Norgate, vol. 2, p. 160).

CHAPTER XIII

THE PLACE AND POWER OF THE NERVOUS SYSTEM AND ITS RELATION TO THE MIND

THE nervous system may be studied under all of the following aspects, namely, in its development both in the individual and throughout the animal kingdom, in its naked eye appearances, in its microscopic structure and finally in regard to its functional activity in health and disease.

The unaided eye can see that it consists of a long central axis called the spinal cord within the vertebral column becoming much thicker as it enters the skull where it is known as the Medulla Oblongata. This part is continued along the base of the skull and is, in man, completely covered over by a great development of what is called the grey matter of the cerebral hemispheres. In the central nervous axis arise all the outgoing or motor nerves of the body, 9 pairs from origins within the skull, and 31 pairs from the spinal cord. Similarly all ingoing or sensory nerve-fibres traverse the central axis on their way into the nervous system.

Under the microscope the " grey matter " is seen to consist of multitudes of nerve-cells, minute living units possessing all possible shapes from a simple sphere to a most complicated figure. The most elaborate forms are in the grey matter of the surface of the hemispheres, a portion called the cortex cerebri. This is significant, for we shall see that here, where the structure is most complicated, the functions are of the highest order. The fish, for instance, has no cortex cerebri : its " mind " is of the simplest.

Every nerve-fibre (white matter) takes its origin in a nerve-cell : there is no such thing as a nerve-cell without a related fibre or a fibre without a " trophic " nerve-cell. Indeed, fibres die if cut away from their related cells. The whole structure, cell-processes and fibre, is now known as a " neuron ".

The nerves may be functionally divided into two great groups—the efferent or those arising in the central nervous axis and ending in the tissues, and those which do just the reverse. The efferent or motor nerves supply the body-muscles including the heart, the muscles of the blood-vessels, the iris of the eye and the muscle of the intestinal tract; they supply the glands of the mouth, the stomach, the intestines, and the great gland, the pancreas, and finally they supply the kidneys and the reproductive organs.

The second great group of nerves is the sensory, those arising in the skin and in the end-organs of the special senses including those of muscles. A great many nerves, which come from the internal organs, are not related to any definite sensation but are only occasionally in activity as nerves of pain. Nerve-fibres are exclusively conductors; they originate nothing, they only conduct nerve-impulses either outwards to tissues or inwards to the central nervous system. The essential structures in the central nervous system are Nerve-Centres—anatomically larger or smaller masses of nerve-cells.

A " centre " is a group of nerve-cells specialized to control or supervise some definite physiological activity in the body. This presiding over a function is called " innervation ", that is, being attended to by the nervous system. As a definite example we might take the respiratory centre in the Medulla. At a certain definite rhythm this centre emits salvos of nerve-impulses to the diaphragm and the other muscles of breathing. In man in health this rhythm is from 18 to 20 in the minute.

The centre, which is bilateral, occupies a relatively small region in the Medulla, so that a quite circumscribed injury here will at once arrest the breathing. It is the sudden destruction of this centre which is the cause of death by hanging. Although the respiratory centre seems to be working all by itself or " automatically ", as we call it, a little study will convince us that the centre is accessible to influences from widely separated regions of the body.

In the first place, if we cut the great nerves coming up from the lungs to the respiratory centre, we shall find the rhythm of breathing to be greatly altered. The animal now breathes very much more slowly, although correspondingly deeply, from which we infer that, in the intact condition, the movements of the lungs themselves are in some way able to accelerate the rather slow inherent rhythm of the centre for breathing. But further, impulses from the skin and from the internal organs can also influence it. A dash of cold water on the skin will cause a gasp followed for a short time by a stoppage of the breathing, while severe abdominal pain will alter the breathing to quite a shallow type.

Let us next consider a far more familiar experience. If we so wish it, we can voluntarily hurry up the rate of our breathing, or on the other hand we can slow it or stop it (for a time) altogether. In physiological language this is that from the cerebrum, volitional impulses are stimulating and inhibiting, respectively, the functional activity of the respiratory centre. Besides volitional influences, the emotions are equally potent in affecting the centre for breathing. Pleasant emotions, particularly in children, can accelerate the breathing; while powerful and terrifying conditions can arrest it altogether, as the phrase goes, " it quite took my breath away ".

Finally the chemical composition and the temperature of the blood traversing the centre are both able to influence the centre directly. Increases of the carbon dioxide and of the heat of the blood increase the depth and the rate of the breathing.

Thus we may infer, surveying all this evidence, that the nervous system is for the purpose of bringing rapidly one portion of the body into relation with another, in fact co-ordinating them. Some other centres in the Medulla and adjacent part of the central axis are for the control of the heart, of the diameter of the blood-vessels, for the production of saliva, gastric juice, and pancreatic juice, for the movements of the stomach and intestine, for vomiting, for the movements of the iris (pupil), and for perspiration. The centres for muscles of articulation in the lips, cheeks, tongue, palate and larynx are also found in this region of the grey matter of the central nervous axis.

Broadly speaking there are two great types of activity in the nervous system, that of the reflex action which does not require consciousness for its performance, and the type where consciousness, either as sensation, volition or emotion, is of the essence of the action.

The reflex is the primitive or fundamental type of action, the earliest both in the life history of the individual and of the animal series.

A reflex action on the structural side involves a sensory nerve, a centre and a motor nerve, such a path being called a " reflex nerve-arc ".

The newly born child is a bundle of reflexes and automatic actions. Put to the breast, it sucks reflexly, and will do so even though its cerebral hemispheres are absent (" acephalic monster "). Reflex actions are elicitable from every portion of the central nervous axis.

The contraction of the pupil when light enters the eye is a reflex carried out from an anterior portion, flushing from heat or blanching from cold is carried out at a lower level, while the jerking of the feet when the soles of the feet are tickled is a reflex concerned with the lowest part of the spinal cord. Our reflexes are literally too numerous to mention.

One characteristic of the reflex action is that the will has no control over it.

When grit gets into the eye, the " eye " waters, that is, the lachrymal gland secretes tears in spite of all our desires to the contrary; when the dentist probes the gums with one of his instruments, the saliva flows in spite of our urgent wish to stop it.

The reflex action is outside our control; we are not responsible for it, it occurs within us but we are not accountable for it; it is physiological activity but not "behaviour".

The other group of actions besides the reflexes is that of those activities of the nervous system which *are* related to consciousness.

The cerebral hemispheres are undoubtedly the physical basis of consciousness; when they are active, consciousness is present, when they are inactive, as in sleep and chemically-induced anæsthesia, consciousness vanishes. The proofs that the cellular elements of the cortex cerebri are the physical substratum of the mind, the material basis of psychical states, are derived from experimental physiology, from a study of the development of the nervous system and from clinical medicine and surgery.

From the remotest antiquity, the powers of the mind have been believed to be related to the brain within the skull. But it is only quite recently in the history of scientific discovery that specific proof has been forthcoming. Complete removal of the brain (which is possible in some animals) reduces them to a state of utter mindlessness; they become inert automata, they feel nothing, they desire nothing, they originate nothing.

It is actually only a little more than fifty

years ago that experimental proof was given that the cortex cerebri *is* the physical basis of sensations and of the origination of all bodily movements. The man who first proved these things was Sir David Ferrier, F.R.S., a Scotsman, long Professor of Neurology at King's College, London. Having (under anæsthetics) exposed the living cortex in one of the higher apes, Ferrier applied the interrupted electric current to the surface of one hemisphere and at once obtained movements of muscles on the opposite side of the body. These were of such a kind as to suggest voluntary actions, had the animal been fully conscious. This representation in the brain of the muscular movements of the body was found to be surprisingly detailed. The converse experiment showed that excision of the area " for " a group of muscles brought on paralysis of that group. Naturally these " motor areas " are often called " Ferrier's areas ".

Ferrier also investigated the central representation of the senses; and in spite of the manifest difficulty of interpreting the signs of an animal's sensations, he succeeded in discovering the localization of the centres for sight and for hearing.

There is no doubt at all that the sense of vision is located in the occipital lobes at the back of the brain, and the sense of hearing at the sides below the temporal bone. Electrical stimulation of the occipital lobes makes an animal turn its eyes about and evince all the signs of seeing something; while stimulation of the temporal lobes makes it prick up its ears and turn its head as though it heard something and wished to hear it better. Human experiences have fully corroborated animal experimentation.

Thus if a tumour presses on the visual centres, the patient may in consequence have visual hallucinations. When as the result of an injury or a wound in war, the occipital lobes are blown away, the man is completely blind although his eyes and their nerves are uninjured. Similarly, if a person has a tumour growing in his temporal lobes, he is liable to hear sounds and voices (auditory hallucinations), a state of things not uncommon in the insane. Finally, if by disease his temporal lobes are destroyed, he will thenceforth be permanently deaf.

When the human brain has been mapped out into its motor and sensory areas, there are left over some comparatively large regions which seem to be neither one nor other.

They are the " association centres ", largest in the human brain, smaller in the higher mammals, and non-existent in still lower types. These are the last parts of the brain to assume their functional activity. They are interesting to the psychologist because they constitute the basis of thought, emotion, volition, speech and memory. They are neither sensory nor motor but higher than both ; they act as co-ordinating centres between these others, receiving impulses from the sensory and emitting them to the motor.

The speech-centres, which are very large in man, are the most important of our association centres. Speech is an intellectual activity which requires an elaborate material substratum. It requires centres in which the memories of both heard and seen words are stored ; these inform the motor speech-centre which in its turn innervates the motor areas (Ferrier's) which finally actuate the muscular mechanisms whereby speech is made articulate.

Thus the cerebrum is the organ of the mind, the physical basis of personality. It is the only organ to which we find consciousness always related. This relationship is remarkable; for whereas it would seem that every conscious state is dependent upon an underlying cerebral condition, yet it appears to be a fact that there can be cerebral activity without the arousing of consciousness. "Unconscious cerebration" would seem to be a case in point. And further, a multitude of experiences can be stored in the potentiality of the subconscious mind.

The modifications of the cerebral substance necessary for the enregistering of conscious experiences have been conveniently called "engrams". These are the permanent material differentiations in the neurons of the cerebrum which are specific and essential for each memory. The longer they have been laid down, the more deeply are they engraved, so that the old man who forgets the events of yesterday can relate to you with perfect detail what happened in his boyhood, for—

> Time but the impression stronger makes,
> As streams their channels deeper wear.

CHAPTER XIV

WHAT THE MICROSCOPE HAS ACHIEVED FOR MANKIND

MOST people have a very hazy idea of the vast extension of knowledge for which science is indebted to the microscope. It should be interesting to recount just what that instrument has enabled us to understand.

In the first place, by the aid of the microscope it was established that a living thing always proceeds from a living thing; that life invariably comes from life.

In all those cases where living things have apparently arisen in liquids without other living things preceding them, the microscope has shown that some—no matter how few—living things were there before. The problem of the arising of life from non-life had narrowed itself down to such a case as this: if a putrescible fluid, broth or milk, be allowed to stand uncovered for a few days, a drop of it viewed under the microscope will be seen to be swarming with minute vegetable organisms popularly called the "germs" of decomposition; but if a similar quantity of the liquid has been boiled and at once protected from the air, then no living things will be found to be growing in the liquid.

In all cases where an observer had believed that he had seen living things which had arisen from non-living material, the microscope was able to show that he had not previously destroyed all the life originally in the liquid, or that he had subsequently allowed the entrance of dust into his "sterilized" liquid. The microscope is always the ultimate court of appeal in such cases, and its verdict is invariably—no life except from life!

This does not mean that at some time in the past, life may not have originated from the non-living, or that in the future some man of science may not be able to bring about this emergence, but it asserts as a matter of fact that in the experience of such men life has never so arisen. Technically put, it is that in our experience there is always biogenesis, never *a*biogenesis.

The next age-long problem which the

microscope solved was the exact mechanism of reproduction. This had been the most tantalizing mystery to all thinkers from Aristotle to Harvey. How and by what means did the young creature or embryo arise? In the body of the female, undoubtedly; but what was the essential part played by the male parent? The microscope showed that the precursor of the next generation was a minute ovum or egg, and that this, unless penetrated by a still more minute male element or sperm, would not develop at all. The rendering visible of the microscopic ovum and of the still more microscopic sperm gave the clue to the whole mystery. It was a Russian physiologist, von Baer, who first saw the living ovum of a mammal (rabbit), just about one hundred years ago.

LIVING TISSUES

The microscope has been of incalculable importance to medicine and to the healing art in that it has given us the conception of the "living tissues". A "tissue" is one of the essential constituents of the body; thus bone, muscle, skin, nerve, and gland are some of the tissues.

Even before these were studied under the microscope we had indeed an idea that they were not all of the same nature because, for one thing, each looked very different from the other even to the unaided eye, but the lens showed in extraordinary detail in what way precisely each tissue differed from the others.

Thus, for instance, muscle was seen to be composed of long, semi-fluid cylinders, nerves of very long, narrow fibres, bone of a most complicated system of canals, skin of many layers of invisible " cells ", and so on. The histologist, as he is called, is able to describe the pattern or system on which each tissue is built up, so that in a few moments, armed with his lenses, he is able to tell whether he is looking at a minute scrap of tooth, bone, brain, muscle, skin or gland.

This knowledge of the ultimate constitution of the tissues of the living animal body is the basis of the new microscopic biology, and of entire departments of medicine whose very names were not invented a few years ago.

Further, it became possible to say exactly in what particulars diseased tissues differ from healthy. Disease, for the most part, has to be long established before the naked eye can recognize it, but by means of the microscope the very earliest stages or phases of disease are revealed. There have in this way been gratifying advances in scientific medicine.

But the microscope did further service to medicine and surgery, for it made it quite clear that such a thing, for instance, as a tumour, was not something composed of a kind of tissue previously unknown but was of the same essential pattern as one of the five or six familiar tissues. A tumour of bone, of muscle, or of gland was merely bone or muscle or gland growing excessively where it ought not so to be growing. It was "exceeding the local" (growth) "limits".

Similarly the microscope revealed a most characteristic plan in the tissues of plants, so that the new science of Microscopic Botany was created. We now know that the invisible structure of a leaf is quite different from that of a stem and from that of a root. The origins of the diseases of plants have similarly been made plain; we understand how to attack the smuts, "rusts" and other parasites of our trees and shrubs.

The crowning achievement of microscopy was the discovery that most infectious diseases are produced by the growth in the body of vast numbers of extremely minute vegetable organisms, each giving rise to a distinct kind of disease. Thus it was made clear that, for instance, diphtheria, tetanus, rabies, anthrax, typhoid fever, plague and tuberculosis were each due to a different kind of germ identifiable by microscopists.

The microscope showed that all such processes as the fermentation of sugar, the souring of milk, the decomposition of a dead body and a large number of the infectious diseases were alike due to the activity of myriads of minute vegetable organisms allied to the fungi. This is sometimes still called the "germ *theory* of disease"; but it has long passed from the realm of conjecture to that of established fact. Only a few ineducable "cranks" still refuse to admit the truth of it.

The microscope has provided the clue as to why so often in the past wounds became putrid and blood-poisoning supervened. Pasteur had shown that milk became sour because minute vegetable organisms had begun to grow in it. Lister, therefore, taking this as a starting point, scrutinized the discharges of wounds, and did, indeed, find in them similar vegetable organisms.

By much patient research he conclusively proved that if all microscopic living matter is excluded from a wound, it will heal without inflammation or putrid discharge. Lord Lister, amid apathy and ridicule, silently and surely transformed surgery from a dangerous art to a safe science.

Finally, the microscope has also been used in the realm of the *non*-living. It has revealed the structure of rocks, precious stones, minerals, and metals. By its aid it has been shown that in a wire over-stretched or over-twisted, the invisible structure has undergone alteration, and this alteration or "fatigue" of the wire has actually been demonstrated under the microscope.

This instrument, the microscope, has introduced us to another universe—that of the infinitely little. For just as the telescope is our introduction to the universe of the infinitely great, after all only a part of creation, so the microscope has been our avenue of entry into a world as abundantly peopled, as wonderful and as incomprehensible as the world of the starry heavens. And as regards mankind this world of the Invisible is far more important for his happiness and far more significant for his well-being.

CHAPTER XV

HOW MANY TASTES HAVE WE ?

THE number of true or pure tastes which we possess is smaller than most people think. We have, in fact, only five true tastes (gustations), namely: Acid (or sour), alkaline (or soapy), sweet, bitter and saline (salt).

Vinegar is sour, baking powder is soapy, sugar is sweet, quinine is bitter and salt is saline. Anything in addition to these that we may perceive in regard to things we take into the mouth belongs either to the group of the odours, to that of contacts, or to that of sensations of heat and cold. In other words, nerves of taste, of smell, of contact (touch) and of heat and cold are all involved in what we call " tasting " anything.

An example may make this clearer. If you are asked what the taste of an apple is like you might reply, " Oh, well, just its own taste, the taste of an apple". But there is no such taste; an apple must be sweet or sour; what we call the " taste " of the apple is its flavour or smell, which can be perceived before the fruit is taken into the mouth at all. The so-called " taste " of the apple is an odour, something volatile, which ascends from the mouth to the nose by the back of the throat and is there perceived through the nerve of smell.

Several sensations are aroused by the eating of an apple. There is the contact with its solid substance, which is mediated by the nerves of touch or contact in the tongue, gums, cheeks and palate. Then if the apple is ripe there is the sensation of sweetness; then the sensation of cold, especially if the fruit has been in cold storage, and, lastly, there is the smell, or odour of it popularly called " the taste ".

All those four kinds of nerves of sensation are generally involved in the " tasting " of our ordinary food. Now one set in this group, the olfactory, can be voluntarily abolished, as when we close the nostrils while eating the apple, in which case no air ascends from the mouth to the nose, so that we cannot smell the apple and therefore cannot recognize it as " apple ". We derive in this case very little so-called "gastronomic" (better olfactory) pleasure from it.

Anyone blindfolded and told to "hold his nose" has the greatest difficulty in distinguishing a raw (if not too sweet) apple from a raw potato. The writer has seen a person thus quite unable to say which was which. A bad cold-in-the-head gives us the same experience; we say our "taste" has gone, whereas the five true tastes are still intact, but the nasal congestion, preventing the ascent of air from the mouth, has abolished our sense of smell. All the five true tastes are retained in a cold.

So important are these odours or flavours in the enjoyment of one's food that when people have a cold they say, "Since I cannot taste anything, it doesn't matter what I eat just now." The pleasure we derive from eating is very largely olfactory. Our enjoyment of the flavour of roast meat, cheese, wine, tea, and fruit all depends on our sense of smell.

There is, for instance, virtually no true taste in roast beef; it is not sour, soapy, bitter, sweet or salt; we add salt to make it more "palatable", and we don't eat beef for the sense of contact. We eat it for its odour, the odour of slightly burnt fat (learnedly called empyreuma); were it odourless we should eat it only from a sense of dietetic duty.

Indeed, so many of the staple articles of our food are devoid of tastes and flavours that we add all sorts of flavourings and seasonings to make them more interesting. Take the case of a milk-pudding: if the vanilla or cinnamon has been left out, how utterly insipid the rice or the tapioca becomes! We should get merely the sense of contact and warmth from the tasteless, boiled grains, not even the most hungry child would eat much of it. The secret of good cooking is by flavourings and seasonings to appeal, not to the palate, but to the inside of the nose.

We speak of a person having a delicate "palate", but we really mean he has an acute sense of smell. The attraction of wine for connoisseurs is in its flavour or bouquet; they sip it slowly, they do not take it "in a mug". Liqueurs, in particular, are sipped so that their flavour may be fully appreciated. Those who are very particular about brandy take it from a large goblet, which becomes filled with the volatile ethers and other constituents of the bouquet that give a massive olfactory sensation.

This sort of thing distinguishes the gourmet from the gourmand; the gourmet eats and drinks—it may be sparingly—and chiefly for the olfactory pleasure of the food. The gourmand eats largely without regard to the flavour of it; he is merely satisfying his large appetite with quantity rather than quality. The gourmet is a gastronomic artist, the gourmand a mere stoker of the vital furnace.

Alcohol has no taste in itself; it is neither acid nor alkaline, sweet, bitter or salt.

A sweet wine or cider is sweet from sugar like any other sweet thing. Beer is bitter from hops, an inferior port from tannic acid. The flavours of the various wines are appeals to the olfactory sensations. *Pure* alcohol has an irritating effect; it stimulates neither the taste nor smell nerves, but irritates the contact nerves in the tongue, palate and gullet thus giving rise to the hot sensation once described by Pat in *Punch* as "going down like a torchlight procession".

Some persons who abuse alcohol take it for this irritant effect on throat and gullet; hence these public nuisances will drink anything that is irritant, such as methylated spirit, or even Condy's fluid. Some drunkards, of course, drink alcohol for the intoxicating subjective effect, and these will drink ether because, being so rapidly absorbed, it intoxicates very quickly. We call those people "nuisances" because, on account of them, other people who know how to use alcohol are worried in a hundred ways.

Exactly the same irritant effect on the touch nerves is produced by pepper, mustard, capsicum and the many condiments. We do not really *taste* pepper or mustard, it is the contact nerves that are irritated by these things. Peppermint, for instance, stimulates the cold-perceiving nerves, so that just after it has been taken, a current of air at the ordinary temperature seems quite cold.

Several sorts of nerves are therefore stimulated by an ordinary dinner; the true tastes are all there with the possible exception of the "soapy", and even of this a banana is a very good imitation.

It is noticeable how we add materials to foods in order to provide them with "tastes"; to get sourness we add vinegar, to get sweetness sugar, to get saltness salt, to get bitterness hops, though it is only rarely that we desire this last taste.

Few foods are in themselves sour—buttermilk is an exception—few are salt, few are soapy or bitter. Hence the insipidity of meat or fish taken by itself is natural; and this is the meaning of the addition of so many accessory materials to food—salt, flavours, relishes, condiments, herbs, garnishing, etc.

The true tastes have different "end-organs", or "taste-buds" as they are called, and they are distributed differently as follows: The sweet-perceiving are on the front of the tongue, the acid-perceiving are at the sides, while the bitter-perceiving are at the back. Thus to taste a sweet liquid it is quite enough to put the tip of the tongue into it, it does not need to be swallowed, whereas a bitter substance is not tasted until it has nearly gone over the back of the tongue. If some time has elapsed since we last took quinine, and we are swallowing our dose slowly, we have time to think it is not so bad after all until it reaches the full development of its disagreeableness literally at "the bitter end".

Some things being perceived on the margins of the tongue are said to "set the teeth on edge", although physiologically they have nothing to do with the teeth. Hence the fine metaphor in the book of Ezekiel—"The fathers have eaten sour grapes and the children's teeth are set on edge". Incidentally it is a poetical description of heredity.

We cannot here give all the evidence that the taste-buds differ physiologically in the different parts of the tongue, but we may refer to the evidence from mechanical and from electrical stimulation and to the effects of drugs.

Tapping the front of the tongue with a clean glass rod produces a sweetish taste, and rubbing the rod against the side of the tongue will give rise to a bitter sensation. Alternating (induced) electric currents, too feeble to affect the retina or the skin, and too weak to cause electrolysis, can produce distinctly different tastes according to the parts of the tongue stimulated.

Lastly, by chewing the leaves of the African plant, *Gymnema sylvestris* (one of the *Asclepiadaceae*), only the bitter-perceiving end-organs are quickly paralyzed, so that a very bitter medicine may be comfortably swallowed. Later on, the sweet taste is also abolished by gymnema.

Cocaine, which in high concentrations

abolishes all the five tastes, as well as touch, temperature-sensations and pain, abolishes the bitter tastes first.

Taste-buds are found only in the mouth, not, for instance, in the gullet or the stomach, so that we cannot taste food when once it has been swallowed. The pleasant taste or odour of food or drink may tempt one to take more of it than the appetite would warrant, and therefore indigestion may be brought on in this way. The appetite is sated before the sensation of smell is.

We appreciate some things for the massive, contact sensation, as, for instance, the thick liqueurs with their non-irritant oily contact.

When, as children, we had to take castor oil, it was not its oily contact we so disliked but its nauseating odour, and so in the nursery we were told "to hold" our noses or had them held vicariously for us. This prevented the odour, not the taste, getting to the nose; for all kinds of castor oil are virtually "tasteless". Sometimes the odour of the oil was masked or antagonized by that of orange juice or sherry, a process similar to that of gilding the pill.

It will be apparent that we can perceive two different tastes at the same time, in fact we can taste two such opposites as bitter and sweet, for we can mix quinine and sugar in the right proportions to stimulate simultaneously the bitter- and the sweet-perceiving end-organs. Lemonade is acid and sweet at the same time; a ripe banana is sweet and soapy at the same time.

Many things other than sugar are sweet —glycerine, saccharine (which is hundreds of times sweeter), and acetate of lead, which is so sweet it is called "sugar of lead". Now the chemical constitutions of these substances have hardly anything in common; we do not know why these things, so different from one another, can all stimulate the sweet-perceiving nerves. Similarly, many things very different chemically are all bitter such as quinine, strychnine, poisonous cheese, unwholesome mushrooms, Epsom salts and bitter almonds. And, of course, the number of different acids known to chemists is enormous, but they all stimulate the same gustatory nerves.

The taste nerves seem to be paralyzed by extremes of heat and cold. Something that may be taken very hot, as, for instance, tea, can easily prevent our getting the flavour of the beverage. Similarly, very cold viands can render the "palate" insensitive to the taste of something taken immediately afterwards, just as great cold renders the gums insensitive to the pain of having a tooth pulled out.

Ginger, besides irritating the contact nerves, also irritates the heat-perceiving nerves to such a degree that the hot sensation long outlasts the stimulus of the ginger; thus "ginger is hot i' the mouth". It also results from this that the tastes of viands taken after ginger or peppermint (which stimulates the cold nerves) are imperfectly perceived.

This sort of thing is really due to contrast in tastes and odours, and hence we know that some things taste well, others badly, after certain tastes and flavours which linger on. Connoisseurs study these things; they do not eat garlic just before a chocolate *éclair*, or an onion before a meringue. The scientific choice of courses and dishes consists in selecting them in such an order that the tastes and flavours shall follow each other pleasantly and without harsh contrasts. We should not go from *crême de menthe* to fried fish, the contrast is disagreeably sudden.

The "smell of cooking", that of hot grease, is to many people so unpleasant that they cannot enjoy the pleasures of the table which, being very largely olfactory, are liable to be overpowered by it. We do not enjoy strawberries and cream in an atmosphere redolent of hot broth. Some few people have survived to this day who do not like to take their food in an atmosphere laden with tobacco smoke. They maintain, correctly, that if their nostrils are full of smoke they cannot perceive the delicate perfumes of certain foods and beverages. Hence having to take a meal in an atmosphere laden with tobacco smoke is to those people an aesthetic outrage.

The flavour of good tea, for instance, cannot be perceived, and therefore enjoyed, when one's nostrils are full of smoke. Smokers, who are notoriously considerate, evidently cannot be aware of the physiology and psychology of the five true tastes.

CHAPTER XVI

THE CAUSE OF COLOUR

COLOURS are made by light, and light—even that of the moon—comes from the sun.

Sir Isaac Newton discovered that when a beam of light was passed through a solid wedge of glass (a prism) it was broken up into a band of seven colours—red, orange, yellow, green, blue, violet and indigo. The band, which is usually so arranged as to have red at the left-hand side, is known as "the spectrum." The rainbow is a spectrum on a gigantic scale in the clouds.

White light, then, is broken up into these seven spectral colours by being bent (refracted) on going through a prism. The colours are potentially present in white light, although the eye cannot detect them. Newton also did the converse experiment of recombining the seven colours by means of a lens into white light again.

Now the colours of objects depend on how the materials of these objects deal with the light that falls on them. If an object sends on to our eyes all the rays that fall on it, it is white; snow does this, a piece of chalk and white writing-paper do it.

We possess an instrument whereby we can tell whether all or some or none of the coloured rays in the light are coming from any given object; it is an arrangement of prisms known as the spectroscope. This breaks up light into the seven colours, but if one of these colours or even a small portion of it is not present in the light, then there is a black band or line in what we see in the spectroscope, and we call that an "absorption" band or line.

When we look at the light coming from snow or from chalk, we find all the seven colours in the spectrum as presented to our eyes by the spectroscope. When, however, we look at a black object with the spectroscope we can see no spectrum at all, for it has absorbed all the light that fell on it and absorbed all of it equally. There is no light left to come on to the spectroscope.

Suppose, now, that we have our band of colours in a dark room, and, taking a piece of red flannel, pass it along the series from red to indigo, it will look red in the red but black in all the others. Evidently, the red flannel is "red" because in white light it quenches all the colours except red, and so allows only that colour to affect our eye. In Nature no flower is perfectly black, because no flower absorbs all the rays of light which fall on it.

Although there are only seven colours in the spectrum, there are thousands of "colours" both in Nature and in the arts. Some "colours" are really dilutions of a pure colour with white light, as, for instance, pink which is red plus white, "eau de Nil", which is green plus white, and so on, we call these "tints".

Then, again, there are the "shades", which are mixtures of black with a particular colour—the so-called dull or "sad" colours —for instance, red plus black which makes a dark red or a brown.

Further, many colours not in the spectrum are formed by the mixing of two or more which are; and these mixed or compound colours may again be diluted with white or mixed with black. Thus purple is a mixture of red and blue, and it may be obtained as a light purple or a dark purple.

CHAPTER XVII

SUSPENDED ANIMATION

THERE is a state into which living things can pass which is a kind of intermediate state between life and death. It is also known as "suspended animation" or "latent life". The living matter (protoplasm) in this state does not show any of the familiar signs of life, and yet it is not dead, because by appropriate means it can be revived and made to show these signs again.

The signs referred to are: (1) the taking in of oxygen, (2) the giving out of carbon dioxide (sometimes called carbonic acid gas) and water, and (3) the production of animal heat. All living things carry out these processes with greater or less intensity. The carbon and hydrogen of the tissues are oxidized by the oxygen absorbed, and heat is the inevitable result of this oxidation. There are other signs of life which for our present purpose we need not examine.

Luckily these three evidences of life are all capable of being measured, for by appropriate apparatus we can estimate the amount of oxygen taken in by the body, the amounts of carbon dioxide and water produced, and the quantity of heat set free in a given time.

There is a further sign of life, the production of an electric current, and this also is measurable, although it requires the use of a very delicate and costly apparatus, the galvanometer.

So long, then, as an animal is alive it is always absorbing oxygen, excreting carbon dioxide and water, and producing some heat and electricity ; if it is doing none of these things, we are entitled to regard it as dead.

Now, excluding the electric sign in the meantime, we find when we come to test certain organisms at certain times that they are giving no evidences of vitality as just described.

Let us begin with some dry seeds in a pill-box ; they are evidently not dead, because, we know, if sown in moist earth they will grow into plants, but all the same they are not showing any of the three signs of life.

The ordinary person could not tell by

looking at them whether they were alive or dead; but if they are able to grow into plants they must be alive. And yet if they are not taking in oxygen or giving out carbonic acid gas they cannot be regarded as *wholly* alive; therefore we are compelled to regard them as in an intermediate state which we name "latent" life. Latent life is biologically purgatory without its punishments.

This intermediate state the Germans call *Scheintod* or apparent death, which is the other aspect of the same fact.

But it can be shown that these so inert seeds, if they be given a sufficiently powerful electric shock, will respond by producing an electric current in the galvanometer, so that this latest discovered sign of life is also the most infallible; it will be given when the other three will not.

It is well known that seeds can for many years remain capable of germinating, although the tales of being able to grow wheat from seeds found in Egyptian mummies are now known to have been Arab deceptions.

Latent life in the animal kingdom is a particularly interesting condition. Desiccation or drying of certain lowly animals will send them into a state of vital latency just as it did the seeds. Ever since the discovery of dried-up wheel-animalcules (Rotifera) by the Dutch naturalist Leeuwenhoek in 1719, we have known that certain animal organisms could enter upon an indefinitely long period of suspended animation. Leeuwenhoek found that those little creatures could remain in dried mud for a very long time without showing any movement, but that they became active on being moistened.

Other organisms which can withstand prolonged drying are "bear animalcules" and "paste-eels" and some of the very simple group of the Infusoria.

Among the cold-blooded animals there are many cases of latent life, for snails, water-beetles, frogs, and fish can all be frozen and yet remain alive.

All life tends to become less active as the temperature is lowered, until at a certain reduction the vital manifestations cease, but even then it does not follow that the life is extinguished.

Sir John Franklin, in his polar expedition of 1820, reported finding carp fish frozen so solid that the intestines of some of them could be taken out *en masse*, and yet on being thawed before a fire some of their companions "revived and moved about actively". A batch of fishes, frozen in a block of ice at minus 15° C., have been known to revive on being thawed, although the bodies of some of the others were so hard that they could be powdered up along with the ice.

A fish has been frozen in a block of ice, then sawn in two along with the ice, and each half, when the ice was melted, performed active movements before it died.

Sir Ernest Shackleton stated that in the south polar seas there are organisms frozen for ten months of the year, and active only during the other two. This is the sort of thing we mean by Latent Life.

A frog can be frozen solid and brought into the lecture-room so stiff that it can be held out by the toes like a stick; and yet after being thawed during the lecture, it will hop about as though nothing had happened. Experiments by the author have shown that so long as ice does not form around the heart, frozen frogs will remain alive.

The hibernation or winter sleep of animals is a state closely allied to latent life.

There is no doubt that the amphibia and the reptiles (snakes, tortoises, etc.) can enter upon a prolonged period of depressed vitality owing to the low temperatures they can endure. As frogs bury themselves in the mud under the ponds and lakes where they pass the winter, it is not probable that they are actually frozen all that time, but they are hibernating.

In the hibernation of the warm-blooded animals, we have a state closely resembling true latent life.

Bears, dormice, marmosets, hedgehogs, and other animals, having laid on plenty of fat against the approach of winter, seek out hiding-places, and retire from the world until the next spring. In those cases of warm-blooded hibernation, though the animal is not breathing, its heart is beating, and its gaseous exchanges are reduced to a minimum. It is living on its fat which it oxidizes for heat, and therefore emerges in the spring very thin and cold.

It need not be pointed out that the warm-blooded animals, by reason of the much greater delicacy of their bio-chemical processes, could not survive the loss of water or the loss of heat which more lowly creatures can endure.

When we come to man himself, we find from time to time cases of such a nature occurring that we can only regard them as closely allied to hibernation and latent life; popularly they are called " trance ", learnedly narcolepsy (a falling into sleep).

Every now and again we hear of persons who fall into a deep sleep or coma in which state they remain for days or weeks, scarcely breathing and with the very slightest action of the heart. The pulse at the wrist may actually be imperceptible, and the heart sounds inaudible.

One of the most famous cases is that of Colonel Townsend, reported on by the well-known Dr Cheyne of Dublin. The unusual feature in this case was that Colonel Townsend could go voluntarily into this state of suspended animation, remaining breathless and pulseless for many hours.

Most certainly this is the nature of the condition of those Fakirs in India who are enabled to undergo such extraordinary feats of endurance announced from time to time in the Press. Some of these are too well authenticated to be attributed to fraud or explained by collective hallucination. A man has allowed himself to have his ears and nostrils stuffed with cotton-wool, to be sewn up in a sack, which was placed in a locked chest, and then be buried for periods as long as six weeks, at the end of which time the doctor who saw the man buried proclaimed him alive.

Now and again persons have been prepared for burial who were not dead but only in this state of narcolepsy; such cases, however, are extremely rare in spite of sensational representations of them, such as those in the famous Musée Wierz in Brussels.

Shakespeare, who has noticed almost everything, has remarked also on this state of suspended animation, for in *King Lear* (v. 3) the king says—

> I know when one is dead and when one lives;
> She's dead as earth. Lend me a looking-glass;
> If that her breath will mist or stain the stone,
> Why, then she lives.

Death is a state of protoplasmic immobility which cannot be recovered from, a state, as it has been called, of "infinite functional inertia". Latent life and not sleep is the "image of death", for just as we awake from sleep, so from latent life there can be a protoplasmic resurrection learnedly called "Anabiosis". In life "the sands of time" are running out rapidly; in latent life the stream has been mysteriously arrested; in death the sand is all in the lower globe never to leave it.

CHAPTER XVIII

SOME LOST ARTS

It would seem an incontrovertible statement that in this age, when science is applied to everything, we should know how to do everything. But do we? Are there no lost arts?

An example that of course occurs to everyone is the building of the pyramids by the ancient Egyptians. Our engineers could pile huge blocks of stone one upon another over a central chamber, but they would do it by steam-driven machinery. We who have made the useful barrages over the Nile could also rear the useless pyramids if we wished. The Egyptians may have employed slave labour and used levers, inclined planes and rollers, but the fact is that we do not know with certainty how they caused these gigantic blocks of granite to rise into the air of the desert.

Passing on to the Middle Ages, what shall

we say of stained glass? We are making coloured glass for churches every day, but antiquarian experts tell us that the glass we make now lacks some quality or attribute which the old glass possessed. Hence it is, for instance, that the pre-Reformation glass is so highly prized by those who have specially studied this subject. We certainly know a great deal about pigments and a great deal about glass, but we have lost the art of combining these as they were combined in the stained glass of long ago so that it came to be a thing of beauty in the haunts of ancient peace.

In the making of varnish we have another instance of a lost art. This is proved by the following quotation from an article which appeared lately in *The Times*:—" Recently the rector of one of Wren's most famous churches was surprised to receive a visit from three varnish experts, two American and one English, who requested permission to examine the varnish in the church. They declared that the oak panels in the famous vestry of the church represented a lost secret in the making of varnish. The varnish employed in the seventeenth century served as a preservative of the wood, but was so transparent that it did not obscure the beauty of the grain. The ingredients which resulted in this quality are not known ". Comment is unnecessary.

Road-making may be taken as our next example. No doubt at the present day our highways are constructed on the soundest mechanical principles; but for hundreds of years the roads in Great Britain were nothing less than scandalous makeshifts. The art of road-making was well known to the Romans. Roads from one end to the other of their vast empire were made in the first instance for military purposes, and were therefore made to last. They carried the heaviest traffic of their time, and they were properly drained. In making them the Romans first dug out the soil to a depth of several feet, and then laid down stones in layers, the largest below, the smallest on the top. The small surface stones were bound together by a top-dressing of soil. Where the road ran through camps or between buildings, the surface seems to have been formed of flat stones placed side by side after the manner of a pavement; the ruts formed by the chariot wheels in such roads can still be seen at Pompeii, and at one or two particularly well preserved camps in England.

After the Romans left Britain in the fifth century, no attempt seems to have been made to keep these highways in repair or to make new ones on Roman principles. Most of the roads in England were mere tracks over the natural surface of the ground, which became quagmires in wet weather and dusty hollows in dry. Where the traffic was concentrated on the main route leading into or out of a town, the road became worn into a deep depression naturally called " the hollow way ". Hence the frequence with which we meet this as the name of a street in many places in England. Holloway Road in London is perhaps the best known of these, but many English towns also have their " Holloways ", pointing back to the time when the traffic had worn the road into a deeper and deeper depression. These undrained, unmade roads of the England of the Middle Ages had no " bed " and no foundation ; the art of road-making had been lost. The roads, in fact, were so bad that travelling was done almost entirely on horseback, and this undoubtedly delayed the development of wheeled traffic. When the stage-coach did come, it was constantly sticking in the mud, as was the huge carriage or "family" coach in which the wealthy moved from one part of the country to the other, for the rest of the people scarcely travelled at all. This was the highwayman's opportunity; he appeared, pistol in hand, at the window of the embarrassed vehicle, and had things pretty much his own way. Well on into the time of the Georges the the roads of Great Britain were a disgrace to a civilized country.

From this slough of despond they were raised by the energy of a Scotsman, one John Loudon MacAdam, a native of "the auld toun o' Ayr". MacAdam, whose name of course survives in "macadamized", was born in Ayr in 1756, and died in 1836 in the little watering-place of Moffat amongst the Dumfriesshire hills. MacAdam reintroduced the Roman method of building up the road from a bed of stones of diminishing size. After making experiments on his estate in Scotland, he published in 1819 his, "Practical Essay on the Scientific Repair and Preservation of Roads". In 1827 MacAdam was appointed General Surveyor of Roads, and the rest of his life he spent almost entirely in England. He declined a knighthood.

The only roads of proper construction in Scotland prior to the macadamized roads were those made in the Highlands by General Wade after Culloden. They are the main roads over the Grampians to-day. Wade's engineers did their work skilfully, building most substantial highways with not too steep gradients or dangerous curves. The admiration of someone who had more Hibernian wit than poetry in his constitution is embalmed in the well-known lines—

> If you had seen these roads before they were made,
> You would lift up your hands and bless General Wade.

Our next example of forgotten arts may be taken from the insanitary condition of the mediæval cities of Europe. Imperial Rome brought pure water for drinking purposes from across the Campagna in a noble aqueduct; and she contrived the opposite of this in a system of sewers the best known of which is the *Cloaca Maxima*. We are so accustomed at the present moment to our cities having plentiful supplies of pure water and possessing excellent sewerage systems that we readily imagine it has always been so. But this is very far from the truth, for the mediæval cities of Europe were very poorly supplied with drinking water, and had practically no sewerage at all: these were two lost arts.

As late as the time of Charles II, the streets of London were in a disgraceful condition; heaps of decomposing garbage polluted the air. The continual outbursts of pestilence were directly due to the insanitary state of these streets which were never clear of decaying vegetable and animal matter. Old Edinburgh was, if possible, in a worse state. Here within the wall built after Flodden, the houses—unable to spread in any but the vertical direction—rose to the dizzy height of ten or twelve storeys. These towering and highly picturesque "lands" had no plumbing whatever. The drinking-water obtained from wells far down in the street below was carried in barrels on the backs of porters or "water-caddies", as they were called, to the top of these immensely high houses. The slop water was disposed of by a "gravity system" conspicuous in its simplicity, for it was merely thrown out of the window on to the pavement below. Hence the ominous cry of "Gardey loo!" a Scottish corruption of *Gardez l'eau,* "beware of the water". It might happen that the lady in her satins and laces, who had just alighted from her sedan chair and who had not looked above, might be splashed by the malodorous liquid; while we may be sure that it was the constant prayer of the bewigged male *not* to "let some drops descend on me". Smollett, who knew Edinburgh well, makes one of the characters in *Humphrey Clinker* explain the phrase "gardey loo" as meaning, "May the Lord have mercy on you". "Auld Reekie, I can smell ye noo", was the familiar exclamation of the traveller from the south on approaching the venerable city if the wind happened to be in the north.

Of baths in mediæval Europe there were none; baths had vanished with the Roman Empire. One of the grievances the Christian Spaniards had against the Moors in Spain was that the Moors took baths. The baths of ancient Rome are amongst the most conspicuous of her ruins. Of course here and there in the Renaissance palaces of Italian princes bath-rooms might have been found; Titian decorated one in the Vatican. Except on the American continent, even at the present moment the bath has not been restored to its proper place in the house. Public baths have been instituted well within the memory of some of us; only the wealthy and leisured few take Turkish baths regularly even now. The spacious times of Queen Elizabeth were not spacious enough to include bathing.

Another lost art is that of heating economically the ordinary dwelling-house. Our methods are miserably inferior to those employed by the Romans centuries before the birth of Christ. No doubt we *can* heat our large buildings, mansions, museums, and churches so as to make them more or less tolerable, but the ordinary house of the ordinary person is far more uncomfortable in an English winter than was a Roman villa here two thousand years ago.

The Romans heated their houses by heating first the floors and the walls, when all was well, calorifically speaking, with the house. We have substituted the open fire which, while it ventilates well, heats very badly, besides being uneconomical and dirty. In the hypocausts of the one storeyed Roman buildings the hot air passed continuously under the floors, and in specially constructed flues through the walls. The same method of heating was used for the water of the baths, a bath being almost always found amongst the ruins of a Roman villa. If our feet are warm, we are warm altogether; if cold, we are cold. The heating of floors, then, is almost a lost art. I say "almost", because it is a fact that a few large buildings in London have quite recently been heated by a system of hot-water pipes laid down within the floor and in the walls and ceilings of the buildings. Before we leave the topic of Roman construction we might remind ourselves that some architects believe that the secret of the admitted excellence of Roman mortar is lost.

There is little doubt that one age forgets what an earlier age knew. Surgery under the Romans reached a degree of excellence which it was not again to attain until the time of Ambrose Paré, the Father of Surgery, who died in 1590. Paré by reintroducing the ligation of blood-vessels which had been in abeyance since the time of Celsus—the reign of Tiberius Cæsar—made the technique of the amputation of limbs practically what it is to-day.

No fewer than two hundred kinds of surgical instruments were found at Pompeii —a far larger number than throughout the entire Middle Ages was considered necessary for a whole college of surgeons. Such operations as herniotomy, the Cæsarian section, removal of the lens for cataract, and those in plastic surgery were all quite familiar to the Romans in the first century of the Christian era.

The eminent medical historian, Dr Fielding Garrison of New York, assures us that from the death of Soranus of Ephesus in the second century A.D. there were no real additions to obstetrics for 1,500 years. Almost everyone who knows anything about medical lore knows that what Galen taught in the second century was the orthodox belief in the medical schools of Europe for 1,400 years; but it is possibly not so well known that a great deal that Galen knew was completely forgotten by these same schools. Galen knew of more than one form of phthisis; he knew of its infectivity, and that a sea-voyage or residence in high and dry altitudes was very beneficial for it. Its infectious character has been virtually re-discovered in our own day. From the death of Galen to the time of Harvey, 1600, there was practically no experimental physiology.

Let our last example be that of the Sun-Cure. Modern medicine is preaching the great value to health of plenty of sunlight.

To the ancients this would have sounded the tritest of truisms. There have been sun-worshippers since the dawn of terrestrial intelligence. The Romans, though providing for shade in the courtyards of their dwellings, selected the sunniest spots, at least in Britain, for their villas. The great religious houses of the Middle Ages were built wherever possible on the open sunny sites so much admired to this day. Think of the abbeys at Fountains and at Tintern. With the castles came in the reign of gloom.

The walled cities of Europe fostered the clustering of houses so close together that from a vast number of the narrow streets the sun was completely excluded. Then came even the worse slums of the towns of the so-called Industrial Revolution, the very high places of all that was contrary to health. To make matters worse, there was actually a tax on the area of glass in the windows of houses which, reducing windows to the smallest possible size, effectually produced the greatest *un*happiness of the greatest number.

Our great-grandfathers never seemed to have realized that the sunlight which they took for granted was in itself a positive factor in the upbuilding and maintaining of a healthy body. And so we had sunless houses, sunless schools, sunless factories, sunless churches and sunless streets, and—tuberculosis, rickets and anæmia. Our forefathers, accepting the sun as a gift to the just and to the unjust, neglected to see that every one of these might really enjoy it. We are now proving tediously in the laboratory that in the free and universal sunshine we have one of the most valuable positive factors in the fostering of national health.

"*Neurodiversity in the Early Years* is an emotive and inspiring book in equal measure. I love how Cheryl generously shares her own experience of raising a neurodivergent child. Readers will find the 'time to reflect' sections especially useful, and Cheryl has also included reflections on intersectionality and the autistic voice. *Neurodiversity in Early Years* is a book that all educators should read to inform and adapt their practice to support the needs of neurodiverse children."

Laura Henry-Allain MBE, *Educationalist, Consultant, Producer and Storyteller*

"This book offers a personal perspective for parents, as well as providing a plethora of invaluable easy-win ideas for SEND leaders in the early years industry, that will challenge your thinking and redefine your neuro-inclusive practice. Cheryl has skilfully collated and embedded case studies throughout that enable readers to resonate with and understand the material. There are clear, user-friendly chapters that can be referred to as and when required. And the recommendations for further learning through Instagram accounts and podcasts are extremely helpful. I would recommend it as a key resource for any SENDCo."

Becky Eckersley, *Lead SEND Advisor, Kids Planet Nursery*

"This inspiring book pushes the reader to reflect deeply on how they might adjust their thinking and practices to better support and celebrate neurodivergent children. Rooted in the author's own life experience, it leans heavily into a range of valuable case studies and quotes from early years professionals, autistic people and their families. The final chapter on what it means to be neurodiversity-affirming feels like an urgent call to action – one that is so important in our increasingly neurodiverse society."

Catherine McLeod MBE, *Chief Executive, Dingley's Promise*

Neurodiversity in the Early Years

How we support children in their early years to understand, to be accepted for their unique differences and to thrive, has a life-long impact. With a neuro-affirming, strength-based narrative running throughout, this accessible book will improve your knowledge, skillset and practical application of high-quality neuro-inclusive practice.

In exploring the best practice to assist young neurodivergent children navigating the world, these eight succinct chapters will:

- Explore key topics, including how to create an environment to enable children to feel safe in your space
- Provide advice on how to work in a connective partnership with parents to enable a family to thrive, and how to create a whole setting approach to neuro-inclusion
- Include a range of first-hand accounts and case studies to bring theory to life
- Suggest a wealth of strategies that can be easily applied and will ensure that all children feel safe, connected and can achieve.

Neurodiversity in the Early Years enables the reader to embrace and embed knowledge and to advocate for a change which will provide neurodivergent children with the foundations of belonging, acceptance and a celebration of who they are. It will be key reading for all early years educators working with children from 2 to 5 years old.

Cheryl Warren is an Early Years SEND Specialist, founder of Aperion Training, and mother to two neurodivergent boys. Cheryl's passion is to inform and enable acceptance of all our children, no matter their strengths or areas of challenge.

Neurodiversity in the Early Years

Practical and Proven Strategies to Enable Neurodivergent Children to Thrive

Cheryl Warren

Routledge
Taylor & Francis Group
LONDON AND NEW YORK

Designed cover image: © thianchai sitthikongsak / Getty Images

First published 2025
by Routledge
4 Park Square, Milton Park, Abingdon, Oxon OX14 4RN

and by Routledge
605 Third Avenue, New York, NY 10158

Routledge is an imprint of the Taylor & Francis Group, an informa business

British Library Cataloguing-in-Publication Data
A catalogue record for this book is available from the British Library

ISBN: 978-1-032-64297-0 (hbk)
ISBN: 978-1-032-63730-3 (pbk)
ISBN: 978-1-032-64299-4 (ebk)

DOI: 10.4324/9781032642994

Typeset in Optima
by Deanta Global Publishing Services, Chennai, India

To William and Stanley, always be you and show the world that you can.

To John, my rock. Today, tomorrow and always.

Contents

Illustrations

Figures

Tables

About the author

Cheryl is an early years educator at heart. After gaining her NNEB in 1996, she has always worked in early education and support and remains passionate about high quality practice and provision within the sector. Cheryl has worked in nurseries, childminder support, further education, family support, as a SENCo, in quality improvement and training and assessing. In 2021, Cheryl founded Aperion Training, which is a training and consultancy company that works across the UK and Europe, enabling educators to develop their skills and knowledge in supporting neurodivergent children to thrive in early years environments. She is often a speaker at events and conferences, delivering webinars, and is also the voice of the 'Not Your Typical Podcast' series.

Cheryl has a wealth of professional experience, but always reflects on her lived experiences in raising her two wonderful, neurodivergent children. She touches the hearts of many who listen to her speak when she talks openly about the highs and lows of navigating a world and systems that don't always recognise, understand or accept her children just as they are.

Cheryl lives in South London with her husband and two boys.

You can find more about Cheryl's work at: www.aperiontraining.co.uk

Acknowledgements

I first want to acknowledge that writing a book was never in my plan! I'm an early years educator, I'm a trainer, I'm a wife and a mum, being an author was not supposed to be added to the list. In 2023, I received an out-of-the-blue email from Routledge, asking if I would consider the possibility of writing a book that reflected the work I do. My first thought was that this was a wind-up, then after many back-and-forth conversations with my husband, me saying I can't do this and him very much saying I could, the process began.

This book is reflective of my very personal journey, alongside my professional one, but I haven't written this alone. I'd like to acknowledge all of those who have contributed with case studies, their own stories and their own personal journeys. Parents and educators have been extremely honest and sincere, and I am truly grateful.

And to the neurodivergent adults who have accepted my request to be heard, and to those who reached out to be a part of it. I am always learning from the lived experiences of others, and to have the neurodivergent voice embedded throughout the book was so important for me.

I owe thanks to the nursery managers, SENCos, nursery owners and childminders who have shared their early years provision with me and allowed me to spend time in their environments with their wonderful children and their teams.

I am always humbled by what I see, the work that our amazing early years workforce are doing day in and day out amidst a tricky time within the

sector at the moment. The dedication to do the best they can for the children and their families truly inspires me every single day.

But ultimately, I would like to acknowledge my two children. My reason for being, my greatest teachers and my biggest inspiration.

1 Neurodiversity and me

Introduction

We know that the early years are the foundation, the building blocks for development and growth and it's during these crucial years that we need to get it right. This time is so important for children learning about the world around us, relationships, connection problem solving, self-regulation, communication and developing a sense of self. This is the case for ALL of our children, every single one of them in our early years settings.

Whether you are in a group setting, a baby room or pre-school room. Whether you are a childminder, a teacher in school or a parent, in this chapter you will hear my story. The start of my journey to becoming a SEND parent, what that looked and felt like and what you can learn from my experiences. You will hear the voices of my amazing neurodivergent children, neurodivergent adults and other SEND parents all sharing their lived experiences that need to be heard.

Many people I have come across who work in the field of SEND have a personal connection. Maybe a relative they have cared for, or a sibling they grew up with, or it could be they have a disability themselves or are raising a child with SEND.

Having that connection can give you a level of acceptance of difference, one that can't necessarily be taught. That acceptance enables a far deeper connection, empathy that is understood on a different level and a greater awareness of the struggles that those individuals face in their day-to-day lives.

And I am no different.

DOI: 10.4324/9781032642994-1

Welcome to our world!

This chapter highlights my personal connection to neurodiversity. How it has come into my life, the ups and downs, the tears and the laughs I've had so far. It will include stories of my lived experiences, of raising two boys in a world that doesn't always understand or accept them. I will share those early signs and indicators, the battles, the sleepless nights, the isolation and the raw emotion that I have felt on this rollercoaster of a journey. This chapter is my story, my experience and my point of view.

As well, I will share some of the experiences of other parents I know to help you to see life through our lens, including the joys, the heartache, the criticism and the hilarity.

Let me introduce you to 'Ortism'

I remember back in 1994 during my first year of the NNEB, (the Level 3 childcare course back in the old days) writing about SEND for an assignment.

We had to write about disabilities that we might see in the children in our nurseries, what they were and how they impacted child development. I can still see the tutors crossing out with red pen on my work. I had written and underlined 'ortism' as a section within my assignment that I was going to write about (whoops!).

Back in mid 1990s, when I was studying, the prevalence, discussion and understanding of autism, specifically, were far from where it is today. This can be seen in Taylor's study of incident rates of autism in the UK between 2004-2010:

> In the present paper we review and update an extraordinary 20-year exploration of the annual rates of autism in young children as recorded in real time and derived from a unique carefully designed medical database in the UK. In a series of formal analyses of the data … [we] have documented that the cumulative incidence of autism in children born from 1988 to 1995 began

> to increase and continued to rise from a low level by more than fivefold during these years.
>
> (Taylor et al. 2013)

In America, the situation was as follows:

> Up until 1990, autism was not included in legislation aimed at guaranteeing an education to individuals with disabilities. In 1990, the Individuals with Disabilities Education Act added autism to its list of conditions covered under the act. Autism had never been tracked as an educational statistic before 1990. Since 1990, the incidence of autism in schools has risen dramatically.
>
> (Rudy 2021)

I'm often asked, why are there more children confirmed as being autistic? According to NICE: 'The worldwide reported prevalence of autism in the literature has increased over time, possibly due to increased general awareness, broadening of diagnostic criteria, and improved access to specialist referral pathways' (Wright 2023).

It's not that there are more autistic children. It is just that over time, the more we are aware, the more we understand. The more we understand, the more we are able to observe the uniqueness of our children, the ways autism presents in them and how we are best able to support their needs.

As Heidi Mavir (2023) so truthfully states:

> I had a very narrow view of neurodivergence. Like many people my understanding of autism, in particular was, largely based on what I'd seen in the media, *Rain Man,* for example. As a result, I thought all autistic people banged their heads on stuff and had learning disabilities.

TIME TO REFLECT

- How well do you understand autism and what is this based on?
- Have you heard the terms 'neurodiversity', 'neurodivergent' and 'neurotypical'?
- Reflect on your current narrative around autism. What language are you using? What language are your team and others around you using?
- When was the last time you had any neuroaffirming training on autism or other neurodivergent conditions, and what impact has your previous training had on your understanding and your practice?

Meeting an autistic child for the first time

In April 2021, I began a new role as a family support worker within a Local Authority nursery. A specialist nursery provision for parents and carers who found raising children a little tricky. A space for children who were in foster care, allowing foster parents some respite. And a setting where children with special needs and/or disability were able to play, interact with their peers and access specialist services such as speech and language and occupational therapy.

It was a wonderful, fun place to work. I was part of a great team of people who all shared the same passion and commitment to provide a safe, enjoyable space with these children and their families. A space for support, growth, acceptance and a space to thrive.

I was key person to several children with a range of cognitive, physical, social, communication and sensory needs. As a nursery we also had autistic children in our care, and this was my first interaction with and connection to autism.

I vividly recall twin boys. Both were autistic; both were pre-verbal and also had other complex developmental needs. We worked hard to settle them with us, ensuring there was a strong emphasis on the parent/nursery

relationship. I also reflect on the fact that I'd had no training at this time, apart from that one assignment back in college.

I remember the team's desire to connect and support these boys the best they could, but it was difficult. At times they would be seen rocking in the corner, screaming uncontrollably, and running out to the garden at any given moment, seemingly through stress or discomfort. But there were also moments of sheer joy and laughter with them as you found a connection with them through the toy they had in their hand.

I then distinctly remember being told of a therapist who would be coming into the nursery to work with them both, as per the parents' request. It was a therapy that has a foundation in behaviour modification, where the child is 'taught' to alter their behaviours to ultimately become more 'acceptable' in society. I won't mention the name of the intervention as I don't want to allow it on the pages of this book, but suffice to say, it just didn't feel right, even back then. Other children in the nursery had a very different autism profile to the twins.

Some traits were similar among them all, autism impacted their social relationships and communication, but the level of impact differed greatly. It was also very obvious to me at the time that many of our children demonstrated a stress response when the room became too noisy, or when they were going through any type of transition.

I was clearly at this time starting to build my knowledge bank, my foundation of understanding that I would need to draw on, more than I ever thought I would need to, in the coming years.

When autism became personal

In January 2008, my first son was born, after a fairly uneventful pregnancy but a very tricky birth, culminating in an emergency caesarean section. He and I spent the first week in hospital receiving specialist care and support before being allowed to go home.

During my pregnancy I did all I could to keep my baby growing well and safe, developing our attachment as he kicked and squirmed around in my belly. My baby was this tiny human growing inside me that I had all to myself. But it was difficult to enjoy my pregnancy as I felt out of control of

the situation. Yet once my baby was born, I really wanted to pop him back inside! Not sure how common this is, but do let me know if it's just me!

I wasn't ready to share him. This was my baby and I needed to nurture and protect him. Little did I know how deep my inner lioness drive would need to be in the future, to continue this level of protection.

My initial observations

My son required brain scans early on due to the complicated birth, with a diagnosis of mild neonatal encephalopathy (decreased blood flow or oxygen to the brain), also due to bruising and a misshaped head. The outcome was reported as 'normal' growth with no obvious neurobiological 'concerns'.

He required physio appointments in his first few months due to underdeveloped midline orientation with his head, trunk and upper limbs and he had poor awareness and preference of his left side. He had increased tone in his limbs and had brisk reflexes in his lower limbs. Appointments with a cranial osteopath had a real impact on this, as well as reshaping his skull, and I would highly recommend it. All while being described as a happy, settled baby. Very sociable and interactive. He was talking at an early stage and there were no differences regarding his speech and language.

After the first tricky two years, backwards and forwards to the hospital, appointment after appointment, and after being discharged from physio, I observed my son to be developing as per my NNEB child developmental bible, *From Birth to Five Years*, by Mary D. Sheridan (1973). (If you know, you know!)

Then he hit 3 years old and I started to make some different observations.

The very first meltdown

I remember vividly a trip to our local theme park. We had an annual pass, and twice a month on a Wednesday afternoon I would collect him from

nursery (aged just 3), and we would take a drive over. Each visit we pulled up to the car park, found a parking space quickly and made our way to the first ride.

I can still tell you now the order we went on the rides. It was the same each week. No deviation. No change. At his request we followed the same path each time and he loved it.

I then recall making arrangements with friends to visit the same theme park in the summer holidays. We were very excited, and we spoke about what we going to do and where we were going for the whole journey. In hindsight (oh what a wonderful thing!), he was being very clear in this exchange that he knew it was going to be different, as others were coming with us. The conversation was to check the order of the day for reassurance.

Just as we pulled up to the car park, the attendant put up his hand to stop us, indicating that we needed to head to the overflow car park just a few hundred metres along the road. This was the start of the first stress-induced meltdown I witnessed in my son.

He began to scream, cry and shake the passenger seat in front of him, he was shouting, 'NO, WE NEED TO GO BACK! WE'RE NOT GOING TO THE BUBBLEWORKS!' I tried to remain calm, assuring him that the car park was full, and we were heading straight to another one. But he couldn't hear me. I then saw out of the rearview mirror his attempt to get out of his car seat as he continued to shout, scream and cry.

Once parked up, I quickly turned off the engine and went to hold him as he sobbed, shaking and in clear distress. I held him so tightly, focusing on him, his needs and the clear connection and reassurance he needed from me at this point.

I proposed that we see the theme park entrance from a different view today. That we were going to meet our friends for a drink and a biscuit. That we were going to be here for as long as he wanted to be, as well as reassuring him that we will be going on everything he wanted to.

We had our day, but, boy, were we exhausted when we returned home!

My experiences are very similar to that of other parents I have spoken to.

THE PARENT'S VOICE

I feel they have all blurred into one. I always knew they were more than a tantrum and I could always see how distressed my son was when having these meltdowns. He is always emotionally exhausted after having one and they can vary from half an hour to 3 hours+. Often it's screaming, shouting and hitting out, throwing everything in sight.

A turning point for me was when he collapsed in my arms after I fell to the floor crying because he had just hit me in the face and caught my cheekbone. I sat on his floor, sobbing. thinking I don't know how to help my son.

He jumped onto my lap and hugged me so tight and sobbed, 'Mummy, I can't stop crying, I don't know how to stop.' After this, everything changed. I knew I had to help him.

(Tara, parent and early years educator)

Hindsight and knowledge are wonderful things, aren't they?

Now I know all the things that my son needs before, during and after events like this. Now I have built up my toolkit of strategies and support techniques, these have become fewer and further between. But this takes time. This takes knowledge of your child, knowledge of their emotional needs and support strategies and knowledge of the triggers, and an understanding of their sensory profile, their signs of dysregulation, and what they need from you as an effective co-regulator.

At this stage I had none of the above. This was not in any parenting manual I'd come across. This was not what other parents had told me parenting would involve. Yes, maybe the stage of the 'terrific twos', but this went on way over 24–48 months and I had so many questions that I just couldn't find the answers to.

The Instagram parent vs my reality

Now I was lucky to have started my parenting journey two years before Instagram was a 'thing' (yes, I am that old), however, by the time my son was 5, it had started to be used by the masses.

Social media is great, it's helped me to connect with like-minded people, collaborate with online projects, find connection and camaraderie with other parents, also helping me to develop my business. However, it also shows me very clearly that my life was/is very different to that of other people.

The Instagram life: the couple with their 2.4 children, their fun, adventurous family Christmases and days out. The awards they receive at school, the parties they've all been invited to, the new restaurants they experience together. All lovely, but that certainly wasn't my life back then. The reality for me was so far removed from this.

Yet another incident was in the supermarket where your child has flung themselves to the floor due to being sheer overwhelmed. Where you are being stared at by other customers. Some offering you that look of, 'Oh, I do feel sorry for you', and others, 'Well, you just need to pick him up and tell him, you need to be firm.' And then those who just walk by, rolling their eyes at you. You know full well you are being judged and critiqued as a parent.

Yes, at last an invitation to a reception class party. But 10 minutes into the magician's act, while the rest of the class are sitting eagerly awaiting the outcome of the trick, will a rabbit appear out of the hat? My son is at the back of the room, pacing the floor with his hands over his ears, chanting to himself and so we leave early.

Having a child (and parent) agree to a play date. Yay! You're in the kitchen preparing tea – and when I say tea, you know I mean putting the chicken nuggets and chips in the oven! You think that they are playing so well upstairs together because you can't hear any arguments or upset. But when you go to check, you realise that your son is upstairs with the door shut playing Lego by himself and his friend downstairs is sitting on the sofa, looking worried and a little fed up.

The haircut! This has always been eventful, and I know that so many parents will relate to this. Two visits I can recall being particularly traumatic. We always went for a very simple haircut and the shorter the better as it meant not having to visit that often. We did, on one occasion, clear the barbers! The screams and cries were so loud, that the customers who had come in for a relaxing afternoon of grooming decided to just go for the quick all-over shave and get out the door asap!

The second was when my son was a little older and therefore stronger. He was so unimpressed and fearful of the clippers being close to his ears, he physically hit the barber in the face. We left pretty swiftly, and we didn't go back there again!

Being a parent is showing your child all of the great things that they could get involved in. Taking them to new places, trying new experiences, immersing yourself in new sports or activities. He had shown no interest in football, like the other 4- and 5-year-olds in his class, when a ball was kicked to him, he always picked it up. Ah ha! Let's try rugby.

We arrived for the first session, he appeared to be interested, he ran a little with the rest of the boys in the session and seemed to be happy following the instructions of the coach. Great, I thought, let's arrive earlier next week and grab a rugby top from the shop, socks and shin pads and get him ready for session number two.

Well, the socks were too tight and the shin pads where far too uncomfortable, so they got thrown away with a scream and a very loud 'No'. It had also been raining the night before and the pitch was now waterlogged, oh, and it was raining slightly too. He was 'encouraged' to go and join his new 'friends' on the pitch, but there was no way that was going to happen. He sat by my feet, under my coat, refusing to wear any of the kit and asking, 'Can we go home now?'.

We never returned to rugby. However, I will never give up. I will never stop supporting and enabling my son to experience success, because '[a]utism doesn't come with an instruction guide; it comes with a family who never gives up' (Magro and Magro, 2019).

TIME TO REFLECT

- Do some of these experiences resonate with you?
- Have you heard similar experiences from parents of children in your setting?
- How did you respond?
- How did you support the parents? What were your next steps?
- It's so important that we hear the voices of parents. We can only support the child holistically if we are able understand their experiences outside of our settings. Parents need to be heard, parents need our support, parents need a safe space to share their own stories with you. How are you providing for this?

Discovering a new identity

As we progressed through those early years, it was becoming very clear that my son was showing the emerging traits of a neurodivergent condition. I recall the feedback one afternoon from his nursery teacher. 'He seems to be doing OK, he seems happy, but he predominately plays by himself, he doesn't seem interested in the other children.' (Doing OK! We will return to this a little later.)

Everyone's reactions to these initial conversations and referrals are different. But for me, it was a trip to the GP. We were lucky enough to have a GP who had been with my family for years, so I felt I could really trust her to listen. I took with me pages of examples of meltdowns that I could recall, also a statement from his nursery teacher. Thank goodness, she agreed to make the referral to CAMHS (Child Adolescent Mental Health Service).

The timescale for us was just over a year from that initial GP discussion to confirming autism. A process that included my son being observed at school, an 'interview' with me discussing the full history of development up to that point. As well as him being observed by a professional in their clinic.

On 3 June 2014, we were called to the clinic and they gave us their feedback.

> In our opinion he has a long-standing history of social and communication issues. He struggles with managing change and has a narrow range of interests. We consider that his difficulties are consistent with a diagnosis of Autistic Spectrum Disorder.

At the end of the report were the recommendations:

- Have a read through the information pack.
- He will need help with understanding ordinary interactions.
- Arrange socialisation in small numbers to build up his confidence.
- Put social stories into your search engine, as these can help with inappropriate behaviour in social situations.
- Have a look at the board game 'Socially speaking'.

Now, besides the horrendous ableist language being used in his report, this was all we were given as a family. A few leaflets and a recommendation to buy a game. I left the clinic upset, confused, concerned and unsure of what to do next.

And this is not just my experience.

THE PARENT'S VOICE

I remember that kick in the stomach and the lump in my throat when being told my children were autistic because of the fear of the unknown, and I cannot even bring myself to say some of the words the doctor used in his report. They should never be used to describe anyone, ever, and it took a long time for those words to stop haunting me.

Although I was aware of my children's autism before the doctors would acknowledge it (I was dismissed several times as an 'anxious parent' before I got fed up, went private and got answers), it still winded and wounded me to hear it confirmed and said out loud. It was as if time stood still, and I wondered whether that feeling would ever really fade or even whether I could erase it from my memory completely. The truth is that I will always remember that moment and the uncertainty that followed. Some days the worry was suffocating. But it passed.

We are now reimagining our futures, and although there are still lingering question marks, I feel optimistic. I am under no illusion that my 'real' children are hiding underneath an invisible veil of autism, and that with time this will be shed.

(Randa, mum to autistic twins)

THE AUTISTIC VOICE

It's in my life and part of my life and certainly when I was younger, it was harder for me. Stuff like loud noises and big objects or buildings that dominated over me scared me a lot. That all has its roots in my autism. The social and emotional impact was and still is tricky, reading people's emotions and understand when it's the right time to do or say something.

It's like a mental spectrum that affects your life and your learning skills and your people skills.

What helps me most is to be able to have a breather when I need it, there is a level of needing to retreat. It boils down to feeling overwhelmed.

It's part of who I am, it's part of me. I'd like people to know that they need to treat me as a normal person, because at the end of the day I am a normal person.

(William, aged 15 years)

Neurodiversity: round two

Now those of you who have been taking all of this in would have remembered that in the opening paragraphs of this chapter, I mentioned that I have two neurodivergent boys! I have two very different boys, two amazing, funny, caring and wonderfully unique boys. So as a parent writing a book, it's only fair and right, that I tell you about my youngest son too!

My youngest son was born 6 years and 9 months after my first. A far less stressful experience with a planned caesarean section. I knew the exact date he was going to be arriving and I was fully prepared (well, as prepared as you can be).

All was wonderful, he was developing well, and his elder brother enjoyed his company, until he'd had enough of the screaming and crying anyway! Then things changed dramatically the night of 23 September 2017, one month before his third birthday.

Just to add some context. It was the night of the Nursery World awards. A great event in the UK Early Years calendar, celebrating the great work of our early years educators across the country. This was my first time at the event, as a nursery I'd been working with were finalists, and it was all very exciting. I was having my hair done downstairs in the kitchen and I had a new dress hanging up ready to wear.

I was suddenly called upstairs as my son had become limp and unresponsive after waking from a nap, and after a call to 999, we were rushed to hospital in the back of an ambulance, as the paramedics suspected an epileptic seizure.

After that first night (and with my hair still up, with lots of clips and sparkles. I was the most glamorous parent on the ward!), we spent a week together in isolation in hospital with many tests and observations taking place. Wires attached to his head to see what was going on in his brain, scans, lumbar puncture, and lots of blood tests. They were unsure at this stage exactly what had caused the seizure and they sent us home. We were told to keep an eye on him and given clear instructions on what to do if he had another one.

Well, that was me not sleeping for the next week or so, watching every movement he made while he lay in his bed. Not taking my eyes off him for a second, making sure my baby was safe.

However, I did have to return to work a couple of weeks later.

The only person I felt he was safe with was my mum. She had him this on this particular Wednesday morning, when she called me, 'Cheryl, he's had another one and I've called the ambulance.' Once again, we were rushed to hospital and more and more tests followed. Because of the short time frame between the seizures, we were assigned to a consultant specialising in paediatric epilepsy and she confirmed my son had epilepsy.

So that was us for the next two years. Medication twice a day. A dosage that had to be monitored closely in those early months as it made him very sleepy and aggressive. Training for me and others, including his childminder, on how to administer the emergency medication should he have another seizure. Remembering to take all his medication on holiday, causing extra wait times at the airport as they had to check the liquid.

It was a tricky couple of years, with night-time monitors recording him as he slept and watching every sudden or strange movement. We had regular appointments at the hospital with the specialist, and always being told that two years seizure-free was the aim.

Well, we made it! After two years of no suspected seizures or panicked calls to 999, he was signed off. According to the consultant, this was 'normal' for childhood epilepsy. Seizures come on suddenly and then they cease by the time the child turns 5 years old. While he is no longer under the epilepsy clinic, and no more medication, it's still there at the back of your mind. I'm still very aware of every vacant moment, or sudden movement, always checking in with him that all is OK.

Lockdown discoveries

Although enjoying being read to, my youngest son had never been one to choose to read himself or showed any desire to write his name. During the COVID-19 pandemic and subsequent lockdown, it became very clear that early phonics and number recall were a challenge for him. And, boy, did we try to do all we could to support this! Between my partner and I, we had almost 70 years of early years practice! So, learning online with worksheets that were being sent over by his teacher, were just not doing it for us.

There were 'castles' being made with numbers put on bottles and placed on top of the turrets. Corresponding numbered Nerf Guns being used to knock them down! We had letters placed on a pile of shaving foam, and when we got the sound correct, we could splat the letter with a spatula, sending foam all over the kitchen! Huge clocks being made with sticks. Number walks and treasure hunts outside.

However, it was very evident that information wasn't being retained. Patterns were not seen. Letters were 'jumping' around the page and when they were written down, they were back to front and tricky to form.

Once he returned to school in year 1, we began the conversations of possible dyslexia. His teacher said that he would keep an eye on him for a while and monitor progress. I wasn't convinced, if my son was struggling with a 2:1 ratio at home, with active learning at its core for 6 months, being back in a classroom of 30 with a relatively inflexible learning environment could be more problematic.

It soon became clear to his teacher that my son would require lots more additional support and the conversations of an assessment for dyslexia began. We were told that he would not be seen by the local authority for an assessment until at least year 3, and with lockdown waiting lists, this could not be until the beginning of year 4. We were not prepared to wait.

After a very thorough private assessment, he was in fact confirmed as dyslexic.

What I needed in those early days and years with my eldest son

What I needed was a sense of understanding, acceptance, support and positivity. I needed to build a community of people around me. A community of trusted people where I knew I could go, to cry. People that I could visit where I knew I didn't need to explain myself. People that I could go out with, with my autistic son and knew they'd have my back when the public tutted or stared at us. People who would allow me to laugh and just talk jibber-jabber with and who wouldn't judge me for it!

And I was lucky, I found those people. Some were online in community groups full of other parents who could help me to understand and who enabled me to realise I wasn't on my own. And others were really good friends and family members with whom I knew I and my son were safe.

What I also needed was to be immersed in the positive language of difference, that neuroaffirming narrative that is so important. This wasn't always the case.

Unfortunately, at the time, the narrative was a little different. Completing forms to gain access to funding or support had to be written on the worst

day ever with my son. The school continually told me that 'we just don't see that behaviour here' and I was actually asked if my son was really autistic! I spoke with his SENCo about the support available for him and the response was, he needed to throw a few more chairs around the classroom to get support. This is not supportive and not how it should be.

The current Statutory Framework for the Early Years Foundation Stage (EYFS) 0–5 years

The statutory framework starts positively: 'Every child deserves the best possible start in life and support that enables them to fulfil their potential … a safe and secure and happy childhood is important in its own right', but then in paragraph two in the introduction; 'The EYFS sets standards to ensure that children learn and develop well … it promotes teaching and learning to ensure children's school readiness' (DfE 2023).

It describes great guiding principles: The Unique Child; Positive Relationships; Enabling Environments: Learning and Development. But these appear to be quickly forgotten within the rest of the standards as there is no mention of connection or belonging.

We need to use the EYFS and place it at the bottom rung of the ladder when we consider designing our curriculum. We need to embed and prioritise the first of the three principles and connection and belonging and move far away from school readiness for our neurodivergent children. We need to push for the child-centred, child-led provision that meets children where they are, provides accommodations and adaptions so that they can experience success. Without that secure foundation in an emotionally safe space, the learning and development will not happen.

The current UK Primary Curriculum

The current UK Primary Curriculum states: 'A wide range of pupils have special educational needs, many of whom also have disabilities. Lessons should be planned to ensure that there are no barriers to every pupil achieving' (DfE 2013).

And this is where I believe the barriers to our neurodivergent children achieving start. In the document:

Pages 17–98 detail the expectations for English, including spellings, word lists, grammar and punctuation.
Pages 99–43 detail the expectations for Maths.
Pages 144–172 detail the expectations for Science.

And just 22 pages in total outlining the expectations and delivery of art and design, computing, design and technology, geography, history, languages, music and physical education – just a total of three paragraphs on that particular subject.

The heavy focus on the academic subjects at the expense of the rest creates a barrier in the first place. It's a barrier that stays high, the need to all be the same, the need to all achieve in those academic subjects at the same level and the need for our teachers to push these above all else.

I hear it regularly. 'Mummy, we didn't do art today, because we have to finish our literacy'; 'Mummy, PE was only a short lesson today because not all the class finished their maths sheet.'

The huge barrier, the concrete block that stands in the way of our children, is that the curriculum being fed to them day in and day out, does not recognise and celebrate difference. It forces our children to all fit into neat little boxes, where they are all having to do the same thing, 'achieve' the same thing at the same level, to the detriment of other subjects they may excel at. All 'behaving' the same way, all with the hands on their lips and walking in line.

The consequence is that children like mine and thousands of others are spending 6 hours of every day with the mindset, 'I can't do it', they are 'not as good as their friends' and what I've heard directly from my son, 'Mummy, I'm stupid'. As well as being in spaces that are so overwhelming and impact their ability to take on new information because they don't feel in an emotionally safe space.

My youngest son's teacher once mentioned that they had a broken classroom door, guess who figured out how to fix it? My youngest son is an amazing artist, loves and comes alive at the project work. I recall the lessons

he had on the *Titanic* and the Romans, a topic that did in fact result in him asking me to get him a book he had seen at school, which we read together at home. He thrives outside with a football, a tennis racquet or in the swimming pool doing lengths and lengths of back stroke and front crawl.

The National Primary Curriculum writes: 'Ensure that there are no barriers to every pupil achieving.' I therefore ask, is the current curriculum push on the academics in fact the barrier to achievement? What is achievement? Achievement in what?

A great quote from the author Mark Twain, 'I've never let schooling interfere in my education' (Seybold 2020). Consider for a minute that the boxes that our children are being placed in, to all achieve the same thing, at the same time, are what is actually hindering their education. The world is full of so many opportunities, so many wonderful experiences to achieve great things. But if we are all taught the same way, the same things, at the same time, what impact does this have on our creativity, our problem-solving, our ability to question life and all that is in it? How does this support individual growth, acceptance of difference, awe and wonder?

I would suggest it is exactly this that is the barrier to our children of difference achieving.

The global dyslexia charity, Made By Dyslexia, rightly states:

> [they] believe in the game-changing power of Dyslexic Thinking. After all, everything from the lightbulb to the iPhone, the aeroplane to the motor car was invented by a dyslexic mind. And our skills are vital in shaping the future too.
>
> (Made By Dyslexia, n.d.)

In fact, did you know the world needs adults with dyslexic thinking skills? According to Hall (2021), '[a]pprentices on GCHQ's scheme are four times more likely to have dyslexia that those on any other programme. The result of the drive to recruit those whose brains process information differently.'. Cavan (2021) states that the GCHQ are actively 'looking for people who can see something that's out of place in a bigger picture, who have good visual awareness and can spot abnormalities. A lot of dyslexic colleagues have those strengths.'

Even their recruitment process allows for those with neurodivergent brains to shine. Allowing mind maps, extra time and other accommodations to allow them to show what they can do. Supporting them to be the best they be, without a standardised, one-size-fits-all process.

So, my son, who sits in the classroom feeling dejected, feeling inadequate, feeling unable to achieve great things, could be called upon to save our country. Why then is he being fed a curriculum that doesn't fit his learning style, his internal narrative or his interests and skills set? Why is it at 8 years old, he tells me that school is rubbish, boring and there are tears most mornings with a refusal to go out the door?

- How can we make education and education for all?
- How can we support ALL of our children to thrive?
- How can we enable ALL our children to achieve?

THE DYSLEXIC VOICE

Dyslexia makes me feel a bit different to everyone else sometimes. I have a disability; it just feels different. But that doesn't matter, I'm still doing what I want to do and living my life. I find sports easy but learning a bit trickier, my brain doesn't work like other people's do, so it's not easy to do it. My brain is very creative. My brain is different and works differently, sometimes other people work faster than me.

If I could make a school for me ... It would just be for dyslexic people. They would teach us things that are easier to learn. Rather than normal maths, they would make it more fun. So rather than write what shape it is, you draw it, rather than having to write it. Instead of coming into school in a boring door, we can have children put things on the wall that we have all made. It would feel like our school. This would make learning fun. We can also have our own desks, for our own stuff.

And instead of English, we can do things where we go outside, we can write letters on paper and step on them to make the words, instead of writing. We can do the same for maths.

(Stanley, 8 years old)

What you can do to make a difference

> *Teachers are there to mould a child's learning journey and not make them withdraw from educational system, as everyone is capable of contributing to society, regardless of having an extra need or not. Autism is not a puzzle or a disease, it is a challenge but not a devastating one. If autistic children cannot learn the way the educational system is carried out, then educators should make it their duty to teach the way they learn.*
>
> (Molly, autistic adult)

There will be lots more coming up in the next few chapters but as a starting point:

1. Consider your own learning on neurodiversity.
2. Reflect on what you know, acknowledge what you don't and find out more.
3. Ensure any training you attend is delivered by a neuroaffirming trainer.
4. Consider the narrative that currently runs through your setting.
5. Be open to a change of perspective.

In my work, I will always mention the New Zealand curriculum. It has wonderful vision and thought-provoking wording that envelops its principles and strands. Te Whariki (woven mat) truly has the children at the heart and ensures children's well-being, sense of belonging, connection and contribution are paramount. It begins by ensuring that educators are always asking the 'child's questions'. And there is a question for each of their strands.

- Do you know me? (Belonging)
- Can I trust you? (Well-being)
- Do you let me fly? (Exploration)
- Do you hear me? (Communication)
- Is this place fair for us? (Contribution)

(Te Whāriki Online, n.d.)

I will be visiting these again in the book but use these as your starting reference point. Can your children, ALL of your children, answer yes to those five

questions. How are you creating a sense of belonging for everyone? How are you supporting the well-being of your neurodivergent children? How are you enabling your neurodivergent children to explore, to be curious, and are you curious with them? Are you supporting their unique communication style? Are you enabling them to be a constant contributor to the environment and all that is within it?

What the future holds

The same as any other parent, who knows what your children will become, what career they might go into, what kind of life they'll have? But it just comes with added anxiety around wanting a future for them, where they can excel, just as they are.

As I write this, my eldest son is just about to start his GCSEs. And if you had asked me five years ago if he would be ready to sit them, or able to sit them, I would have said I wasn't sure. But here is he, taking it all in his stride and telling me not to worry!

What my boys, and all of those other amazing neurodivergent children need, is a connection to others and to live in a world where they see their contribution as important and valid. Where they can be their true authentic self, where they belong and where they can thrive. And where they can be happy.

And we are able to make that happen. We are able to play a part in creating that world.

Are you ready to take on that role?

TIME TO REFLECT

- Consider the emphasis you place on phonics and early writing in your setting. Is it relative to all the other curriculum offers you provide? Is the drive still for being 'school-ready'? What about other strengths, other areas of interest, are they given the same value?

- Do we truly reflect the children's interests in our early years provision, are we enabling our children to achieve in all areas?
- Do you still use the term school readiness? Readiness for what? What does being ready for school mean?
- Do you provide the balance required in your classroom to ensure all children can achieve their individual potential, in their way, in their time?
- Do you celebrate neurodiversity in your setting?

Final reflections

All parents and carers of neurodivergent children will have different lived experiences. What we need to remember is that ALL these lived experiences need to be heard. Parents and cares would have been on a huge personal journey before those initial conversations with you and it's important we support them, hear their story and provide a space with empathy and advocacy.

The parent voice is an important one. A valid one. Let's enable the parent and carer voice to be heard as part of the team around each child we are supporting in our early years spaces.

You can make the difference in your early years setting, you can BE the difference for your children and families.

Resources

Further reading and research

Sara Alix (2024) *The SEND Handbook for Parents and Carers.*
Mine Conkbayir (2023) *The Neuroscience of the Developing Child.*
Heidi Mavir (2023) *Your Child Is Not Broken.*
Barry Prizant (2022) *Uniquely Human.*

Instagram

@aperion_training
@childhoodunderstood
@elliemidds
@Heidi Mavir
@jodiewarren
@ruth_jones_slt
@StoriesaboutAutism

References

Alix, S (2024). *The SEND Handbook for Parents and Carers*. Abingdon: Routledge.

Cavan, J. (2021) Available at: www.gchq.gov.uk/news/dyslexic-thinking-skills

Conkbayir, M. (2003). *The Neuroscience of the Developing Child*. London: Routledge.

DfE (Department for Education). (2013). National Curriculum in England: Primary Curriculum. Available at: https://assets.publishing.service.gov.uk/government/uploads/system/uploads/attachment_data/file/425601/PRIMARY_national_curriculum.pdf

DfE (Department for Education). (2023). Early Years Foundation Stage Statutory Framework: For group and school-based providers. Available at: https://assets.publishing.service.gov.uk/media/65aa5e42ed27ca001327b2c7/EYFS_statutory_framework_for_group_and_school_based_providers.pdf

Hall, R. (2021). People with dyslexia have skills that we need, says GCHQ. *The Guardian*, 3 May. Available at: https://amp.theguardian.com/uk-news/2021/apr/29/people-with-dyslexia-have-skills-that-we-need-says-gchq

Made By Dyslexia. (n.d.). Available at: http://www.madebydyslexia.com/

Magro, K. and Magro, K. (2019). Autism doesn't come with an instruction guide. it comes with a family who will never give up. Kerry Magro. 5 July. Available at: https://kerrymagro.com/autism-doesnt-come-with-an-instruction-guide/

Mavir, H. (2023). *Your Child Is Not Broken: Parent Your Neurodivergent Child Without Losing Your Marbles*. London: Pan Macmillan.

Prizant, B. (2022), *Uniquely Human: A Different Way of Seeing Autism*. New York: Simon & Schuster.

Rudy, L. J. (2021). Why autism diagnoses have soared. *Verywell Health*. Available at: https://www.verywellhealth.com/is-there-a-real-increase-in-the-incidence-of-autism-260133

Seybold, M. (2020). The Apocryphal Twain: 'I have never let schooling interfere with my education.' Center for Mark Twain Studies. Available at: https://marktwainstudies.com/the-apocryphal-twain-i-have-never-let-schooling-interfere-with-my-education/

Sheridan, M. D. (1973). *From Birth to Five Years*. London: Routledge.

Taylor, B., Jick, H., and MacLaughlin, D. S. (2013). Prevalence and incidence rates of autism in the UK: Time trend from 2004–2010 in children aged 8 years. *BMJ Open, 3*(10), e003219. https://doi.org/10.1136/bmjopen-2013-003219

Te Whāriki Online. (n.d.). Te Whāriki Online portal. Available at: https://tewhariki.tki.org.nz/

Wright, J. (2023). Autism prevalence in the United States, explained. *Spectrum | Autism Research News*, 2 March. Available at: https://www.spectrumnews.org/news/autism-rates-united-states-explained/

2 What is neurodiversity anyway?

In this chapter we are going to unpick the terminology around the neurodiversity affirming movement. By looking closer at and exploring the vocabulary, you will feel more confident as an educator in referencing and embedding this shift in language across your setting. Let's take the word 'neurodiversity' apart:

neuro – relating to the nerves or the nervous system, including the brain and the spine.
diversity – the state of being diverse; variety.

These are the online definitions and the breakdown of the word 'neurodiversity'. The word itself is defined as: 'The range of differences in individual brain functions and behavioural traits, regarded as part of normal variation in the human population.'

Neurodiversity itself is a relatively new term; it 'refers to the virtually infinite neuro-cognitive variability within Earth's human population. It points to the fact that every human has a unique nervous system with a unique combination of abilities and needs' (Neurodiversity Hub, n.d.).

And here is where we need to examine our own internal, subconscious understanding of difference, shifting from seeing autism, attention deficit hyperactivity disorder (ADHD) and other neurotypes as problems, deficits and disorders. And we should consider them more of the individual, wonderful uniqueness that represents Earth's population and consider both abilities and needs.

DOI: 10.4324/9781032642994-2

Variety, difference, normal variation, let's consider those words above for a moment – when did those words shift in narrative and become linked to 'problems', 'deficits', 'disorders' or 'challenges', all then connected to intervention, a need to change a person to become more neurotypical and less neurodivergent?

We need to ensure we are embracing all that difference brings to the world, acknowledging that this difference is not less. It's simply differences within the brain, just like we see differences in height, eye colour and shoe size. In Dr Rebecca Wood's (2019) book, she collected the thoughts of autistic adults. Jon says, 'Autism is an innate way of thinking. We're a variation on humanity's wonderful diversity. Nowadays what would really help is an understanding that neurodiversity is just another form of being human.'

Nason (2014) writes:

> In the neurotypical world we tend to focus on the different being a negative, rather than unique. We measure 'goodness' by how it compares to the norm, and whether it matches our view of value. If the qualities are out of the norm, then we immediately see the negative that blinds us from the positive characteristics. We do not look at differences as something to value, understand and marvel at.

This should be our starting point, the vision, aims and execution of all SEND policy and practice: looking at difference as something to value.

Neurodiversity

Take a group of individuals, maybe a team you work with, or you and a group of friends. You are a diverse group of people. You will think differently, you will process information differently, you will have differing cognitive abilities and take on board information in different ways. Your nervous system (we will see what this means a little later in the chapter) will respond differently in different situations than those around you. This is diversity.

You are a group of neurodiverse individuals and within that group, some will be neurotypical, and some may be neurodivergent.

Neurotypical

Within the same group of people there will be those individuals who are neurotypical. Those who follow a typical trajectory of brain development. And in our early years settings you will see children who will reach their milestones at the 'expected' time. Children who you are able to describe at parents evening as meeting the developmental markers within the assessment tool you are using. These children would be described as neurotypical.

Neurodivergent

Within the same group of people there will be individuals who are neurodivergent. Those children who are following a divergent pathway, children whose development diverges from expectations. Those children with a neurotype of autism, ADHD, PDA, dyslexia (and many others we will look at) will be described as neurodivergent.

Both our neurotypical children and our neurodivergent children will have differing needs, strengths, capabilities and traits. But it does not make one group more or less than the other. They are just different.

Remember that difference is not less. Therefore, the role of an educator is never to provide support for neurodivergent children to become more neurotypical. Far from it. It's understanding their neurotype and ensuring they are understood, accepted and celebrated for that.

What are the numbers?

According to Neurodiversity Experts at LexxIC (2023):

4% of the global population are identified and confirmed ADHD.
2% of the global population are identified and confirmed autistic.
10% of the global population are identified and confirmed dyslexic.
6% of the global population are identified and confirmed with dyspraxia.
5% of the global population are identified and confirmed with dyscalculia.
1% of the global population have Tourette's syndrome.

Therefore approximately 20% of the population has a neurological difference (just based on the conditions listed above). A quarter of the current world's population: 1 in 4. And that relates to those who have their differences confirmed, it doesn't cover those who self-identify nor those currently on the long waiting lists for assessment.

TIME TO REFLECT

Now is the time to consider where you are at right now. Remember we are all on a learning journey and will be at different points in our understanding, and the reason you are now reading this chapter is to learn and understand more.

- What is your current understanding of neurodiversity?
- What are your experiences?
- What about your team? Are they all at the same stage? Where might the gaps in knowledge be?
- Can you start to consider your preconceived ideas of neurodiversity and neurodivergent conditions? Once you have done this, you will be able to analyse where these may come from and start the process of a change of thinking and a change of narrative. For you and your team.

What are the different neurotypes?

In this section of the chapter, we are going to focus on those that we predominately see within our early years settings.

Identify preferred language

With all of the neurotypes that I am going to be referencing, we need to always ensure that we support individual preference on the language we

are using. Many neurodivergent adults have a preference for identity first language, i.e. autistic adult rather than adult with autism. This is felt to be preferred and it clearly clarifies that autism is part of who they are, it's their identity and not something they carry around with them. However, it's important that you ask and seek clarity on individual preferences.

Co-existing conditions

Many of our children have neurodivergent conditions that are not standalone. Many overlap and these are considered co-existing conditions. Some suggest that this is due to conditions similarly impacting the central nervous system, with many conditions impacting the brain response and reaction to stimulus, impulse control and focus. You therefore may find that the support you provide needs to be considerate of a range of needs, crossing over one or more neurotypes. Some adults are confirmed and identified autistic and also ADHD (AuDHD), and they often refer to the battle in the brain due to the contradictory nature of the conditions. Autism requires routine and structure with ADHD enjoying spontaneity and impulsivity. It's a big ask to find the balance and the equilibrium and greater support for environmental factors is often required. As Elkin (n.d.) writes:

> There is a significant overlap between ADHD and both DCD [developmental coordination disorder] and dyslexia. Studies looking at DCD in people with ADHD have reported that as many as 89% of people with ADHD also have DCD. When looking at populations with DCD, around 50% of people with DCD also have ADHD. It is, therefore, very clear that these conditions commonly co-exist, making life more complicated for those in which they occur.

This can mean that individuals are less likely to be identified and confirmed as one type, or it is confirmed later as an individual may not present as typically autistic.

Autism spectrum condition

As defined by the National Autistic Society: 'Autism is a lifelong developmental disability which affects how people communicate and interact with the world' (National Autistic Society, n.d.).

Autism is a wide spectrum that presents differently in each autistic individual. Yes, there are some common traits that support the identification pathway; primarily those traits will impact sensory, social and emotional development. However, the presentation of these traits will differ for each person. There is a great quote from Dr Stephen Shore, 'Once you've met one person with autism, you've met one person with autism' (Flannery and Wisner-Carlson, 2020). He then goes on to explain that educators and carers need to understand each child, based on the evidence in front of them.

Therefore, it's imperative that we make sure we continue to understand each child who comes into our care. Understand how their autism presents for them, their unique sensory profile as well as their triggers, need and their strengths and capabilities, ultimately accepting their uniqueness.

Some common early indicators

A caveat, these indicators may differ as per each child's autism presentation.

- Predominance and preference for solitary or parallel play
- Observed safety in routine, structure and the familiar
- A strong connection to one main educator
- Observation of sensory preferences or avoidance of sensory stimulation
- Parents'/carers' indication of food aversions or disturbed sleep patterns at home
- A need for sensory feedback through repetitive behaviours
- Communicating using echolalia (when children repeat back the words spoken to them by another), as a gestalt language processor (when children learn language in chunks, memorising whole phrases or scripts they may have heard in stories, songs or films), or preferring the use of gesture or signs to indicate need
- Distressed behaviours linked to any of the above if these are not supported or provided.

We do not take any of these emerging traits in isolation, our role as educators is to ensure we build a picture, in clear, transparent and supportive relationships with the child's main carer. We are also not in a position to confirm any child's neurodivergence in our care.

We need to remember too that we don't just offer the support to our children once their neurotype is confirmed. For many in our early years settings, they leave us without the confirmation as the processes can take a while or they may be too young.

We are here to support the child in front of us, their needs right here, right now. So, let's get to know and understand that child, their autism presentation, their sensory needs, their regulation needs, their special interests, their way of viewing the world.

What is hyperlexia?

Hyperlexia is a co-existing condition with autism, one which presents as a keen interest, or fascination in letters, or numbers. Children are observed as being early readers and writers with an amazing memory, however, still with minimal verbal language and demonstrating different social interactions with their peers.

Attention deficit hyperactivity disorder (ADHD)

According to ADHD UK (2023):

> ADHD is a (disorder) 'condition' that is defined through analysis of behaviour. People with ADHD show a persistent pattern of inattention and/or hyperactivity–impulsivity that interferes with day-to-day functioning and/or development … With a total estimate of 2.6 million people in the UK with ADHD (694,000 children).

Inattention, being hyperactive and impulsive are the common themes among educators in their descriptions of children in their care when I'm called in

to offer support. They are 'fidgety', 'bouncing off the walls', 'won't sit still', 'always on the go', they 'can't focus'.

Now what I would like to add here is expectation and understanding of development, specifically the development of boys. Our boys and girls develop differently, no one way right or wrong, just different. Many of the behaviours we see in our settings may be indicating a boy's natural pathway of development. A child not focused, a child not sitting still, could be an emerging trait of ADHD, however, we always have to look at the wider picture of gender developmental differences.

There are disparities in the research as to whether at the age of 4, boys have a huge testosterone surge, but those agreeing with it, report on the differences we may see in our boys and girls. With this surge of testosterone comes the need to move the body, be ready to run, fight, and protect. They want to be the fastest, the strongest and the best. And with the nerve endings tingling with this hormone, it's little wonder our boys can't sit still. Therefore, it's can't, not 'won't' sit still. Focus can be fleeting and due to the need to move, therefore, there is little room for concentrating on anything else.

Research is now starting to show us the fundamental differences within the functioning of the brain for those with ADHD. Some of the structures, predominately those we would link with working memory and emotional control, within the brain take longer to fully develop, and therefore children can present as immature or their behaviours not reflective of what we would typically see in children of the same age. And in order for our brains to complete multiple tasks, or shift focus, we need strong neural connections. Again for those with ADHD, these can take longer to develop or be less efficient. The way the brain network functions is that it's made up of brain cells that pass information along from neuron to neuron. To do this, 'the tail end of one neuron releases tiny amounts of chemicals called neurotransmitters. These chemicals have to cross a small gap — called a synapse — to get to the tip of the next neuron' (Rawe, 2023).

Therefore, ADHD can affect this process in a few ways:

- The sending neuron may not release enough neurotransmitters.
- The receiving neuron may have trouble 'catching' the neurotransmitters.
- The neurotransmitters may get sucked back up by the sending neuron too fast, before a good connection is made with the receiving neuron.

Some common early indicators

A caveat, these indicators may differ as per each child's ADHD presentation:

- May shift attention regularly
- Will spend brief amounts of time with activities or resources that are of little interest
- Prefers to listen to instructions when they are ready
- Demonstrating a preference to stand for activities
- Requiring a resource to play with when sitting for a period of time
- Requiring regular movement breaks
- Needing support to take turns

Dyslexia

The immediate response to the question, what is dyslexia?, is a difficulty with spelling, reading and writing. And that isn't wrong, but we also have to understand how it impacts other skills. There are common links to executive function skills, namely, retaining information, working memory and processing information. The British Dyslexia Association (BDA) has adopted the definition of dyslexia: 'Dyslexia is a learning difficulty that primarily affects the skills involved in accurate and fluent word reading and spelling. Characteristic features of dyslexia are difficulties in phonological awareness, verbal memory and verbal processing speed' (British Dyslexia Association, n.d.).

Great early years practice supports and celebrates the wonders of early mark making, providing children with a range of resources to make those early marks. Big chalk writing on brick walls in the garden, using wooden spoons and tools in shaving cream and gloop. All of which are supporting the development of the hand muscles that will enable children to hold a pen or pencil when they are ready to.

We don't push the 'correct' forming of letters too young, we don't insist on children learning to read and write in this critical play-based stage of development. Therefore, we may not identify this neurodivergent condition in our settings. But it's still worth noting some of those early indicators.

Some common early indicators

- Some confusion between positional language, e.g. up, down
- Understanding one instruction at a time
- Can find it tricky to keep focus and attention
- Forgetting names of known people
- Some words may appear muddled
- Mixing up the alphabet or numbers 1–10
- Finding self-registration difficult

CASE STUDY: PERSONAL EXPERIENCE OF DYSLEXIA

I was diagnosed dyslexic as a child and as an adult diagnosed autistic. To me, it means being the ultimate square peg in a round hole. It makes me who I am in all the good ways, but also an understanding that being neurodivergent does cause some challenges in daily life.

My education experience was turbulent, I started to fall behind in year 3 and the school I was at was unwilling to offer any additional support for reading, writing and spelling. I tried a couple different schools until we found one that suited me, as I seemed to be a magnet for bullying. At the school I went to from year 5 to year 11 did wonders for my academics, with a lot of hard work, it paid off. Although socially I didn't quite fit in.

When I went to college, I found it difficult emotionally, with the lack of structure and the not working towards a final exam date. I left education for a while and returned to do an Access to Higher Education in Biosciences, which was extremely challenging and the mental health struggles I was going through at the same time, led to me gaining my autism diagnosis, but the course leaders were extremely supportive and helpful.

When I got to university, it was different. The support for me had been put in place which was amazing for me. However, we were in a pandemic which meant that I was working remotely which really suited me. For me, the higher I got in the education journey, the more I enjoyed the learning, because as an individual you are in charge of your learning, and you can work in a manner that works best for you with the support being available when needed.

(Rebecca, neurodivergent adult)

Dyspraxia

Dyspraxia is a developmental coordination disorder (DCD) and affects movement and coordination in both fine and gross motor development, for those with the condition. The challenges are faced in the planning and processing of motor tasks.

The Dyspraxia Foundation (n.d.) describes the condition as 'a disruption in the way the messages are passed between the brain and the body' and impacting, movement, organisation and planning and speech and language. It's often referred to as the 'clumsy child syndrome', with parents and professionals describing children as regularly bumping into things, running with an awkward gait, or often falling over.

Some common early indicators

- Finds activities like stacking and building blocks challenging
- They may show preference eating with their hands rather than using a knife and fork
- They may regularly fall or bump into furniture
- Can find it tricky to ride a bike or scooter
- You may see a different hand grip and they may find writing or mark making a challenge
- Find stairs or climbing equipment tricky to manage

Pathological demand avoidance (PDA)

I want to start by addressing the words used within this condition. The National Autistic Society now reference it as just demand avoidance, debating the usefulness of the full label. Other groups, individuals and parents of children with PDA have referred to it as Persistent Drive for Autonomy, which I feel more comfortable referencing.

According to the PDA society,

> [PDA] is widely understood to be a profile on the autism spectrum, involving the avoidance of everyday demands and the use of 'social' strategies as part of this avoidance. PDA individuals share autistic characteristics and also have many of the 'key features' of a PDA profile.
>
> (PDA Society n.d.)

Those with PDA experience many intense emotions as demands are placed on them, described as a need for control over events and situations. When this is not felt, there is an overwhelming feeling of anxiety and a threat response perceived by the nervous system. The demands can be seemingly low to others; however, rules, questions, commands, requests, expectations and even visual instructions can trigger stress, anxiety and panic. As with many of the sensory aversions of the autistic profile, children with PDA *can't* complete many tasks, rather than they won't complete tasks.

I am often asked how to support children with PDA in terms of ensuring their safety and emotional well-being in settings, and I always refer to the PDA Society's PANDA guidance:

P = **P**ick battles
A = **A**nxiety management
N = **N**egotiation and collaboration
D = **D**isguise and manage demands
A = **A**daption

Some common early indicators

Some forms of resistance might be shown:

- Saying no, even to things they seemingly enjoy
- Finding and using excuses not to do something
- Physically resisting, going floppy or sitting down
- Aggressive behaviours and emotional meltdowns

In her YouTube video on demand avoidance, Purple Ella describes her own experience:

> If I put something in my diary, as soon as it's in black and white and it's a demand, I feel anxiety. I feel anxiety as I put it in my diary; I feel anxiety in the lead-up; I feel anxiety on the morning when I wake up and that thing is in my diary. It makes me experience demand avoidance, even if it's something I wanted to do. Ditto putting a task on my 'To do' list – as soon as the demand is on my 'To do' list, it's a demand and it causes anxiety.
>
> (Purple Ella, 2020)

Sensory processing differences (SPD)

SPD is the term used for those whose find being overwhelmed, discomfort and difficulty in processing the sensory input their brains and bodies receive. At present in the UK this is not confirmed as a stand-alone identity, however, it is one that is added to the criteria for the DSM-V (the *Diagnostic and Statistical Manual of Mental Disorders*), the medical reference guide for clinicians for assessment for autism spectrum condition.

Neurotypical brains can receive sensory stimuli, filter out what they don't need and take in what they do, and the messages from this stimulus are sent from the sense organs to the brain. The brain processes the information and quickly makes a judgement on whether that stimulus is safe, and what to do with the information.

CASE STUDY: PERSONAL EXPERIENCE OF SPD

I see the world in black and white ... and I struggle to see that there are numerous colours in the world. With my sensory needs, I can easily get over-stimulated by sights, sounds and smells that those who are neurotypical may not. Imagine being in a shopping centre and entering a clothes shop and what do you experience? I will sense the smell from the clothing to each person's unique smell. Hear the way they speak, every sound from talking and the music to footsteps and hangers being put out on a rail and cash being exchanged in the till. I will feel the ground beneath my feet, each person brushing past me, the fabrics of the clothes and the way the air is against my skin.

(Molly, autistic adult)

Our children can quickly become overwhelmed by the sensory input around them, display sensory sensitivities to noise, visual stimulus and touch or display behaviours that indicate they are seeking sensory input. Many of us are aware of the five main senses, but do you know about the lesser-known three that give us a great knowledge base of the why behind some of the behaviours we may observe in our children?

Let's make a start on the ones we know more about and how sensory processing disorder may impact these.

Tactile: how things feel when we touch them

- Children may not be able to wear certain clothing, it may hurt or feel uncomfortable on their skin.
- They may avoid messy play because of the need to wear a harsh plastic apron with tight sleeves.
- Children may also avoid messy play because of the actual messy bit. It can feel uncomfortable or unsafe to have sticky or dirty hands.
- Avoidance when washing or being over-sensitive to being hot or cold.
- Children who are not comfortable with hand holding or hugs when dysregulated.

Gustatory: how things taste

A common one seen in early years settings, children who have a limited or restricted diet.

- Avoid brushing teeth.
- Children who seek strong tastes, pickles, spicy food, etc.

Auditory: how things sound

- Children who are the loudest in the room, making sharp, sudden or continuous loud sounds.
- Children who avoid loud or sudden noises, they may place their hands on their ears when the room gets too loud, or prefer to wear noise cancelling headphones.
- They may not respond to their name being called.

Visual: the things we see

- Children who are overwhelmed with lots of bright visuals in the space.
- Children who are impacted by harsh lighting.
- Children who seek comfort in dark, low arousal spaces.

Olfactory: how things smell

- Children who are impacted by strong smells, perfumes, or they may not notice unpleasant smells.
- Children who find it tricky to sit at the dinner table with the food smells from the other children's plates.

Let's now have a look at the additional three senses that are really important for us to understand.

Vestibular: the sense of movement

The vestibular system is located in the inner ear and supports our coordination, our balance and special orientation. Our brains and bodies receive stimulus through our eyes, ears and our vestibular system (balance and

movement) and all of this input combined allows us to work out where we are. Are we too close to something? Are we moving or standing still?

Greutman (2023) tells us:

> When your child has an underdeveloped vestibular system, their brain is not getting the correct information from their eyes, ears, sense of gravity, or movement in their bodies. This, in turn, makes their brain and body feel unsafe. When they do not feel safe, their arousal level, attention, and survival mode responses kick in. This leads to a fight-or-flight response in the body.

So, what might we see?

- A child who suffers from motion sickness
- Avoiding the swings in the park
- Children seeking to spin, roll, be upside down or craving movement

Proprioception: the sense of body position

This is located all around us, within our skin, our muscles, joints and ligaments. Our bodies use the receptors in these areas to send the messages to the brain to tell us what pressure we need to carry out a task, where our limbs are in relation to the rest of our body and also helps us with coordination. As such,

> [p]roprioception is crucial for motor control, postural stability, and the ability to identify weight, size and pressure. The proprioceptive system can be a good tool for calming, organising and self-regulating the brain and nervous system. Proprioception is essential for maintaining a level of alertness and as a result can impact positively on levels of attention and learning.
>
> (NHS, n.d.)

So, what might we see?

- A child may appear clumsy, they may bump into things, fall over often
- They may misjudge how heavy or light an object is
- They may seek touch and deep pressure across their body

Interoception: the internal senses, what's going on inside

This is the sense that sends the signals from the receptors located within your inner organs to the brain and tells us how to respond. Telling us if we are hungry, if we are too hot or cold or if we need to go to the toilet. Children with sensory processing disorder find it difficult to interpret the messages and therefore respond the way we would expect them to.

This can also link to emotions, they are not as tuned in with their body's messages and therefore its needs, this can therefore impact regulation.

This can have a huge impact on children's ability to keep safe, they may not be tuned into unsafe situations as they may misinterpret the cues for danger (faster heart rate, etc.). They could potentially go all day without eating or drinking as the cues for hunger and thirst are not given the appropriate response. They may not know to take a layer off if they are too hot, or feel the sense of the hot floor on their feet and burn their soles.

SPD has two elements to it: those children who are sensory-seekers (hyposensitive), and those children who are sensory-avoiders (hypersensitive), and those children who show signs of both. We need to be aware of each child's sensory profile in order to offer the best support for them.

TIME TO REFLECT

- How well do you understand the different senses and the impact of SPD on children? How do you currently respond to the behaviours that may be linked to SPD? Do you ensure your team are aware of these behaviours and always seek to ask why?
- What strategies do you use to help you and your team get to know your children's sensory profile?
- How do you currently support your sensory avoiders? How do you support your sensory seekers?

The nervous system

The neurodivergent brain is like a maze of different shapes, sizes and colours, our paths to the end may not match up, but with some

> *nurturing from those who take the time to understand us as individuals, we can function in society. Just because our brain mazes are different to neurotypical brains, we are not crazy, we are unique but still human.*
>
> *(Molly, autistic adult)*

The nervous system is made up of the brain, the spinal cord and nerves. It controls much of what you think and feel and what your body does. It allows you to do things like walk, speak, swallow, breathe and learn. It's an extremely clever system and as well as the above, it also controls how the body reacts in an emergency. It is, in fact, the control centre of the brain and needs to be in good working order to be able to survive the world around us.

Imagine a car. If you have the right amount of oil, water, diesel and air in your tyres, it runs smoothly, your car is working efficiently and effectively. However, if you are low on diesel, or your tyres are decreasing in pressure, your dashboard lights up and tells you that you need to address the issue.

As humans we don't have a dashboard that lights up to tell us that something isn't quite right and this may be the reason we don't feel great, or we can't function effectively, or we are a little more emotional than normal. If we understand how our nervous system functions, what it needs to stay balanced and stable, we can 'feed' it with what it needs to help us regulate.

In our nervous system we have these 'sub systems' and it's crucial for us to understand what these are and how they work.

In order for us to stay calm, to experience connection, to be a rationale thinker and to be creative and expressive, our nervous system needs to be in a *parasympathetic* state. The parasympathetic nervous system is there for rest and digest, helping us to regulate and settle.

When we feel unsafe, either from real or perceived danger, it activates the *sympathetic* nervous system to keep us safe and enable us to prepare for action. This can look different for different children but in essence, it's how they are able to remove themselves from the situation by the following actions:

- Screaming
- Running away
- Fighting to get out of the current position they are in
- Meltdowns
- Hiding and retreating

Conkbayir (2021) explains:

> The brain sends warning messages down the spinal cord and into the nerve fibres that connect to glands and organs. Stress hormones like cortisol and adrenaline are then released into the bloodstream. These trigger other physical reactions, for example, our heart pumps faster and our breathing quickens. Sometimes, these changes are helpful. They make us alert and give us the energy to tackle or escape from a dangerous situation. But repeated stressful experiences are not good for the mind or body, especially for young children.

This is the fight, flight or freeze response you may have heard of before.

Many of our neurodivergent children who I have described in this chapter can face many perceived dangers on a daily basis. The room being too noisy, being given food that to them is unsafe, being in crowded places, transitions, a change in routine or structure of the day or having to wear shoes. The neurodivergent brain goes into immediate survival mode.

The fight, flight or freeze response (the sympathetic nervous system)

Our brains are very wonderful, very clever things. They have been built and designed to keep us safe, always seeking the path of survival. Therefore, when it comes to our perceptions of what is a dangerous situation, the brain's survival mode takes over, in a fight, flight, or freeze response.

Now this was great back in the cavemen days when we saw a bear heading towards us. The nervous system sensed danger, the stress hormone cortisol floods the brain, the heart beats faster, sending all of the oxygenated blood to the big muscles, that then enable us to run or fight our way our of the situation, that keep us alive.

However, the brain can't distinguish between a bear chasing us, and a neurodivergent child's nervous system sensing danger from a crowded, noisy space. The response is the same.

Our three brains

We can use neuroscientist Paul MacLean's 'Triune Brain' model to understand the division of the human brain. In the 1960s, MacLean separated the brain into three hierarchal regions which is based on an evolutionary view of the brain's development. The three regions are as follows:

1. Reptilian or Primal Brain (Basal Ganglia)
2. Paleomammalian or Emotional Brain (Limbic System)
3. Neomammalian or Rational Brain (Neocortex)

(Interaction Design Foundation, 2023)

Our reptilian brain is the brain that senses any perceived or actual danger. Once it does so, the messages that are sent to the limbic system (the emotional control centre) are to respond in a way to get us out of the situation; this often results in dysregulated behaviours as everything is telling us to run, fight or freeze. Once this happens, this is the area of the brain in control, and therefore the neocortex, the brain that is there for reasoning, language, rational thinking, is not able to function.

Ultimately, we need to provide a space, an environment, and experiences and opportunities that feed the reptilian brain with messages of safety, a sense of belonging, a place where needs will be met, a space of calm. Only then, can our children explore, be curious and navigate our enabling environments where they will then thrive.

What we might see from our children

Fight

- Yelling
- Blaming others
- Hitting
- Demanding
- Aggressive behaviours

Flight

- Fidgeting
- Running away
- Avoiding situations
- Procrastinating
- Being unfocused

Freeze

- Being absent
- Being isolated
- Being zoned out
- Being unresponsive
- Hiding away

Once we understand some of these behaviours as a fight, flight or freeze response, we can then begin to more consciously consider what might be a contributory factor in these behaviours. Once we identify the triggers, we can remove or diffuse these, therefore resulting in reduced stress, and then reduced meltdowns.

Final reflections

Once we embrace this new terminology and perhaps new ways of understanding our neurodivergent children, we can enhance our provision. As educators, our role is ever changing, always moving forward and there is always new knowledge, ideas, theories and strategies to learn.

When I think back to 30 years ago when I began my early years career, things were very different. But the fact that this is a sector that is continually evolving, continuing to strive for better, is why I love it.

Commit to learning more. This isn't the end of your learning journey with neurodiversity, this is just the beginning, I know each and every day I am seeing things differently and developing my understanding and knowledge all the time.

And once we know a few strategies and guidance that can support us to deliver effective and quality-driven neuroinclusive practices, a child will

come along and blow all of that out of the water! And that's OK. We start the journey again of knowing, of growing and doing all we can to enable every child in front us to laugh, learn and thrive in our care.

Resources

Further reading and research

Heidi Mavir (2023) *Your Child Is Not Broken.*
Kerry Murphy (2022) *Supporting the Wellbeing of Children with SEND.*
Barry Prizant (2015) *Uniquely Human.*
Monique Thoonsen and Carmen Lamp (2015) *Sensory Solutions in the Classroom.*
Rebecca Wood (2022) *Learning from Autistic Teachers.*

Instagram

@aperion_training
@Heidi Mavir
@jessie_and_the_family
@jodiewarren
@simoninclusionteacher
@stephstwogirls
@StoriesaboutAutism
@tsw_see_beyond_the_clouds

References

ADHD UK. (2023). What is ADHD? About ADHD.. Available at: https://adhduk.co.uk/about-adhd

British Dyslexia Association. (n.d.). What is dyslexia? Available at: https://www.bdadyslexia.org.uk/dyslexia/about-dyslexia/what-is-dyslexia

Conkbayir, M. (2021). *Understanding Neuroscience and Self-Regulation in Early Years*. New York: Hallmark.

Dyspraxia Foundation (n.d.). Dyspraxia at a glance. Available at: https://dyspraxiafoundation.org.uk/what_is_dyspraxia/dyspraxia-at-a-glance/

Elkin, R. (n.d.). The overlap between dyspraxia, dyslexia and ADHD. Available at: https://psychiatry-uk.com/the-overlap-between-dyspraxia-dyslexia-and-adhd/

Flannery, K.A. and Wisner-Carlson, R. (2020) .Autism and education. *Child and Adolescent Psychiatric Clinics of North America* 29(2): 319–343. doi: 10.1016/j.chc.2019.12.005

Greutman, H. (2023). How the vestibular system affects your child's behavior: A guide for parents & educators. Growing Hands-On Kids. Available at: https://www.growinghandsonkids.com/vestibular-system-affects-childs-behavior.html

LexxIC. (n.d.). Neurodiversity experts: Neurodiversity in the workplace. Available at: https://lexxic.com/

Mavir, H. (2023). *Your Child Is Not Broken: Parent Your Neurodivergent Child Without Losing Your Marbles*. London: Pan Macmillan

Murphy, K. (2022). *Supporting the Wellbeing of Children with SEND*. Abingdon: Routledge.

Nason, B. (2014). The Autism Discussion Page on the core challenges of autism: In *A Toolbox for Helping Children with Autism Feel Safe, Accepted, and Competent*. London: Jessica Kingsley Publishers

National Autistic Society. (n.d.). What is autism? Available at: https://www.autism.org.uk/advice-and-guidance/what-is-autism

Neurodiversity Hub. (n.d.). What is neurodiversity? Available at: https://www.neurodiversityhub.org/what-is-neurodiversity

NHS (n.d.) Sense – proprioception. Available at: https://sensoryprocessinghub.humber.nhs.uk/sense-proprioception/

PDA Society. (n.d.). Katie. Available at: https://www.pdasociety.org.uk/

Prizant, B. (2015). *Uniquely Human: A Different Way of Seeing Autism*. New York: Simon & Schuster.

Purple Ella. (2020, July 17). Demand avoidance [Video]. Available at: YouTube. https://www.youtube.com/watch?v=aUeeyivGuW8

Rawe, J. (2023). The ADHD brain. Understood. Available at: https://www.understood.org/en/articles/adhd-and-the-brain

The Interaction Design Foundation. (2023). The concept of the 'Triune Brain'. Available at: https://www.interaction-design.org/literature/article/the-concept-of-the-triune-brain

Thoonsen, M. and Lamp, C. (2015). *Sensory Solutions in the Classroom.* London: Jessica Kingsley Publishers.

Wood, R. (2019). *Inclusive Education for Autistic Children: Helping Children and Young People to Learn and Flourish in the Classroom.* London: Jessica Kingsley Publishers.

Wood, R. (2022). *Learning from Autistic Teachers.* London: Jessica Kingsley Publishers.

3 When we know more, we can do more

Those reading this who have completed any training qualifications, or who work in early years or primary education, will have attended a training session on safeguarding. It takes us through the categories of abuse, the signs and features that could indicate a child is being maltreated as well as the steps we should follow to ensure we are sharing our concerns in the right places, with the right people.

We are categorically told that safeguarding is everyone's responsibility. And it is, there is no other narrative to be had, it is absolutely everyone's responsibility. But what if we placed the same expectation, the same insistence, and the same narrative on neuroaffirming and neuroinclusive practices? Just imagine for a minute, what impact this would have? I do! And I do this every single day. And when we all do, it is having impact.

There are two key areas we need to ensure we fully understand prior to embedding this change in narrative. We need to understand inclusion, and we need to understand uniqueness. Let's go ahead and look at these.

Understanding inclusion

We are all aware of this key definition of inclusion:

> a universal human right. The aim of inclusion is to embrace all people irrespective of race, gender, disability, medical or other need. It is about giving equal access and opportunities and getting rid of discrimination and intolerance (removal of barriers). It affects all aspects of public life.
>
> (Hudson, 2022)

DOI: 10.4324/9781032642994-3

Under this definition, we give equal access, remove barriers and remove any level of discrimination. But do we just pay lip service to this with regards to our neurodivergent children in our early years and school spaces? Are we there yet in its truest form, ensuring we have these practices fully embedded in our provision?

Inclusion is doing the following:

- ensuring all children are given the tools to access our full curriculum offer
- embedding neuroinclusion in our whole provision
- offering adaptions and accommodations
- providing neurodivergent children with the same opportunities as their neurotypical counterparts

But what does this mean in practice? Is this the reality?

CASE STUDY: THE MISSED TREAT

I remember visiting a school several years ago. When the children were arriving in the morning, they were greeted by the teacher and asked to begin the task that was outlined on the whiteboard. There was lots of chatter and anticipation for the beginning of the day and hustle and bustle as the children began to gather their equipment and take a seat at their table. Once the registration had been completed, the teacher informed them of a very exciting assembly that would be taking place that morning. A company of actors were visiting the school and were going to be treating the children to an excerpt from their newest play. An instant excitement took over the classroom, with lots of chatter about what it would be like.

A minute or so later, the teacher stopped the children completing their current task and began to invite them to line up by the door to go down to the hall for assembly to watch the play. However, four children, whom she then named, were to stay behind with

the teaching assistant to complete a reading task as part of their programme.

Consider just for a moment the impact of this scenario. It may well be that these children required some additional support, but did this need to take place at this moment? Those four children who were involved in the initial excitement were now told that they were unable to go with their peers, to experience this great play put on by the visitors. Not only would they be missing out in the immediate event, but they could also be excluded from the subsequent re-enacting of the play in the playground, or the group huddle discussions about what the majority of children had just experienced.

TIME TO REFLECT

- Does this demonstrate inclusive practices?
- Can you think of any further deeper level exclusions from this?
- How would this have impacted confidence, self-esteem, the sense of belonging?
- Could this have a far-reaching impact on social exclusion?
- Has this situation increased the divide between those who can and those who find education challenging? How has this impacted the wider understanding and acceptance of difference?
- What could have been done differently?

If the desired result of inclusion is 'a sense of belonging and membership, positive social relationships and friendships, and development and learning to reach their full potential' (DEC/NAEYC, n.d.), then we need to ensure we are not excluding our children from events, situations or opportunities that could go a long way to achieve this.

How can we do this? We can use the word INCLUSION to help us.

Include and involve

Always start with the 'how'. How can we ensure that every child can be involved in this activity, in this experience? What do we need to do to enable everyone to take part? Which accommodation or adaptions need to be considered? What support does each child need to complete and achieve a given task and to be involved.

Never exclude

On a basic level the notion of inclusion is to include, therefore the opposite would be to exclude. This is not just referring to the provision and opportunities to be inclusive of every child in the setting, but to also make sure that any specific support programmes take place, for the most part within the classroom or early years space. According to Department for International Development (2019), that is the basis of successful inclusion. And this doesn't require a huge refurbishment or extensive building works, it might just need a little outside-the-box thinking. Where can a little nook be created, where can a space for small group work be set up, how can the group or class be split into working groups where children can support each other, where you can better deploy the adults, you have in the room?

Consider each child's specific requirements

I understand that within the early years space some may feel unable to take children with SEND. This could either be due to needs being too complex, or they feel unable to meet the safety needs of the child, or they do not have additional resources to provide a potentially required, 1-1 for the child. However, we have to consider 'how can we?', not 'we can't' (check out the next section on assessing need).

Listen

Listen to what the child's parents/carers are telling you, they are their first and main educator and know their children best. However, they may not yet be in a position to know what they need to tell you, they may be only at their start of their journey to understanding their child's neurotype. So, our role to support inclusion is to be aware of the additional messages that can come through your conversations with them.

Also listen to the child's behaviour. This can tell us all about how they are feeling, how they are coping with a situation and aid our understanding of their stress response to overwhelming experiences.

Understand the barriers to inclusion

Is it a lack of staff training skills, lack of perception or an understanding and knowledge gap? Is it an environmental barrier? Is it a barrier linked to routine and expectation? Is it a policy barrier? Is it an embedded culture that needs to change? First, identify the barriers, physically, culturally, practically that exist and move to the next phase.

Seek support to break them down

It's one thing to identify an area that is creating a barrier, the next is to work out how to break this down and remove the barrier completely, so that you can impact change. However, it may be that we can't do this on our own. So, who can we connect with? Seek training and support from an external, neuroaffirming consultant, access help and guidance from your local authority, connect with other settings or schools who do this well. Tune in to podcasts and/or social media accounts that promote inclusion, connection and affirmation of all neurotypes.

Include the whole team around the child

This must be paramount. The child needs to remain at the centre, and we form part of their team around them, with all other professionals and their parents as part of that team. In meetings, in discussions about ongoing care, considerations and need, we must play our role within that team.

Offer adaption and accommodations

Always ensure you are providing those adaptions and accommodations where required. Continue to reflect and review these to ensure they are still required and still relevant and supportive to that child's needs, right now. It's not a one-time-only assessment, its ongoing. They also have to be consistently carried out and provided by the whole team, not just when the SENCo is in the room.

Neuroaffirming

We *MUST* always assume competence. For the majority of our neurodivergent children, it's not that they can't, it's that they 'can't yet', so let's do all we can to support them to achieve and to reach their full potential. Let's provide a strength-based approach to all we do and an affirming narrative where we always meet our children where they are, never forcing them to become more neurotypical to 'fit it'.

Consideration of specific requirements: assessment of strengths and needs

Many of our neurodivergent children can access and thrive in mainstream settings. With the best environment, an understanding of need, purposeful adaptions and accommodations, a knowledgeable, flexible and committed team, our children can settle and achieve great things in their early years spaces.

The points below will enable you to highlight your key areas of strength in providing this, alongside your challenges, and ensure that you have done all you can to accommodate a child of difference. Only once you have consistently completed the steps below will you be in a position to discuss whether or not your setting is able to keep that child safe and facilitate a positive early years' experience for them. Under the Equality Act 2012, every public sector has a responsibility to provide accessibility, as summarised in 'Reasonable Adjustments: A Legal Duty' (DfE, 2020). This might 'mean alterations to buildings by providing lifts, wide doors, ramps and tactile signage, but may also mean changes to policies, procedures and staff training to ensure that services work equally well for people with learning disabilities' (DfE, 2020).

Before a child starts at your setting

The first thing to do is gather all the evidence you can from the parent/carer or previous setting to ensure you start with providing the right space for them, right from the beginning. Consider gathering data about the child:

- What are their strengths?
- Current interests/play type – how do they play or engage in their current or special interest?
- Communication – what is their method of communication?
- How do they manage in different environments – home/out in public/at family gatherings/crowded spaces?
- How do they sleep – patterns/current challenges?
- What is their current diet/any food aversions/where and how they like to eat?
- How do they currently manage with transitions or a change in routine?
- Behaviours – are there any consistent/current triggers? What can cause a child to become dysregulated? What does this look like for this child? What support do they need to become regulated?
- Any indicators of their current sensory profile? Are they a seeker or avoider? Do they have any sensory sensitivities? How are these supported?

Once the child has started with you

Environmental

Have you completed an environmental audit of your setting? An environmental audit is a way of assessing the physical environment to ensure that it provides a safe and supportive learning space for all children. In particular: noise, temperature, smells, lighting and visual stimulus have been found to have an impact on engagement, felt safety and participation. Adult and child perceptions of their environment may differ. What some people take for granted can be overwhelming and upsetting for others. If you have access to an outdoor space, use it and use it often, in all weathers!

Staff training needs

- Have you identified gaps in the knowledge and skills set of your team?
- Do they understand neurodivergent behaviours, play types, communication styles? Knowing these and providing for these can help to connect with and understand the child in front of us. Only once we understand all of this can we provide effectively for them.

Behaviours

- Do you understand the neurodivergent behaviours in front of you?
- How are you responding to these behaviours?
- Are you aware of the impact of sensory processing differences on a child's behaviour?
- How are you currently supporting self-regulation?
- Are you providing a sensory diet?
- Do you offer a place of escape where that child can retreat to, to decompress?
- Do you offer weighted blankets, cosy spaces, fidgets, dim lighting, ear defenders?

A sensory profile

- Have you completed a sensory profile for the child?
- Is every team member aware of the child's sensory profile?

- Is the child a sensory seeker or avoider, and how are you accommodating for this?
- What adaptions are in place to enable the child to access the full curriculum?
- Are you providing them with a sensory diet to support their sensory needs?
- Are you aware of the behaviours that may indicate a sensory need and how to support this?
- Are your team knowledgeable in the lesser-known senses of the proprioception and vestibular input? Once known, this can be a game-changer in our understanding of the needs of the child in front of us.

Transitions

- How are you supporting transitions?
- Is this an area the child finds difficult?
- What have you done and what are you doing to support this?
- Are you consistently using visuals, objects of reference to support a child?
- Are your team flexible and adaptable in their thinking around whether all children tidy up, or whether a toy of interest can go outside with the child, or be placed on the lunch table?
- Do children have time with a trusted adult during difficult transitions, an adult who is highly aware of their needs and requirements during any change?

Removing other stressors

Our early years spaces are filled with stressors that impact our neurodivergent children and their ability to be regulated, calm and ready to explore and discover. Many stressors can be environmental, but we also need to consider group dynamics. Consider the children you already have in on certain days, would a new child joining be able to settle and thrive more on other days?

Food and expectations

- What snacks are you providing?
- Are you always offering a child their safe foods?

- Do you allow them to eat when they are ready and where they feel comfortable eating?
- Expectations: sitting for carpet time, sitting for a story, accessing imaginary play, messy play, connections with peers, singing, all MAY be activities that can be tricky for our children. Consider the accommodations and adaptions you can make to enable them to participate, when they are ready, in their way, and when they feel safe to do so.

Understanding uniqueness

Knowledge is power, and now we know more, we can do more, '[t]he language of inclusion is changing, and we are repositioning children with special education needs from problems back to learners' (Heiskanen et al., 2018). Below are examples of exactly this, once these educators knew more, they did more.

EXAMPLE 1

We listened to your webinar last night, it opened our eyes and we changed something today in the nursery and I wanted to share it with you.

We have a little girl who is autistic and has not been eating while she has been with us, however, her mum does say that she eats at home. Today, I sat at the table with her, just me and her, away from the group, but as you said, where she could still see her peers. The girl sat and let me feed her and she ate all of her lunch, and then most of her pudding. We have all been celebrating her amazing achievement, we are so proud of her.

This was in response to a discussion around understanding the sensory overwhelm of lunch time, the noises, the smells, the closeness of peers sitting right next to us, scraping their plates. Just a small adaption enabled this little girl to feel safe with her trusted adult, enough not just to try a little bit of food, but eat the whole plateful.

(Nicola, nursery manager)

EXAMPLE 2

Your visit has helped us to understand that children who are neurodivergent do not need to conform or be cured but in fact be supported and encouraged to be their own selves, and that we needed to focus on being in their world rather than changing their world. This has had a great impact on our ability to enter their world and see the world through their eyes and adapt our practice accordingly.

We have taken on board your advice and taken a step into the children's world and have been overcome by the progress we are seeing. Not only have we encouraged a child to eat a full meal which he has never done before, we have also supported him to the point where he can comfortably play with others around him when before this would have been a trigger.

(Nursery SENCo)

EXAMPLE 3

A child began attending my setting, she settled well but showed a dislike to any change. One day, not long after she had started, we chose to take the children to the woods for a nature hunt. The weather was slightly warm, she was very quiet and holding my hand, I spoke to her to reassure and discussed with her our surroundings.

The other children were running around excited, collecting twigs, feathers and leaves to put into their bags. She did not speak a word until we arrived back to my setting where she broke down crying. She had a meltdown, and we were unable to reassure her through verbal communication or cuddle her, as this increased her distress, only to make sure she was safe and let her know we were here for her when she was ready. Eventually she calmed down and retreated into the cosy area after asking to go home and for her mummy.

In hindsight, we did not take her needs into consideration, we assumed because she was happy that she was settled. When, in fact, she needed predictability before she was confident enough to explore

a new space and feel safe. She was tired, hot and overwhelmed with the surroundings, temperature and children shouting.

The next time we went for a walk in the woods, she had more of a bond with me as her trusted adult. We went during a cooler time, with fewer children and provided her with noise-cancelling headphones. We also had a prior discussion of where we were going and what we were going to see using picture cards as a visual aid. With these small adaptations, she was less anxious, more prepared and happier to explore her surroundings.

(Nikki, childminder and parent)

Understanding to acceptance

CASE STUDY: FAIRY DUST!

I remember supporting a nursery several years ago, a well-established nursery with a great staff team. They asked me to observe a boy in their baby room, they told me that they felt that they needed more support as they were unsure how to engage with him. They reflected on what they felt was a lack of eye contact from him, limited interest in any activities or resources and difficulty with transitions. The SENCo had been observing him, had already been in conversation with his parents and as he was now over two years old and pre verbal, so a referral had been made for an assessment.

I observed him for a while, there was little connection with the space, the areas within it, the other children and with the staff. He appeared disengaged and any attempt to connect with him to engage interest in what was available, was met with clear communication, as he walked away.

It was time for the group to move towards the garden area. He was unsure of what was taking place and became distressed at the transition. The team managed to calm him enough to encourage him to follow them into the garden. Once outside, he immediately found a

plastic animal, lay on the floor in the middle of the garden and began to move it around in front of himself, making noises and laughing occasionally as he did so.

I sat nearby, observing this play for a while. I noticed he was very engaged in his solitary play, not affected by the other children running near to him, he was focused and playing to his agenda. I moved a little closer, ensuring that I watched for any adverse response from him, as I didn't want to distress him any further. Once I felt he was comfortable with me closer, I moved to directly in front of him, collected a toy animal like his, lay on the floor and began to mirror his play. As he moved the animal, I moved my animal, as he made a sound or gesture, I did the same.

After several minutes, he looked up at me, he gave me direct eye contact, then quickly looked away again, and I continued to follow him. This was his play, at his pace, his agenda and with him in complete control of how it went.

After several more minutes, he looked up again at me and smiled, I looked and smiled back. Then to everyone's surprise, he began to engage physically with me, climbing on me, laughing and continuing to smile. We played like this until it was time to transition inside, at which point he took my hand and walked back into the room with me, with no distress.

So, what did I do?

Did I sprinkle magic dust in the air? (as the team asked me if I had!) No.
Did I say or do anything that was new or revolutionary? No.
Do I know something they didn't? Possibly, so let's explore it a little more.

Prizant (2022) explains:

> I made the case that autism is not an illness, but a different way of being human. I have always believed that the best way to provide support is for non-autistics, and society in general, to collaborate with autistic people, to listen

and better understand each person's experience, and change what we do in providing appropriate support if it's needed.

And this is exactly what I did, I collaborated, I listened, I connected with him, right where he was. With no neurotypical agenda to my connection or my play with him. I validated his play, I said, through this connection, I hear you, I see you, I understand, and I will follow you. I made him feel safe to be with me. We developed a trusting relationship where he felt safe to be his true authentic self. I understand and I accept.

TIME TO REFLECT

- Are your connections affirming their neurotype?
- What do you understand about neurodivergent play? (See Chapter 4 for more on play.)
- Consider reflecting with your team on the whole setting approach to the differing neurotypes of the children you have. Where can you learn more?

The role of the Special Educational Needs Co-ordinator

At the beginning of this chapter, I mentioned that SEND provision needs to be everyone's responsibility, and I stand by that statement. However, within early years settings and schools there is someone who takes on that overall responsibility. In many cases, one member of staff who co-ordinates the delivery of implementing the best practices for children with SEND: the SENCo.

The role of the SENCo is to ensure that the SEN Code of Practice 2015 is adhered to in England and Wales only, for Scotland: it follows the Education (Additional Support for Learning) (Scotland) Act 2004.

Within the SEND code of practice, it makes it very clear the responsibilities and duties placed on early years settings and school with regards to the

SENCo role, including 'ensuring all practitioners in the setting understand their responsibilities to children with SEND and the setting's approach to identifying and meeting SEN' (DfE, 2015).

But what does this look like in practice and how does the SENCo support their team? We need to consider where SEND provision touches everyday practice to enable us to deliver effectively on quality neuroinclusion. As SENCo, it's worth considering the following as your starting points for reflection to determine where the setting currently is with regards to the 'settings approach' as described above in the code of practice.

Policy

To look at the approach within the setting, we first need to consider the directive coming from the top:

- What does your policy say?
- How neuroaffirming is your policy?
- Is it one the setting has had for a while that is looked over briefly each year and a new date placed at the top or the bottom of the document?
- When was the last time you really read it over and reviewed its content?
- Does it mention neuroinclusion and neuroaffirming practice and the expectation for all to deliver it?

The application process

- What is this asking from parents and/or carers and, more importantly, how is it worded?
- Does it ask about special educational needs or disability? If it does, is that where the information gathering stops? Take a look back at earlier in this chapter regarding the assessment of need. Ask the right questions to gather the information you need right from the start. But also, be aware of how you are asking those questions. If it mentions 'concerns', 'worries', 'developmental delays', or other negative language, then it may be time to consider this narrative right from the start.

The show-round

- What is the narrative from that initial connection with a parent?
- Would a parent/carer, who may be seeing some differing traits and behaviours in their child's development but is not yet ready to discuss these with other professionals, feel able to discuss these freely with you?
- Are you mentioning 'red flags' or 'delays' that place a negative connotation on SEND?
- Or is your show-round filled with the following narratives?:
    - Celebrating uniqueness
    - Understanding, supporting and celebrating children's different pathways of development
    - Creating a sense of belonging for each and every child
    - Ensuring each child feels safe, heard and accepted, just as they are
    - Supporting parents/carers of children following a differing pathway of development without judgement
    - Working in a transparent and consistent way with parents/carers of children who are requiring some additional support in their early years

The skills set and knowledge of the team

To ensure consistency in a high-quality early years setting, neuroinclusion has to be embedded within the team. And for us to do that, each and every team member needs to have had the training forming their foundation and building on knowledge gained, to be effective as a whole setting. A training audit of skills, competencies, knowledge and practice is a clear way of identifying gaps and ensuring you are meeting the training needs for everyone. As a starting point, take a look at:

- Sensory processing and the impact of the environment
- Basic neuroscience
- Understanding neurodivergent behaviours and traits
- Schematic play

Alongside training, as SENCo, your role is to lead and mentor your team. This should include regular observations; modelling of neuroinclusive practices; SEND delivery added to the agenda of each staff meeting and room meeting; keeping yourself updated on neuroaffirming practices and local authority processes.

BEING THE MODEL

To know you need to model best practice with regards to neuroinclusion is one thing, but knowing what to model is another. First, as SENCo, as well as auditing your team's knowledge and skills, ensure you are self-reflective too. Where are the gaps in your knowledge and confidence in neuroaffirming practices? Once identified, don't be afraid to reach out to develop your own skills set.

What to model?

- Joining the child right where they are
- Following the child's lead in play
- Making a holding space for the child during your interactions
- Identifying and planning for schemas in play
- Effective serve and return interactions
- Building a trusting and safe space
- Identifying and meeting sensory needs
- Understanding and responding in a calm and understanding manner to behaviours that may challenge
- Flexibility in routine
- Adaptions and accommodations.

Environment

I wrote about this earlier and will continue to do so, as it's so vitally important. However, an audit of the environment and the training and skills gap of the team really do go hand in hand. You can complete an environmental audit (which I would encourage you to do) but to make the changes that may be required, the whole team need to understand the 'why'. Why are we

discussing the sensory environment, why is it important, what impact does it have on the children in my room, what impact will the changes make, why do these need to be consistent? Once we know the 'why', we are more likely to embed the alterations. Also, as SENCo, ensure that you are making changes 'with' the team, not 'to' the team.

Neurodivergent children become neurodivergent staff

I know, who would have thought it! We can make all of the adaptions and accommodations for our wonderful neurodivergent children. We can ensure that our practices are neuroaffirming, that our environments are low arousal for the children and that we provide adaptions and accommodations for our children to feel calm, settled, safe, supported and understood. But what about your neurodivergent team members and colleagues?

Ensure that your settings are just as supportive, accommodating and accepting of your wonderful team. You may have staff who have identified and confirmed neurodivergence, inform you right from the start and then the dialogue is open regarding their strengths and their support needs. However, for many, it's only once they are working in the education arena where children are being identified with a differing neurotype and discussions are being had about their strengths and needs, that an individual may identify similarities for them. How are you supporting both pathways? What level of accommodations and adaptions do you have in place for them? Do you know their sensory profile, their triggers, their communication style, their distress signals?

For example, autistic teacher Madge Woolard explains:

> Schools are frequently noisy, smelly places, full of sensory bombardment. I often spend hours in a windowless room with fluorescent lighting, which gives me a headache. I'm asked to change rooms at a moment's notice … I have to lug the keyboard across the noisy playground to teach in the dining hall, where staff are still clearing up after dinner … I often spend my evening in almost total silence to recover.
>
> (Wood, 2019)

Executive function

Executive function is the higher-level functioning of the brain's organisational processes, as well as helping us to have a level of control over our impulses, our attention and focus. It touches on working memory, using previous knowledge to develop new skills, time management, and allows us cognitive flexibility. It's the part of the brain that allows us to plan ahead, prioritise, organise and complete a task. Neurodivergent children, or staff, can face the following challenges:

- Find it difficult to stay on task or complete an instruction
- Face challenges in organising what they need for a task
- Find a change in routine or task tricky to manage
- Need a lot of clarity and repetition of a task given in order to complete it
- Will often lose belongings
- Face difficulties with time management
- Find asking for help challenging

So how can we support our staff within the early years and education space, ensuring we are providing accommodations and adaptions that will enable them to feel safe and flourish throughout their career?

As I have discussed before, we need to understand the specific needs of the child or adult in front of us. Don't make assumptions based on an identity on paper, allow time and space to understand the needs, strengths and challenges faced by your team member. Remembering that if they are in the category of just figuring out their own neurowiring, they may be seeking clarity and understanding from you to help them understand themselves. Create a space where they are able to talk openly with you, without judgement or consequence, especially if they are finding things a little tricky. Create an environment where asking for help is a strength.

Creating a safe working environment

- Embed neuroaffirming practices across your early years environment and ensure all staff, parents, children and visitors are aware of your approach
- Create an open culture of discussion around difference

- Provide opportunities for new staff to share their unique differences, well-being needs and required support, adaptions and accommodations
- Add well-being support discussions to every staff meeting, supervision and appraisal
- Ensure celebrating and acceptance of difference are always on the meeting agenda

When setting a task, or giving an instruction, make sure you are very specific, nothing is left with a hidden agenda, or an unwritten expectation. You may need to break down a task into smaller chunks, with clear time frames and instructions. Using visuals can be of real benefit, or alternatively a real example of the end product you are wanting them to complete.

With time management being a potential challenge, offer assistance, tools or resources to help. Can you provide an online or physical calendar, a daily planner or specific task master resource? By discussing together a way of overcoming this challenge, you are acknowledging and accepting the need for support, validating their executive function needs and being their advocate.

Allow the need for breaks. For our neurodivergent team members, this could be a sensory break when things become too overwhelming, a time for them to decompress, regulate and breathe. All of which can go some way to preventing burnout. Support them in understanding the times of the day when they may need to take a short break or breather and support their need for this.

Communicate with them in an open, honest and transparent way, also enabling the discussion to be held with the rest of the team. Provide a space where everyone who needs to know is aware of the accommodations and adaptions that are in place to support all staff to thrive, personally and professionally, within your early years setting.

> *In my opinion, those who are neurotypical should come to understand that myself and others who are neurodivergent are no different to themselves. We only see the world in a different perspective, but our perspective is not incorrect.*
>
> (Molly, autistic adult, early years educator)

Taking the team through this change in practice and the importance of managing change

Kristie Parkins, a qualified change manager, gives the following guidance when making these changes and embedding this culture shift.

MAKING A CHANGE

Many people do not like change. It may be that they are happy as they are and cannot see why there is a need to change. Some do not understand the change and others simply don't want to change.

It is normal to be unsure of stepping out of our comfort zone. This is why it is important to give our team the right tools or/and support to make the change as smooth as possible. We also need to accept that people adopt change at differing speeds.

As a manager or team lead, it's important to know really your team members or get to know what makes them tick. You need to understand them as individuals, understand their unique needs, to know what kind of support they all need to adopt something new.

By doing this, you'll be able to use those that embrace the change to try and influence those that don't find it so easy. There are also some ways to work together to introduce new things, for example:

- *Pilot one new thing as a team or to an individual* to use for feedback before rolling out more change. Like a new set of procedures, or policy, do them by level of importance and ask for feedback on how well it went before you roll out the next one. You may find there is a better way people want to accept change of questions that need answering before you move on to the next element. You may also find that one size does not fit all, and you need to make changes for individuals rather than a team.
- *Try to be able to assess readiness for change*. Rather than do something like a survey or a questionnaire. Maybe try to do a fun task or icebreaker to try and gauge how people are feeling about particular changes. This can be quite useful when it's a larger

change before you go into the change. By doing this, you'll be able to see the areas where people may need a bit more help or time to accept change.

- *Do not overload people,* maybe appoint a change champion to help with the change and support the roll out to team members. Often people listen to other colleagues before a manager and accept change faster. Once others see the successful implementation of change and the benefits it can bring, they will want to be involved.
- *Offer rewards* like a team lunch or activity when they have managed to successfully implement a change.
- Throughout the implementation of any change, it's really good to be able to let colleagues *anonymously provide feedback* or their worries. Not everyone is confident enough to share their views with the rest of the team or directly with managers. It may be a good idea to provide some kind of feedback box or area where each person can feel safe to share feedback, be it positive or negative.
- *Share the plan with the people who will be going through the change.* Create a visible one-page plan that can be shared throughout the team so they know when you're hoping to implement the changes and how they're going to get there. A timeline with all the activities is great to show to your managers and your colleagues so that they can prepare themselves for the days, weeks or months ahead. It does not have to be complex, it can be very simple, nice visual drawing with some fun attached to it.
- *Involve people in the journey* rather than dictate what and when the change will happen, this shows how much you are invested in your people, and that their opinions matter. Set them up for success and support them throughout the journey as you are all in it together and they need to see this.

Final reflections

My view is that we shouldn't need inclusion officers or inclusion support, nor policies that reflect inclusive practices. Controversial? Maybe. But while we still have staff employed in those roles, it shows it's something we are not yet doing well.

Inclusion should just be what we do, and inclusive practice should be part of the DNA, the foundations and the ethos of any early years setting.

This chapter has provided information, guidance and suggestions to begin the process of change, change towards an approach that focuses on inclusion and equitable practices across the early years space. It may feel like a larger piece of work than anticipated, however, change has to start somewhere.

Focus on each of the areas of the INCLUSION concept as your starting point. Use this to guide you towards being that neuroaffirming educator. Start with one area of the setting, it may be policy, it may be the environment, it may be learning more about the sensory needs of the children currently in your setting. But make a start. Start the process of change, bring those around you on the journey too and know that this is the way forward to better support your neurodivergent children and families.

Resources

Further reading and research

Heidi Mavir (2023) *Your Child Is Not Broken.*
Barry Prizant (2022) *Uniquely Human: A Different Way of Seeing Autism.*
Monique Thoonsen and Carmen Lamp (2015) *Sensory Solutions in the Classroom.*
Rebecca Wood (2022) *Learning from Autistic Teachers.*
www.aperiontraining.co.uk to download my free environmental audit tool.

Instagram

@aperion_training
@elliemidds
@Heidi Mavir
@jessie_and_the_family
@jodiewarren
@reframingneurodiversity
@ruth_jones_slt
@sensory.slp
@shauntheteacher
@speechdude
@stephstwogirls
@StoriesaboutAutism

Podcasts

Childhood Understood
Eu-Hu podcasts
Not your typical podcast
Reframing neurodiversity
The hidden 20%
The SENDCast

References

DEC/NAEYC (National Association for the Education of Young Children & Department for Early Childhood of the Council for Exceptional Children). (2009). *Early childhood inclusion: A joint position statement of the Division for Early Childhood (DEC) and the National Association for the Education of Young Children (NAEYC)*. Chapel Hill, NC: The University of North Carolina, FPG Child Development Institute.

Department for International Development. (2019). Implementing inclusive education. Available at: https://www.gov.uk/research-for-development-outputs/implementing-inclusive-education

DfE (Department for Education). (2015). Special educational needs and disability code of practice: 0 to 25 years. Available at: https://assets.publishing.service.gov.uk/media/5a7dcb85ed915d2ac884d995/SEND_Code_of_Practice_January_2015.pdf

DfE (Department for Education). (2020). Reasonable adjustments: A legal duty. Available at: https://www.gov.uk/government/publications/reasonable-adjustments-a-legal-duty/reasonable-adjustments-a-legal-duty

Heiskanen, N., Alasuutari, M., and Vehkakoski, T. (2018). Positioning children with special educational needs in early childhood education and care documents. *British Journal of Sociology of Education*, 39(6), 827–843. https://doi.org/10.1080/01425692.2018.1426443

Hudson, K. (2022). What does Inclusion mean? Inclusion. Available at:. https://www.inclusion.me.uk/news/what-does-inclusion-mean

Mavir, H. (2023). *Your Child Is Not Broken: Parent Your Neurodivergent Child Without Losing Your Marbles*. London: Pan Macmillan.

McLeod, S. (2023). Maslow's hierarchy of needs. *Simply Psychology*. Available at: https://www.simplypsychology.org/maslow.html#Educational%20Applications

Prizant, B. (2022) *Uniquely Human: A Different Way of Seeing Autism*. London: Souvenir Press.

Thoonsen, M. and Lamp, C. (2015). *Sensory Solutions in the Classroom*. London: Jessica Kingsley Publishers.

Wood, R. (2019). *Inclusive Education for Autistic Children: Helping Children and Young People to Learn and Flourish in the Classroom*. London: Jessica Kingsley Publishers.

Wood, R. (2022). *Learning from Autistic Teachers*. London: Jessica Kingsley Publishers.

4 Consideration

In my work, I refer to what I call the 3 Cs for neuroinclusive practice:

- Consideration
- Connection
- Consistency

This and Chapters 5 and 6 will explore what I mean by these, and how all early years' educators can use them to reflect, examine, and reframe their work., and in doing so, support and enable neurodivergent children to feel safe, secure, be curious, investigate, play and learn in surroundings where they feel able to be their true selves.

So, the first of my collection of the 3Cs to support neurodiversity in early years, is consideration. Consideration is 'careful thought, thoughtfulness and sensitivity towards others' (*Cambridge English Dictionary*, 2024) Now this isn't a bad place to start, ensuring we take careful thought of and have thoughtfulness and sensitivity towards others. A great foundation to the 'why' we need to be doing something. And just like Eeyore from the *Winnie the Pooh* stories by A.A. Milne says, 'A little consideration goes a long way'.

Consideration focuses on:

- The environment
- Sensory needs
- Play and engagement
- Narrative
- Training needs

DOI: 10.4324/9781032642994-4

We have touched on all of the above in Chapters 1–3, however, this is where we will go deeper, breaking down each area and really looking at how we can deliver on it and embed consideration in everyday practice. We need to ensure we take a thoughtful view of this potential change in practice, this new way of working, to enable us to have this running through the veins of our setting.

Maslow before Bloom

You may or may not have heard of this saying before. It suggests that in order to effectively engage higher-level learning and thinking skills, humans first need their basic needs met. Abraham Maslow created a hierarchy of needs, with basic human needs as the foundational basis, a very holistic focus on effective support for children in the classroom. McLeod (2023) explains this in more detail:

> Our most basic need is for physical survival, and this will be the first thing that motivates our behaviour. Once that level is fulfilled, the next level up is what motivates us, and so on. The human body cannot function optimally if physiological needs are not satisfied. Maslow considered physiological needs the most important as all the other needs become secondary until these needs are met.

In essence, we need to feel comfortable and safe in the environment we are in, our nervous system needs to be in that optimal balanced state before any level of critical thinking, engagement or learning can begin to take place. Early years focuses on learning through play, for our children to explore, engage with the environment and access our full curriculum offer. Playing independently, and with a trusted adult, maybe developing connections with peers. All of which supports cognitive growth and holistic development. But if our children feel in a constant state of distress, anxiety, fear, panic and generally unsafe, none of that can happen. Therefore, our first and main priority, as an educator, is to ensure physical safety, alongside emotional safety and security.

Environment

Have you seen the 'Can you make it to the end?' YouTube video from the National Autistic Society: Can you make it to the end? (youtube.com)? Do make this your starting point as it highlights very powerfully why we must start with the environment. It will allow you, as a neurotypical adult, to see, hear and feel, in just a small way, how the sensory experiences and input from seemingly everyday tasks can greatly impact many neurodivergent children and adults. This 1.29 minute clip, with few words, demonstrates why this is the first area of focus for this chapter, and why we just must get it right.

So, what do I mean by environment? We need to look at our sensory spaces right from the start of the daily journey for that child:

- Is your setting on a busy road or high street?
- Does the child arrive at a busy time of day?
- How cluttered, busy or bright is your entrance?
- How many other areas/rooms/busy spaces does the child have to navigate before they to get to their room?
- When they arrive, how crowded, busy and noisy is their room?
- Do they arrive at the start or middle of a meal time?
- Do they arrive just at the start or middle of a transitional period?
- How do the other children and staff greet them as they enter the room?
- What does the room look like, feel, sound and smell like?
- Do they see their preferred activity or a regulation space they can head to?

A child can experience all these environmental touch points within the first 10–15 minutes of every single day. And all of these ten considerations can impact the start of each day with regards to their regulation and their emotional safety. Some of these factors we may find tricky to change, it could be that it relates to the actual structure of the building or the location of the setting. But what can you change? What do you have an element of control over as an educator, where can you make it better?

CASE STUDY: ROBBIE'S SAFE SPACE

While I was working at a nursery in South London, 'Robbie' was in the toddler room. Robbie was a quiet child, preferred solitary play, had a very close connection with his parents and took a while to settle each day. His parents took him away for a week one summer, a holiday that involved his favourite thing to do, visiting train stations.

When Robbie returned to nursery, he was extremely distressed at drop-off. He would be holding onto his parents, screaming, crying and trying to escape the room. We worked hard with his parents and took a gentle approach to a re-settle, to support him to return fully to nursery, when he was able.

I began to speak more to his mum and in that conversation discovered some new information that we were not aware of before. Robbie seemed 'afraid', as mum put it, of the hand dryer in public places, as the weather had got a little brighter and warmer. She had begun to push him to nursery in the pushchair and she had noticed the closer they got to the busier roads, he put his hands over his ears. She started to mention more and more about his overwhelm in heightened sensory situations.

Before I knew much about sensory sensitivities and sensory processing challenges, I was beginning to pull together all of this information and make a plan for Robbie to support this transition from home to entering his room at nursery.

I created a safe space for Robbie. We had a pop-up tent that I found in the back of a cupboard and I set this up in a corner of the room. In there I placed soft cushions, pictures of Robbie with his mum and dad at the train stations he had visited, ear defenders and some of his favourite story books. As his key person, I asked mum to call the nursery when they were 5 minutes away. This gave us time to reduce the noise level in the room, turn down the lights, turn off any music that may have been on in the background, and ensure I was available to greet him at the door. We had the handover at the main front door to the nursery rather than in the room, as it was quieter. When Robbie and I entered the room, other staff members acknowledged his arrival

with a smile and positive body language, but no overwhelming verbal welcome and we went straight to the tent together.

We spent time looking at his pictures and chatting together. During which time Robbie was scanning the room to check who was in and what was available to explore and discover that day. Once he acclimatised to the space, he slowly came out of the tent and continued his day.

Robbie just needed time. He needed that reassurance from a safe and trusted adult that everything was OK. He needed to adjust and sometimes decompress from the journey to nursery that had already overwhelmed him, before he'd even entered an over-stimulating toddler room with noise, busyness and lots of people.

Autistic writer Donna Williams described autism as:

> an internal human 'normality' with the volume turned up. We all have experienced moments when we are not quite aware or when we are too aware to handle the world ... we all have had times when we've hardly any awareness of our bodies, even being out of them, or let so in, weighed down by them, that we become hypercritical, eager to escape, tune out, disappear.
>
> (Williams, 1998)

For Robbie, he was eager to escape the sensory feedback his body was receiving in that moment. It all just became too much for his brain and body to handle and this was seen in his behaviour. His crying, his screaming, his need to run away, were all telling us, 'I'm in distress.' So, rather than adding to the noise with the narrative, 'It's OK, mummy will be back later. Let's go and see what's in the room today, your friends are waiting for you. Look, there's George, he wants to come and say hello. Let's go and play with the trains over here, you like trains, don't you? Don't worry, mummy will be back after tea', alongside all the people in a small space, the bright lights, the nappy-changing smells, the humming of the heating and children playing.

I stripped it right back for Robbie. I took him calmly and quietly after saying goodbye to his mum, we entered a calm, quiet, low-arousal space, we retreated to a place of safety together, with me as his trusted adult. And we just sat. No agenda. No discussion. Just

calm in the space for Robbie to decompress, adjust, feel safe and be given the autonomy to head out into the room when he was ready.

For Robbie, there were several key factors impacting his central nervous system and therefore his ability to regulate. There are elements that as an educator I have no control over, but where I did, I needed to consider what I could change to make him feel safe. While I couldn't change the location of the nursery and Robbie's route to get here each morning, I could suggest to his parents a buffer. I offered them a pair of noise-cancelling headphones, these would remove the harshness of the sounds of the traffic and busyness in the street.

I was then aware that as his key person, I was Robbie's main and trusted adult. For the next couple of weeks, I ensured that I was the constant who greeted him outside and brought him into the space. Offering that considered approach to the handover, and I'm aware that this supported his mum too. Just this alone had a profound impact, ensuring familiarity, routine, structure and predictability, all of the things that Robbie's nervous system required to regulate.

The physical space

As educators working within the same space, day in and day out, we can reach a point where we no longer notice. The displays become wallpaper, the noises and sounds fade into the background, we get used to the smells and just how it is in the space. But for a neurodivergent person, this may all be a lot to process, as 'they can experience sensory overload, or information overload. Too much information can cause stress, anxiety, and possibly physical pain. This can result in withdrawal, distressed behaviour or meltdowns' (National Autistic Society, n.d.b). But this is where our children need to you to start.

An environmental audit is a great way to determine the space from a sensory perspective, allowing you to consider points that may have not even entered your mind. It can make us see the space from a different lens (Figures 4.1 and 4.2), from a neuroaffirming lens. Let's go back to some of those initial questions?

Figure 4.1 Before – a large open space

- *What does it look like?* – Is the space filled with busy displays, children's artwork suspended from the ceiling, lots of unnecessary bright colours? Do you have harsh strip lighting on all day, is there any natural light, is the space cluttered and filled with unnecessary 'stuff'? As the child walks in the room, how overwhelming could that visual stimulus be?

Figure 4.2 After – cosy, calm space, ideal to support regulation

- *What does it sound like?* – Are there constant noises from background music, when are the noisier times of the day? How loud are the staff, are voices raised to gain attention from others? Is there a doorbell or are staff communication tools being heard constantly in the background? Do you offer a buffer for children when you know you are going to be testing the fire alarm?
- *What does it smell like?* – What cleaning materials are you using to wipe down surfaces, do you use an air freshener? Are staff aware of their own smells, perfumes, aftershave, body spray, shampoo? Do you change nappies in the room? Are meals and snacks prepared within the room or do those smells waft into the space at certain times of the day?
- *What are the touch points?* – Do you have resources that support children who are sensory seekers? Are you offering messy play, but without the option to get involved without getting messy, are you providing an adaptation or accommodation for sensory needs? What are you expecting children to wear, either as a uniform, or as a protection for messy play?
- *What are the taste points?* – What are you offering at meal and snack time? Do you offer and allow for children's safe foods?

Safe foods in the environment

Many neurodivergent children have preferences for familiar, safe foods. Take a plate of blueberries as an example. Each blueberry will look different, feel different, some will be firm, some will be soft, some will be sweet, some will be tart, some will be hard, some will be squishy. Therefore, there is that unpredictability of what they are going to get when they put it in their mouth. With a breadstick, for example, each one is the same. Each breadstick looks the same, smells the same, crunches the same and tastes the same. It's predictable, they know what they are getting and there are no surprises. Indeed, '[t]his need for sameness could also explain a person's preference for processed foods. Processed foods are predictable, designed to look and taste the same each time. In contrast, there will always be natural variation in fresh food' (National Autistic Society, n.d.a).

A place of escape

> *The child had not wanted to return to the busy nursery room after a nappy change as the noise level had increased. We created a place of escape for him, to use when he needed to. An area that enabled him to regulate. This has helped him so much.*
>
> *(Tracey, nursery manager)*

A place of escape, a calm corner, the regulation zone. So many different terms for essentially the same thing. Where can your children go to decompress, to regulate, to breathe and reset when things get too overwhelming? This doesn't have to be a big area, filled with expensive sensory room equipment. It could just be a pop up tent, some voile hung from the ceiling with a few cushions, ear defenders, fairy lights and a box of fidgets tools. Just ensure you provide the space within your space, that it is easily accessible, available and purposeful.

TIME TO REFLECT

- Have you provided your children with a place of escape?
- Where could you add an area?
- Consider placing it in a space with less 'traffic', and ideally near natural light. Also with an obvious backing to create a sense of safety.
- It is open or enclosed
- What could you provide within the space?
    - Bubble lamp
    - Ear defenders
    - Fidgets
    - Weighted blanket
    - Images of safe and trusted adults
- Special interest toys and resources

Figure 4.3 shows a space that was created for a child who was demonstrating that he was not feeling safe to return to the main play space. They used what they had and set up a table on the other side of a joining door. This was his table, with his picture on it and his familiar resources and fidgets. This was just what he needed to take some time, either with a safe adult, or a space he went to by himself and regulate. Once he did, he returned to the main space within the nursery.

Figure 4.3 A child's place of escape within a pre school room

Sensory needs and behaviours

We are learning more and more from neurodivergent adults about the importance of knowing and understanding the impact of the sensory environment on regulation, learning, behaviour and the support mechanisms that should be in place to support our children within the education space. We need to know and understand the impact of over-responsive and under-responsive sensory systems, why our children 'bounce off the walls', why they place their hands on their ears, why they have a limited diet and why they may take their shoes and socks off. And once we understand all of the above, we understand the impact and importance of us getting the space right for our children.

As human beings, we are continually processing the sensory stimulus around us, and our brain and body are figuring out what to do with the information. We are working out if we are safe with the information we are being given and, if not, our brain and body will respond to ensure we are safe and kept away from harm.

Activation vs calming

Not all children require a calm, sensory space. Not all behavioural responses require a retreat, stillness and quiet. Sometimes our children need their senses activated due to under-developed sensory systems (Table 4.1).

Table 4.1 Activation vs calming

If a child is …	*Sensory system*	*Support needed*
Running around and jumping	Proprioception	Activation
Placing everything in their mouth	Gustatory	Activation
Pulling and stroking children's hair	Tactile	Activation
Spinning round and round in circles	Vestibular	Activation
Putting their hands on their ears	Auditory	Calming
Covering their eyes, placing their head in their hands	Visual	Calming

Sensory input – and how we process it all

- *Registration* - We receive the input via our sense organs. Our ears hear the child crying or our nose smells that lunch has been brought into the room.
- *Arranging* – The sense organs will then decide which input is priority and figure out which one do we need to act on immediately and which are not necessary right now. Is the child crying the immediate reaction required, or do I need to respond to the child crying first?
- *Processing* – Once the sensory input is deemed appropriate and important enough for action. it will be passed to the cerebral cortex for action.
- *Action/behavioural response* – This is where we see the actionable response to the sensory input. Let's go and find where that crying sound is coming from and respond by comforting the child.

And the way we process information will lead us to take action. For many of our neurodivergent children with sensory processing challenges, this action may not be what we would expect nor understand.

I remember taking my son to a friend's house as we had been invited to a party. Now we had been to this house lots of times before. It was a close friend of mine; she understood him, and his needs and it was a safe space for me and my son to visit for play dates. So, I figured that this would be an OK place to go on a Saturday afternoon. I prepped my son prior to leaving the house, where we were going, how it may feel a little different as there would be other people there, I was also warned about furniture being moved around to accommodate the party guests, so we chatted about that too.

We got to the house, knocked on the door and were greeted by my friend, as the prior arrangement (familiarity and predictability were required as much as possible). But my son then froze (*Registering*). I managed to support him to get into the house for us to shut the door behind us, but he

wouldn't go any further (*Arranging*). He told me – very loudly I might add! – that the house smelt funny and he didn't like it.

Now he was right, maybe it wasn't a 'funny' smell, but it did smell different. What I hadn't taken into consideration was that my friend's mother-in-law had prepared a lot of the food for the party, she was Ghanaian, and while I was loving the smell of the curry, Jollof rice and yam, my son wasn't so keen. Therefore, he didn't get any further than the bottom step in the hallway, the furthest away from the kitchen as possible (*Action*). It was just far too overwhelming, it was causing distress and therefore he was unable to regulate, focus on anything else and ultimately, debilitating, restricting his ability to go any further (*Behaviour*).

Many parents will tell you of the preparation required ahead of going anywhere, doing anything and for any expected and known change in routine. Understanding the sensory needs of our children is a huge part of that. Once we are aware, once we see ahead, we can plan to mitigate the impact.

And the same applies in an early year's environment. Understand sensory sensitivities, understand the impact of the sensory environment, understand the behaviours associated with sensory overwhelm and those distress signals. And then go ahead and create that sensory safe space.

Play and engagement

Play is a child's fundamental right and the primary delivery of early learning. Neurodivergent play has just the same purpose. However, it looks different to what we may have seen before and what we are more used to seeing as we observe our children play. But neurodivergent play, needs to be understood, accepted and validated.

The definition of play is an activity that is *led by the player* without an agenda or instructions from an outside source. Therefore, if we are 'forcing' our children to play our neurotypical adult-directed way, because we feel we need to 'teach' or to show our neurodivergent children to play the 'right' way, is it play at all?

What if, while you were playing pop-up pirate with your children, you were told by an outsider that you were playing it wrong? What if you were

told you had to start with the pirate up and you had to pop him down into the barrel? That really wouldn't make any sense, would it?

What if you were told that even though you love to dance, the way you dance, to the music you love dancing to, wasn't 'right'? Your steps were wrong, the music wasn't right, and you moved your arms in a way that wasn't quite correct. Are you still then playing? Are you still the player? So, is it play?

There is a misconception that autistic children, specifically, do not know how to play or they do not play properly, and our children are told daily, sometimes several times a day that their play is wrong, that their play doesn't matter. This isn't always as blatant as I have put it, but through directions given, by play being stopped, by 'forcing children' to play differently, this is exactly what we are doing.

They do play, they just explore and play in their environment differently to the dominant neurotype. However, when we are in our early years spaces observing our children., the way our neurodivergent children play often can make little or no sense to us. Some would suggest that our children need to be 'taught' to play. However, does this sound neuroaffirming to you? Does this say autonomy, meeting them where they are, or validating their play needs and play types? I think not!

Appropriate play is not play

We need to avoid the urge to shape or change the child's play with our neurotypical play agenda. By participating right there with them, we are engaging, we are creating trust, we are validating their uniqueness, we are saying, 'I trust you, I believe in you.' This build the relationship, this supports the connection, this says, 'I've got you and the way you play, who you are and how you are is just right, because it's right for you.'

Types of neurodivergent play

For us to be able to support and engage our neurodivergent children in their play, we need first to know and understand the different play types they may be engaged in.

Solitary and parallel play

The Bright Autism blog explains this type of play well, stating:

> During parallel play, [an autistic child] can choose when to engage and when to retreat, giving them control over their social environment. This form of play respects their need for personal space while still exposing them to the rhythms and dynamics of social interaction. In this way, parallel play acts as a bridge between solitary play and more interactive forms of play, allowing children to learn from their peers in a low-stress setting.
>
> (Api, 2024)

Schematic play

Schemas are those patterns of play that we observe our children engaged in. Our role as educators is to observe what this schema looks like, how we can interpret this play and what the children are learning and exploring by playing this way. Then considering, how can we support them further? We may see the following actions:

- Positioning schemas – arranging or lining things up
- Transporting schema – taking objects from one place to another, carrying objects inside something to take them to a new place
- Enveloping schema – being covered in blankets, or scarves, or covering toys in materials or other resources
- Rotation schema – an interest in things that turn, spin, roll, or spinning themselves
- Trajectory schema – moving objects by throwing or dropping

They are often described at urges to do something, creating their own opportunities for learning, supporting the development of those neural pathways and strengthening the synaptic connections within the brain. It is deep, fascinating, interesting, child-led play, one which is vital to understand and follow. Once understood, it can be used to scaffold learning and can be used to plan for and to connect with each child.

Repetitive play

Play that is on a constant loop, over and over, again and again play is observed quite often with neurodivergent children. Once again, it can provide the notion of safety, regulation, and provides predictability. All of which we know support our children in unpredictable, overwhelming environments. I'm sure you have seen children that will gravitate to the same area, the same resource or the same play type each morning when they arrive in the setting. This forms part of their routine, it's what they do, they connect the setting with that resource or process, therefore creating a sense of familiar, and in the familiar is safety. Our role is to provide that safety, provide for that routine, follow that desire and need for regulation.

Special interest play

They are not obsessions, they are special interests, we all have them, it's just that for our neurodivergent children, these can go to a deeper level. In any early years environment I have worked in over the years, or have been supporting, the policy is that we follow the interests of the children. Our setting is child-led, we plan around the current interests, observed trends or patterns in play. That is, until we feel they have a differing neurotype. We see these repetitive behaviours in their play and feel we need to, somehow, divert their attention to something else. We need to see them engaged in 'other things'. Why? We just need to go with it and embrace it, but if the interest observed is in cars, don't just flood the setting with cars. Really observe what it is about the cars:

- Are they categorising by make and model?
- Are they organising by engine size?
- Are they informing you of the recent rankings in Formula One?
- Does a relative fix cars and that is what they are seeking to explore?

Or if it's dinosaurs or trains or European countries, then your homework for the weekend is to find out all you can about these things. Use them to plan activities, to extend learning and to ask questions. But more importantly, use these interests to connect with them.

CONNECTING WHEN A CHILD IS ENGAGED IN THEIR PREFERRED PLAY

- Approach neurodivergent children with ease, and respect
- Understand and see the value in their play
- Meet their play needs by understanding the purpose they serve
- Model and show alongside them, how *you* play, without forcing them to do the same
- Understand the importance of their play type

Our narrative

We can create an amazing low sensory environment, we can understand sensory needs, we can support different play types. But if the narrative and the language in the environment do not connect to this strength-based approach, affirming approach, then we will be unable to embed the change required to be a truly neuroaffirming early years space.

And our narrative isn't just in what we say. It's within the environment we create. It's the way we support play, it's the displays around the setting, it's the outside professionals we work with, it's the content in our reports, the message within our policy. It's also the narrative we use for the show-rounds for new parents, the chatter in the staff room, the support we provide for our neurodivergent colleagues. Our narrative is the heart and soul of what we do.

So, what does your narrative say and/or suggest?

CASE STUDY: IT BEGINS WITH THE POLICY

A nursery school, a beautiful outdoor-focused nursery, had a wonderful environment. Children had continual access to the outside, as well as regular trips to their forest school. The inside environment was calm, with low visual stimulus and they regularly invested in developing their team through training. They had a very knowledgeable

and experienced SENCo, however, she was frustrated at the lack of consistency in their approach to neurodivergent children. She felt that while some understood the need for the use of visuals, flexibility in delivery, a full understanding of the children's sensory needs, this was not shared among the whole team.

I was asked to take a look at their SEND policy. And here lay the issue. The foundation on which practice is built, the guide that everyone in the setting is asked to follow, did not reflect the ethos and the strength-based narrative they were wanting to be consistent in offering. Any new staff starting their role at the nursery were being shown one way within the rooms, while their policy and procedures were informing them of a very different narrative. On reflection with the team, many were honest in saying that they hadn't read it for a while, were shocked at how different it was to what they were being told by the SENCo and were being verbally asked to deliver.

So, when we are looking at consideration, we need to start with the foundation message that is being read by new staff and apprentices as part of their induction.

Check the language, does it mention any of the following?:

- You are committed to ensuring all children thrive by having full access to your curriculum offer
- You understand the need for children to play and learn in an emotionally safe space
- You provide this through an understanding of each unique child, that is shared with those caring for the child
- You will truly hear the voice of the child, through observing their responses, their behaviours and their interaction in the environment to understand their unique support needs
- You will provide a flexible offer, one which tunes into the needs of each child
- You will work with the parents/carers to gather all the information required to provide an environment where the child can have a sense of belonging
- You provide environments that support all children to thrive, spaces that are calm, support regulation and where children's

unique ways of learning, thinking, communicating and playing are valued and validated through positive connections
- You allow self-expression, validate the way children communicate and play and will always enable them to be their unique selves

Once the policy is in place, it's vital to review and reflect that this is embedded across the whole setting. Your narrative is also in your show-rounds, your staffroom, your displays.

Training needs

Early years is an evolving sector, one which never stops changing as the world develops more knowledge, more understanding, more awareness and as theories develop and new ones come into fashion. That's why I love it, like me, it never sits still. However, this does mean that we need to ensure that we are on that wave of change, right alongside it.

Here are some things I have learnt that have changed my thought process as well as my practice over the years:

- *Identity-first language*: Autistic adult, rather than an adult with autism. This is because '[p]erson-first language belongs to the pathology paradigm and, as such, implicitly accepts and reinforces the assumption that Autism is intrinsically a problem, a Something-Wrong-With-You' (Walker 2012, n.p.).
- *Behaviour*: This is a response to an unmet need, and so refrain from using the term 'challenging behaviour'. It may be challenging to us as the adult, but the child is not displaying challenging behaviour. For many of our children, the behaviours are a survival response, and it should be down to us as the adult to respond with care, consideration and understanding, not with an immediate consequence.
- *Sensory processing*: I wasn't taught about this during my level 3 childcare qualification. This was first brought to my attention, after my son's neurodivergence was confirmed, which is crazy! This has changed so

> much for me. We NEED to know about sensory sensitivities to ensure we understand and can support our children in the best way possible.

Dr Stephen Shore famously once said, 'Once you've met one autistic person, you've met one autistic person', going on to say, 'This is why some [autistics] are good at mathematics while other may be good in their arts, sports, or writing – just like the rest of humanity. Autism is an extension of the diversity found in the human gene pool' (Meredith, 2020). We need to understand each child's presentation of their neurodivergent condition, not to place them all inside one box.

We therefore need to continually be open to learning and understanding more and part of that includes time for self-reflection. Time to identify gaps in knowledge, skills and understanding in relation to neurodivergence. Ensure that there are regular opportunities to analyse your own training needs, as well as those of your team. The four key areas to start with are:

- Neurodiversity and how to embed an affirming culture
- The sensory environment and providing a safe sensory space
- Neurodivergent play
- Behavioural responses to unmet needs

Start with yourself. How would you rate your knowledge, skills and execution of the above on a scale of 1–10? How would you rate your ability to share this knowledge with the team you are working with? How would you rate your ability to model this with your team? Do your seniors have the knowledge and skills to mentor and guide their teams to ensure effective delivery of the above?

And then once you have identified your gaps, how do you ensure that the trainers, or the training courses you send your team on, are sharing in your policy of neuroaffirming practices and can help you move towards that culture change in your setting?

Finding neuroaffirming trainers and courses

Simply ask the questions! Find out about more on the content and style of delivery, don't just join the cheapest 'behaviour management' online course.

Ask for a breakdown of the content and check the language being used. Research the trainer or the company, are they advocates for neurodivergence and the neurodiversity paradigm? If you are seeking training specifically on autism, ADHD, PDA, dyslexia, what is the connection with the trainer and these conditions? Are they sharing their personal, lived experiences, or are they training from textbooks? Ask them about their understanding of neuroaffirming practices and how these are embedded in the content of the training.

Inspirational poet, author and human rights activist Maya Angelou is often quoted as saying, 'Once we know better, we do better' (Hannah, 2024) This could not be more important to understand. If we know more, we do more and we do better.

Final reflections

All of the areas discussed in this chapter, using consideration, give a chance to reflect and review. Remember that consideration is to 'give careful thought'. Consider your practice as an individual and consider the practice across your team. It's a simple activity to audit across the early years space, but it allows us time to review and see all of the areas from a different perspective.

Consider the narrative, 'we do it this way, because we always have', is that helpful?

Consider the changes required, and while potentially tricky at the start, these could ensure you work smarter, and your children and families benefit. Looking inwards can provoke many feelings, but diving deep into our own narrative and practices can support change in a positive direction for everyone.

Resources

Further reading and research

www.aperiontraining.co.uk/free-audit, for my free environmental audit tool and one-page sensory profile on my website

Instagram

@aperion_training
@elliemidds
@Heidi Mavir
@jessie_and_the_family
@jodiewarren
@mrgteacher
@neurowild_
@reframingneurodiversity
@ruth_jones_slt
@sensory.slp
@shauntheteacher
@speechdude
@stephstwogirls

Podcasts

Childhood Understood
Eu-Hu podcasts
Not your typical podcast
Reframing neurodiversity
The hidden 20%
The SENDCast
The SEND network

References

Api, S. (2024). The role of parallel play in children with autism. Bright Autism blog. Available at: https://brightautism.org/blogs/news/the-role-of-parallel-play-in-children-with-autism (accessed 19 January 2024).

Cambridge English Dictionary. (2024). Consideration. Available at: https://dictionary.cambridge.org/dictionary/english/consideration

Hannah, T. (2024). *When You Know Better Do Better, Maya Angelou – Poetry & Poets*. Explore the Beauty of Poetry - Discover the Poet Within. Available at: https://www.poetrypoets.com/when-you-know-better-do-better-maya-angelou/ (accessed February 2024).

McLeod, S. (2023). Maslow's hierarchy of needs. *Simply Psychology*. Available at: https://www.simplypsychology.org/maslow.html#Educational%20Applications

Meredith. (2020). Interview with Dr. Stephen Shore: Autism Advocate & on the Spectrum. IBCCES. Available at: https://ibcces.org/blog/2018/03/23/12748/ (accessed 12 May 2020).

National Autistic Society. (n.d.a). Eating – a guide for all audiences. Available at: https://www.autism.org.uk/advice-and-guidance/topics/behaviour/eating/all-audiences

National Autistic Society. (n.d.b). Sensory differences – a guide for all audiences. Available at: https://www.autism.org.uk/advice-and-guidance/topics/sensory-differences/sensory-differences/all-audiences

Walker, N. (ed.) (2012). *Loud Hands: Autistic People, Speaking*. The Autistic Press

Williams, D. R. (1998). Autism and sensing: The Unlost instinct. Available at: https://openlibrary.org/books/OL460713M/Autism_and_sensing

5 Connection

Introduction

There are many definitions of connection, some that mention a link or an association with something or a relationship between two things or people. For me, these do not define or reflect the true meaning of connection between the adult and the neurodivergent child. Then I came across one that brought tears to my eyes, that sent a shiver down my spine and brought a moment of clarity on what exactly it is we need to do in our early years settings. How we need to be, for our children, the relationship we need to build, the foundation of all we do.

The Calm Editorial Team have given this heartfelt definition: 'Emotional connection is about sharing feelings, being vulnerable, seeking to understand each other and meeting one another with trust' (Calm Editorial Team, 2024). Please just take a moment to read that over and over again. Sharing feelings, being vulnerable, seeking to understand each other and meeting one another with trust. I truly believe that this is the greatest definition and one that I am going now to break down, to ensure that we can dive deep into this statement and make it the bedrock of our work. Ensuring that connection centres on advocacy, support, and is neuroaffirming for the whole family.

Emotional connection

This starts right at the beginning through the relationships between baby and caregiver and how this can form the foundations of emotional connection

DOI: 10.4324/9781032642994-5

between child and adult. Erik Erikson's theory of eight life stages of human growth from infancy to later adulthood can help us see the importance of trust right from the outset, with the first three important for us to understand when it comes to connections and relationships we have with children in the early years (Stages 1–3).

Stage 1 Trust vs mistrust (0–18 months)

Babies need to come to the conclusion that they are in a safe place, with safe people. Somewhere their basic needs are being met and when they are in distress, they are being responded to by an attuned and connected caregiver. This gives the child the initial learnings of self-regulation as the caregiver soothes and supports them through effective co-regulation.

Obviously then, the opposite can happen, that when a child's basic needs are not being met, when their dysregulated nervous system is not being responded to with a calm and considered connection, the baby quickly learns that they are to mistrust the adults around them and mistrust themselves, which then can continue throughout future relationships.

Stage 2 Autonomy vs shame and doubt (1–3 years)

This is where our children are beginning to figure out who they are in relation to others and the world around them. Starting to develop independence with toilet training and feeding, making their own choices, which ultimately come with an outcome, some positive, some not so much. It's the reactions and responses from the adults around them that can twist that wonderful sense of achievement through autonomy and therefore growth and confidence, that can shift the course towards shame and doubt.

If they are made to feel guilty about their choices. If they are made to feel shame through their mistakes, it can impact their future confidence, their sense of self, their resilience which again can continue to impact throughout life.

Stage 3 Initiative vs guilt (3–6 years)

This is where our children continue to develop independence, develop their initiative through their own ideas and critical thinking. We are supporting our children to find their identity, to support their true sense of self, to enable them to try and try again, with support and encouragement.

If they are made to feel guilty about their choices, made to feel that their decisions or ideas are not validated or accepted, this will in turn shy a child away from using their initiative or want to make future plans of their own.

Our role through a positive emotional connection, support, guidance and a trustful relationship is critical for the growth of an independent, critical thinker; someone who can use their own initiative to make decisions, be OK with making mistakes as they trust those around them. Conkbayir (2023) argues:

> Humans are wired for social connection, with holistic wellbeing suffering in the absence of relationships and consequent difficulties in trusting others. Left unresolved, this can pave the way for unfulfilling adult relationships which are littered with mistrust, insecurity, anger and jealousy.

Connection and trust are key to providing a sense of belonging which is basic for emotional growth. With a sense of belonging, we are able to be our true authentic selves and with that ability to be just who we are comes a feeling of freedom of expression, awareness of self-identity and strength in the notion of 'this is me'. To this end,

> [Educators] are not only instructors but mentors and guides who can raise the confidence of their students, help them find a sense of direction, and empower them to believe in themselves. The best way to effect daily change as a teacher is to commit to integrate these values into your everyday practice.
>
> (Robinson and Robinson, 2022)

TIME TO REFLECT

- How do you allow children to express exactly who they are?
- How are you enabling that true sense of self identity?
- What strategies have you embedded in your early years setting that allow children to make choices and be safe with those choices?
- What emphasis do you place on emotional connection across your setting? How do you do this, and what does that feel and look like for the children and the team?

In their exploration of belonging, Allen et al. (2021) write, 'A sense of belonging may be just as important as food, shelter, and physical safety for promoting health and survival in the long run.'

What does this mean for our children?

This means providing a space where they feel heard, seen, accepted as their true self and enabled to be their true self. Where your policy states that children's needs are met, their interests planned for, their uniqueness embraced, this has to be the same for ALL children. Brene Brown (2015) talks about fitting in being the opposite of belonging:

> Fitting in is one of the greatest barriers to belonging. Fitting in is about assessing a situation and becoming who you need to be in order to be accepted. Belonging, on the other hand, doesn't require us to change who we are; it requires us to **be who we are**. Belonging gives us a sense of security because we feel known and valued. Trying to fit in, on the other hand, makes us feel anxious and constantly on edge because we sense that if we slip up, we're out.

And this is what many autistic adults agree with and say it is masking. That feeling of being on edge, trying to comply to rules that don't make sense, trying to hold in a suppressed stims (repetitive behaviours or movements that many neurodivergent children and adults use for regulation) because of the responses from others around you.

I have been supporting early years settings in the past, observing children in the space, who are masking. Masking comes in many forms and can be difficult to identify, however, it's important that we know what to look out for. Let's take carpet time, a time where children are all asked to sit on a carpet to listen to a story or for a moment of adult input. I have observed carpet time where the team believes the child is 'behaving' but are unaware of some of the slight nuances in movement, the alertness in their eyes clearly looking for an escape route, fidgeting, as they are clearly uncomfortable in the space, the body wriggles that suggest a need to move for regulation.

So, is this child feeling on edge, do they have the fear of slipping up in case they are pulled up for it? Their behaviour would suggest so. Therefore, returning to Brene Brown's definition, this is fitting in, which is the opposite of belonging.

And to ensure we are truly connecting and provided that space for connection our children need to have, a sense of belonging. I would encourage you to observe, and really observe, your neurodivergent children. Really look at those subtle differences or changes in their behaviours to determine whether or not they are doing all they can to fit in rather than feeling safe in the space and being their true self.

So, how do we provide that space that promotes a sense of belonging that does offer connection and grants the child that sense of belonging?

Let's start with respect. Respect for them as an individual, respect for them as a human being. Respect for their neurotype, their interests, their communication preferences, their play type and preferences. Respect for difference. If a child feels heard, accepted, valued and respected for exactly who they are, then they will feel they belong.

Connection and trust create a sense of belonging and belonging is vitally important for emotional well-being and psychological safety. Indeed, '[c]onnection is a child's deepest need and an adult's highest influence' (Schott, n.d.).

If we continue to push our children to be someone they are not, to push verbal speech over their preference of gestures, signs or the use of augmented, alternative communication (AAC) devices. If we push them to play our neurotypical way, because we feel they should. If we continue to force them to learn 'appropriate' social skills or 'learn' neurotypical behaviours of attention and focus, we are not affirming who they are, we are not validating them as a wonderful and unique individual who has amazing things to bring to the world.

We are saying, you don't do it right, you need to be different to who you actually are. What this then results in is masking. Masking is hiding your true self and being someone else to fit in. The National Autistic Society defines masking as 'a strategy used by some autistic people, consciously or unconsciously, to appear non-autistic in order to blend in and be more accepted in society' (National Autistic Society, n.d.). In her own experience of masking, Purple Ella (2023) explains:

> Masking happens in the context of being given the message at quite a young age that who you are and your natural, instinctive way of being are not okay, and that you will only be accepted if you shape yourself into something else ... I think as an autistic child, I was given the message that my entire job in life was to make other people feel comfortable. And I never thought about making myself feel comfortable.

Similarly, David Gray-Hammond describes masking as

> a survival mechanism in a world that actively oppresses and abuses us for being different to the majority ... Society taught me that the majority were better than me, more worthy of love and acceptance. I pushed down my autistic identity because I wanted to be accepted.
>
> (Gray-Hammond, 2020)

Our neurodivergent children need to feel that sense of connection, just as their neurotypical peers do. I would go as far as suggesting that they need it more. Connection through play, connection through communication, connection through our interactions, connections through mutual respect and validation of each other and meeting one another with trust.

TIME TO REFLECT

- How does it feel for everyone in your early years environment?
- Are they seen, heard, validated and affirmed for exactly who they are?
- Do you allow self-soothing regulatory behaviours?
- Do you affirm all play, do you affirm all communication, do you allow flexibility in your routine and curriculum that enables autonomy and respect for every child?

Positive relationships

We seek and make connections through positive, collaborative and respectful relationships. In our early yeas spaces, we make these relationships on many levels and with many different people. Yes, with the children in our care, but also relationships with our colleagues, the wider senior team, the parents and the outside professionals we engage with. These relationships will look and feel different, but one thing they have all have in common is the need for honesty, respect and trust. Our environments just won't function well without these key features being reflected in all we do.

From a parent's perspective, I want to feel that sense of a positive relationship with those who are caring for my child as well as the need to know that my children have that positive relationship with them also.

I will now share a case study and then consider its perspective from two viewpoints.

Positive relationships with parents

Understanding and empathy will go a long way in your relationships with parents. Understand that life can be tricky, understand that we are fighting continually, understand that we may feel a sense of anger, isolation and fear, in various ways, at various times.

As my son began Year 4, as with any other year, there was that dread and fear of what was to come. How would this teacher make my son feel, will his needs be met, will he feel supported, will he continue to grow in confidence or will the impact of one person send him down a different path? I felt I needed to develop a connection with his teacher in the first few weeks, I needed to feel that he had my son's back, that my son was in a safe space.

As a parent with a son who had already been through the school, I was acutely aware of the impact that a poor relationship and connection can have. And his teacher felt this from me, he really tuned in with empathy and understanding for what I was telling him.

I asked for a meeting with his teacher, Mr Davies, and instantly knew my son was in a good, safe place. Already, in the space of a couple of weeks, his teacher 'got him'. I felt heard as a parent, I felt that he wasn't just telling me what I wanted to hear, this was genuine. He understood the need to get to know my son from the outset, already picking up on his interests and what kind of teacher he needed to be for him. He told me that the focus was going to be on building trust and faith in him as a teacher, creating that space where my son felt comfortable in trying new things, possibly making mistakes, but in the knowledge that this was OK.

Honestly, I cried. This was so key for my son. Due to his anxiety and fear around school, he needed this trustful and connected relationship. This created the sense of belonging that was key to his growth and confidence within the classroom. The emphasis was not on the academic outcomes, the emphasis was on a truthful, relational approach: 'a way of interacting or communicating with others that embodies core values such as respect, inclusiveness, honesty, compassion, cooperation and humility' (Brookes, 2008).

CASE STUDY: THE YEAR 4 EXPERIENCE, THE RELATIONAL APPROACH IN ACTION

At the heart of it all as a teacher you are entering an academic and (supposedly) nurturing relationship with each child in your class so, like each relationship, you must undergo a 'getting to know you'

phase. During that phase, learn what excites each child, find out about the things they love, relate to those interests, mention them or ask questions of them often. Relate, bring your own experiences of these things no matter how trivial to the child. With Stanley, it was the technical and scientific world and it was football. Two things I also find extremely interesting. It was so important to engage with Stanley in these things. I wanted him to be able to build up enough trust to approach me and initiate his own conversations based on his thoughts and interests rather than me probing all the time.

A teacher must try and foster organic relationships with their children and that can only be done with a genuine heart. You've got to find common ground with your children. That's what I did with Stanley. When that was established, it was so important to let him know that he (like all his peers) was important and that he had a voice and that I, as his teacher, was always going to be there for him, that anything that did not work for him in the past was forgotten and that anything in the future that seemed daunting was going to be seen through with me standing next to him.

It was vital for me to earn Stanley's trust. From all my years of teaching, this approach has always been successful. It instils self-esteem and self-confidence in a child. It empowers a child – especially if they are self-aware. Every tiny step forward is to be celebrated in that child. Each celebration just empowers a child to keep moving forward. Suddenly learning is no longer scary or a challenge if you can break it down into manageable chunks. Someone once told me that bravery is a muscle. Everyone has it but the moment you decide to start exercising for the first time, it's scary, you don't know what you're doing but you do it anyway. The more you do it, the easier it gets, the stronger you become, the more confident and empowered you become. I love that very obvious analogy. This is what worked for Stanley, the little and often approach backed up with a lot of praise from a teacher he trusted.

In this post-COVID-19 world, it is of paramount importance that we as teachers see our children, their learning and their family life

as whole. We must take into consideration every factor of a child's life when it comes to their learning and school progress. We need to teach at the child's pace, we need to slow down, not worry about our colleagues' disapproving looks. We need to make our children feel safe and valued at school, we must want our children to walk into school excited about the day ahead and happy as they leave at the end of the day. If we succeed as teachers in doing this for our children, then half the battle has been won. A happy child is a successful child.

(Giles Davies, primary teacher)

Dr Mine Conkbayir writes about the relational approach with regards to supporting behaviour. We often think of 'behaviour' in the negative sense. A child is behaving a certain way and therefore there needs to be consequences. However, behaviours are also how we are internally behaving and seeing the world depending on the situation and experiences we are having. Conkbayir (2023) writes: 'Relational approaches emphasise the importance of adults gaining trust by building empathetic and nurturing relationships with them.' For myself and my son, the adult (teacher) gained trust, by building that empathetic and nurturing relationship with us both.

What does this relational approach and connection look like for parents of neurodivergent children in an early years setting?

Time

There is never enough of it, is there? But for parents of neurodivergent children, an offering of connection in an unhurried space, giving them time to

talk, to share, to offload, to vent, to be heard is so crucial. I know that in the midst of a busy beginning and end of each day, time is not afforded to early years educators. But when you are able to offer it when needed, the trust and connection built between you and the parent/carers can make the difference.

Just the time together to navigate the next part of the journey, the assessment process, or the funding criteria. Time to hear how their weekend truly was, not just a quick, 'Yeah, it was fine.' Time to ask how they really are, so that they are able to respond with honesty and feel able to share the current challenges.

Empathy and understanding

Raising neurodivergent children in a neurotypical world is hard. You feel continually judged and criticised, you can feel that you and your family don't fit in anywhere, that somehow you are not afforded the same level of acceptance and understanding as others. If we feel we are in an early years setting that has the relational approach embedded within it, we feel a sense of connection. We feel truly able to share what we need to, when we need to do it, safe in the knowledge that we won't be judged, or our parenting questioned. We feel safe.

Being heard

Within that relational approach and that positive connection, our feelings, our thoughts, our worries and anxieties, our wow moments as a family, are all heard. This has such an impact on families. We know our children best; we are living daily with the challenges of difference in today's world. We need our voices heard; we need to be believed when we tell you how things are at home. We need and want to work in collaboration with those caring for our children in the early years setting.

What does this relational approach and connection look like for neurodivergent children in our early years settings?

> *Mr Davies was different because he helped me, he helped me when I was struggling. He was a teacher that took notice of me. He helped me with my confidence and was the best teacher. He knew I liked football and spoke lots to me about that which was good.*
>
> *(Stanley aged 9)*

It's critical for our children to feel safe in any environment they are in. Creating that sense of belonging where our children feel seen and heard is vital for their mental health and well-being. This provides this emotional security and connection that everything else needs to be built upon.

What does this relational approach and connection look like for neurodivergent staff in our early years settings?

> *As a neurodivergent adult working in early years settings I have had a varied experience; ranging from being fully supported to develop my skills and abilities in a larger team as part of a nursery chain, one where I felt my voice was fully heard. I supported autistic children to develop and thrive.*
>
> *On the other hand, I have also had a disastrous experience in an independent nursery where I was bullied and had to resign as all the staff saw me as an outsider and somebody different who they did not wish to engage with.*
>
> *As a neurodivergent adult, I feel connected in the early years environment when my voice is heard and respected, my points of view are addressed and needs accommodated into everyday practice, knowing that I am not being judged for me. Connection is feeling fully supported and encouraged to thrive.*
>
> *(Molly, autistic adult)*

The way we are changing practices and our approach for our children also must extend to our team. Our team are our best resource and with data, 'estimating that around one in seven people (more than 15 per cent of people in the UK) are neurodivergent' (Business Disability Forum, n.d.) and a 'Worldwide prevalence of 15% to 20% of the population is considered to be neurodiverse' (MyDisabilityJobs, 2024), we can't shy away from adapting our early years settings and offering adaptions to our neurodivergent staff members.

And this starts through an embedded practice and ethos of connection. Connection through being seen, connection through being heard and connection through being allowed to be your true authentic self, safe in the knowledge that this won't be judged or criticised.

Connection though play

In Chapter 4 we looked in detail about play, the need to understand neurodivergent play, alongside the different types of play we might observe and how to support and validate that play. It's a path to connection with our neurodivergent children, to join them and connect with them, right where they are.

CASE STUDY: JOIN THEM WHERE THEY ARE

I was working with a nursery where they had asked me to observe a child they were currently caring for and offer strategies of support. The child in question was 3 years old, pre verbal, and was confirmed as autistic. She was given funding for a 1-1 member of staff for the mornings she attended nursery. After speaking with the manager, I was invited to observe the child who was in the garden.

She was moving around the space, playing independently. She was clearly avoiding areas that were busy and was indicating a preference for sensory input in the activities she was spending more time at. I stood back to observe further, this time her 1-1 support worker was with her. She first moved to the water tray that had boats, scoops and

funnels. Her 1-1 followed and knelt down at the tray beside her. The child was splashing the water, smiling and laughing, at which point, the adult picked up the scoop and began to tell her that she was scooping the water into the red boat. The child walked away.

She then went to the small stones in one area of the garden, sat down and lifted and slowly dropped the stones, watching closely. Again, she began to laugh and smile. The adult again followed her, sat down and started to count the stones. The child walked away.

The adult was doing what all childcare educators instinctively do, she was narrating, commenting and using these moments as teachable moments. Nothing wrong in that. However, by doing so, the child was not validated in her play, she was not able to connect through her play preferences and therefore walked away from the adult who, she felt, was pushing her play agenda onto her.

The child then noticed me and walked over. She began to clap her hands in front of me. I popped my pen and paper onto the floor and without saying anything, copied her movements. She then placed her hands on mine, indicating for me to stop. I just said stop. She then opened my hands again, indicating her desire for me to continue, and as I said, more, I began to clap. At which point she smiled and gave me eye contact. This back-and-forth exchange went on for several minutes. With me following her lead, repeating my actions and keeping my language simple.

It was clear that there was a connection, with the staff commenting on behaviours and communication they hadn't seen before. It was through play that we connected: through 'sharing feelings, being vulnerable, seeking to understand each other and meeting one another with trust' (Calm Editorial Team, 2024). It was my desire to meet her where she was, to follow her agenda instead of mine, that validated her and it communicated to her that she was seen, heard, and accepted.

She placed herself in a vulnerable position by reaching out to a stranger. She didn't know who I was, nor did she know how the exchange would work out for her. We were seeking to understand each other through this connection and met one another with trust.

I have adopted an approach to play that has connection at its heart. As I have said in previous chapters, our neurodivergent children need us to join them in their play and not place our neurotypical play agenda onto them. Our children need us to understand that their play is OK, their play is important and that their play is valid. By joining in their play we seek and gain connection in new and wonderful ways. Let's link connection and trust again when considering play with our neurodivergent children. How? By meeting them right where they are by providing a **TRUSTful** play experience (Figure 5.1).

T for True

Join children in their play in the true sense of the word. Join them, don't force them to join you. Offer your unhurried time and honesty as you play together. Ensure you are sincere in your connection, authentic in your relationship with them and are a natural and affirming play partner

R for Responsive

Respond on their time and by their cues. Be guided by them and follow them. As they make sounds or movements in their play, you follow. Connect with them as the true leader of the play.

U for Understand

Understand their preferred play type and style. Remember that it doesn't have to make sense to you, just know that it makes sense to them. Continue to join and follow them.

S for Shared and Sustained

Work together for a joint cause, contribute to the play alongside them. Join them in their play goal and their agenda. Problem-solve together and share in the experience. Keep your focus with them and offer moments of extension and support when needed or asked for (remember this can be by the use of gestures or other communication cues).

T for Together Time

Just enjoy the moment. Be truly together with the child, see this moment as a collaboration and an opportunity for connection and developing a deeper relationship.

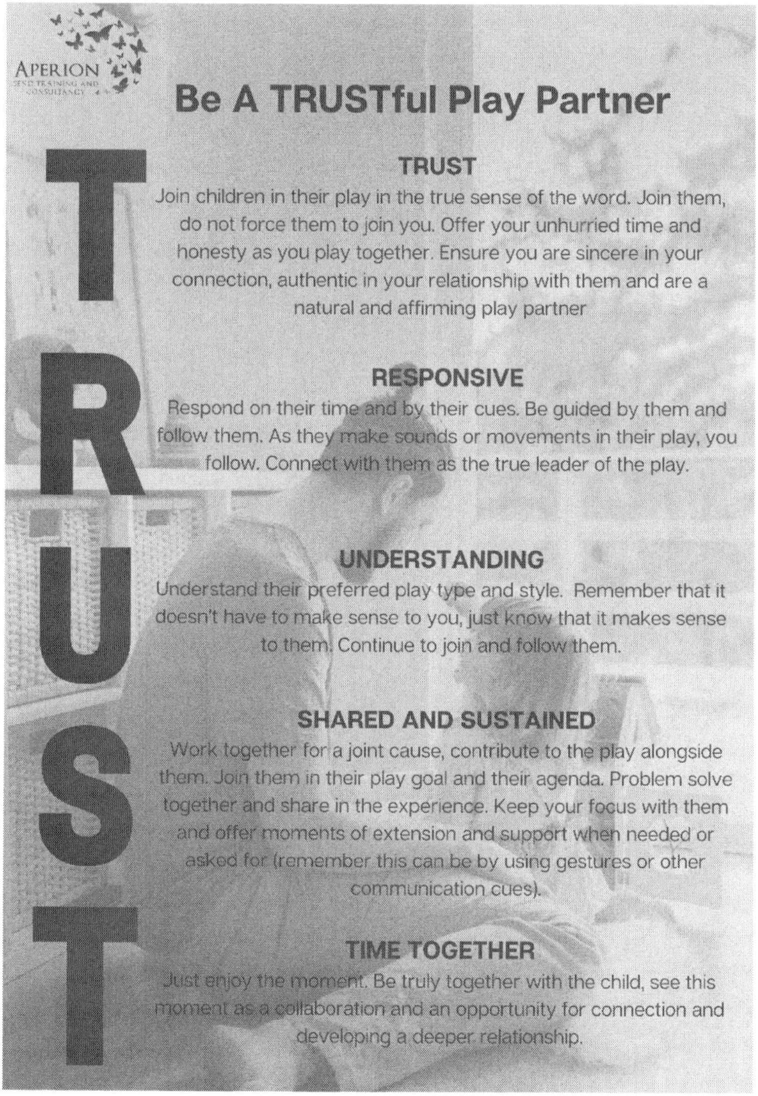

Figure 5.1 Be a TRUSTful play partner

Connection through co-regulation

Babies are not born with the ability or skills set to self-regulate, they are reliant on positive connections and attuned adults to teach them. When our toddlers share their big feelings and emotions with us, it's our job to always share our calm rather than join them in the chaos. They learn from responsive, engaging, trustful, connected relationships with the adults around them.

Self-regulation is the ability

> [to] regulate (or manage) our thoughts, feelings and behaviour. Being able to self-regulate helps us to remain calm and attentive and helps us to respond, rather than react in the face of our many strong emotions and responses to stressors in life.
>
> (Conkbayir, 2023)

We also know that the ability to self-regulate is an important predictor of mental heath and well-being (Compas et al., 2017).

We need to be an effective co-regulator for our children to learn from us as a key mentor for self-regulation skills. The first step in our role as co-regulator is to consider the stressors currently in our environment. As discussed in Chapter 4, we are responsible for providing a safe space, first of all, for our neurodivergent children, a space of calm, where we eliminate sensory stressors, therefore providing an environment conducive to self-regulation.

We then need to understand the triggers that cause our children to become dysregulated and offer accommodations to defuse or diminish these.

Then we need to understand what support our children need from us to 'teach' them a way to return to a calm state. It's these that we model for our children, we become a mentor and a coach in these high moments of stress and anxiety.

Ways to co-regulate:

- Provide a nurturing and supportive relationship, seek and foster a relationship built on connection and trust
- Pre-empt what might prompt dysregulation and be available for closeness and connection
- Support children to learn about emotions, to be able to label and express them safely

- Model calming and regulatory practices such as deep breathing and mindfulness
- Coach and support children to find solutions
- Provide a clear place of escape for when things become too overwhelming

TIME TO REFLECT

- What strategies do you adopt to model co-regulation?
- What strategies do you use to teach self-regulation?
- Do you provide support to aid understanding of big feelings and emotions?
- How do you help children to locate and label their big feelings?
- How do you coach children to find solutions?

Connection through communication

Communication skills are important for ALL children, indeed '[s]peech, language and communication underpin everything we do – making our needs known, expressing our likes and dislikes, interacting with others and building relationships' (I CAN CHARITY, n.d.). However, verbal communication is not the end goal. The goal is always to provide our children with the chance, opportunity and resources for them to share their voice with us, and for them to be heard.

Neurodivergent children may use language differently, they may use non verbal communication differently and they may express themselves, their thoughts and feelings through their behaviour. We may have children in our settings who are non-speaking, or we may have children who are extremely articulate with their verbal language skills, but who may find difficulty with social communication. But either way, with any child, we need to ensure we validate all communication and use this effectively to connect with them.

The use of visuals is a great resource in our early years spaces. Visual timetables in sight of the child, the routine depicted on images on a lanyard for the child and adult for reference. Now and next boards, to demonstrate expectations or routine and visuals as a choice board.

PECS (Picture Exchange Communication System)

The Picture Exchange Communication System® (PECS®) is a system of communication which aids people with lower levels of verbal communication skills to communication via images.

> [People are] taught to approach another person and give them a picture of a desired item in exchange for that item. By doing so, the person is able to initiate communication. A child or adult with autism can use PECS to communicate a request, a thought, or anything that can reasonably be displayed or symbolized on a picture card.
>
> (PECS, n.d.)

While PECS is widely used across nurseries and schools in the UK, it has attracted some negativity and concern from the autism community as a communication aid, as its original aim was for it to be used for punishment and reward-based practices. When using the PECS®, children must give 'a picture to a communication partner (trainer) in order to receive a concrete outcome (high-value reinforcer)' (Bondy and Frost, 1994, cited in Roberts, 2023). Such practices are not in line with neuroaffirming approaches and are not ones I would recommend or approve.

Any preferred communication preference, tool or resource MUST have the child's voice and autonomy as its foundation. They shouldn't be used as a way to 'tell' children what they need to do, they should provide them with an opportunity to share their views, their thoughts or their ideas with us. We have to advocate for choice and freedom for communication, with a move away from compliance-based practices.

Ruth Jones, a neurodiversity-affirming speech and language therapist, informs us:

When we are using tools to support children to learn how to use language, we can think about teaching them in a natural way. This means we are not training them to use language in certain situations by rewarding their attempts. It means we are filling their world with language, to make it communication-rich and seeing 'what sticks' in terms of the approaches we are using. We have to use these methods of communication in order to teach them, so when you want to say something about what's going on, sign it, point to the symbols on a core board or device.

Neurotypical children learn language by listening to it, and over time (12-18 months), we then start to hear them begin to use the language that has been filling the world around them. We have to apply the same process of teaching and patience when we are thinking about different communication methods being taught to neurodivergent children.

Visuals used in any early years setting will always be there to support and aid understanding and provide a voice for each child. We need to ensure these are consistently used and used in the right way, also understanding that each child will have their own communication preference and profile. In order for us to know what a child's communication preference is, we need to allow them the opportunity to use a range of methods. As well as ensuring we are continuing to observe their use of language and communication during the day, in different situations and respond positively without judgement or critique.

Connection through celebration

Celebrating the small wins, I cannot emphasise the importance of this, for children and for the family as a whole. You know when a child first uses the potty or toilet, the whole family and setting go crazy! Mums call the aunt, dads contact the grandparents, the older sibling tells everyone at school, and the child has the hugest grin on their face! The same applies for our neurodivergent children. It's the small wins that show progress when some days you're struggling to find any, it's the moments where you feel that your child is going to be OK. When the world continues to tell you there is a 'problem', those moments can make all the difference.

CASE STUDY: HE LICKED A BANANA!

I remember being at a nursery, where I was asked to observe a boy that they needed support with. They were wanting to support him and enable him to fly, but needed some guidance on how they could do that. While I was on the floor (which is where you will regularly find me), a child and his parent arrived. The child's key person went to the door to greet them and to complete the handover. All of a sudden there was this excitement, there were hugs, smiles and so much positivity coming from the front door. I gave time to the member of staff to settle the child and then asked her what had happened, what had prompted the celebration.

What she told me brought a tear to my eye and left me in no doubt that this team 'got it', they understood how to support children and families of difference, they knew the importance of connecting through celebration and those small wins. The key person told me that they were celebrating together the fact that the child had licked a banana for breakfast!

Now to many, this would seem a little odd to be celebrating and insignificant. But that key person understood the importance of this huge milestone for that parent. She knew that this was a big deal and that it needed to be given the time and support to share in that moment. It was in this moment that a connection was made. Not necessarily a connection with the child there and then, but certainly with the parent. That parent felt safe enough to share this moment with that staff member, she felt she could tell the story without judgement. She felt heard and validated as a parent.

This connection will live with that parent for many years and this one moment could make the difference for the support that is put in place for that child due to the trust between parent and key person.

Make a point this week, after reading this chapter to highlight a 'win', with one of your parents. Celebrate alongside them, join in with the joy in that moment. Feel the importance of that connection.

Final reflections

It's a fundamental need as a human being to connect with others. And while many (wrongly) assume that many of our children are just in a different world and they are not wanting to engage, they seem 'happy' on their own, and they are not wanting to be close to others, they still do seek connection.

As I have said in this chapter, you will see our children play, learn and respond differently in situations to their neurotypical peers, and the same can be seen for connection. They will connect in their time and in their own way. Keep this in mind while you engage with them, be mindful of your presence in their space, be aware of your impact on their play, observe the nuances in their behaviours that show you they are seeking connection from you.

Continue to reflect on your learning from this chapter to support the development of your own practice. Understand the importance of connection for our neurodivergent children and adults and always remember that 'meeting one another with trust' is the foundation to this.

Resources

Instagram

@aperion_training
@expectingandaccepting
@jessie_and_the_family
@jodiewarren
@mrgteacher
@neurowild_
@reframingneurodiversity
@ruth_jones_slt
@sensory.slp
@simoninclusionteacher
@speechdude

Podcasts

Childhood Understood
Eu-Hu podcasts
Not your typical podcast
Reframing neurodiversity
The hidden 20%
The SEND network
The SENDCast

References

Allen, K.A., Kern, M.L., Rozek, C.S., McInereney, D., and Slavich, G.M. (2021) Belonging: A review of conceptual issues, an integrative framework, and directions for future research. *Australian Journal of Psychology*, 73(1): 87–102. doi: 10.1080/00049530.2021.1883409

Brookes, D.R. (2008).What Is a relational approach? Relational Approaches. Available at: https://relationalapproaches.com/approaches/

Brown, B. (2015). *Daring Greatly: How the Courage to Be Vulnerable Transforms the Way We Live, Love, Parent, and Lead*. London: Portfolio.

Business Disability Forum. (n.d.) Research: Neurodiversity statistics infographics. Available at: https://members.businessdisabilityforum.org.uk/neurodiversity-toolkit/resource/research-neurodiversity-statistics-infographics/

Calm Editorial Team. (2024). How to build emotional connection in relationships. Blog, 9 February. Available at: https://blog.calm.com/blog/emotional-connection

Compas, B.E. et al. (2017) Coping, emotional regulation, and psychopathology in childhood and adolescents: A meta-analysis and narrative review. *Psychology Bulletin*, 143(9): 939–991.

Conkbayir, M. (2023). *The Neuroscience of the Developing Child: Self-Regulation for Wellbeing and a Sustainable Future*. Abingdon: Routledge.

Gray-Hammond, D. (2020). The cost of autistic masking. Emergent Divergence. December 27. Available at: https://emergentdivergence.com/2020/12/27/the-cost-of-autistic-masking/

I CAN CHARITY. (n.d.). About SLCN. Available at: https://www.icancharity.org.uk/about-slcn/

MyDisabilityJobs. (2024). Neurodiversity in the workplace | statistics | update 2024. Available at: https://mydisabilityjobs.com/statistics/neurodiversity-in-the-workplace/

National Autistic Society. (n.d.). Masking. Available at: https://www.autism.org.uk/advice-and-guidance/topics/behaviour/masking?trk=public_post_comment-text

PECS (The Picture Exchange Communication System). (n.d.). Available at: https://nationalautismresources.com/the-picture-exchange-communication-system-pecs/

Purple Ella. (2023). Autistic masking & romantic relationships.[Video]. YouTube. Available at: https://www.youtube.com/watch?v=vOMDSQ5Dc28

Roberts, J. (2023). The problem with PECS®. Therapist Neurodiversity Collective. Available at: https://therapistndc.org/the-problem-with-pecs/

Robinson, K. and Robinson, K. (2022). *Manifesto*. London: Penguin.

Schott, L. (n.d.). Parenting | positive discipline | trauma recovery | attachment theory. Synergy Parenting. Available at: https://www.leliaschott.com/

6 Consistency

If you are wanting to make any change, alter anything in your professional or personal life, then consistency is key. The definition of consistency is, 'the quality of always behaving or performing in a similar way, or of always happening in a similar way' (*Cambridge English Dictionary*, 2024) Gretchen Rubin (n.d.) tells us that what we do every day matters, more than what you do once in a while.

I love working in the early years setting because no two days are ever the same. It all depends on the children, what they are wanting or needing to do, how they want to play, which team members are in that day, and sometimes even the weather can make an unplanned change to the routine. I could not work in an environment where it was always exactly the same.

However, while in early years setting, it's important to go with the children in the moment, to change things up sometimes, to teach resilience in change; but this is not always supportive of our neurodivergent children and their needs.

Again, it always comes back to knowing your individual children, their needs, their preferences, their thoughts and their views. We may have a child in our care who is identified and confirmed as autistic. Their preference could be for familiarity, consistency in structure and routine. However, we may also have a child with Attention Deficit Hyperactivity Disorder (ADHD) who, for the most part, finds comfort in the familiar, but may also have the desire for spontaneity to express their creativity and feed their need for instant movement.

While this seems to contradict the notion of consistency, what we need to provide for is consistency in our practices and support strategies that enable us to know what our children need and what supports them best.

DOI: 10.4324/9781032642994-6

- Consistency across our teaching and learning offer that always have connection and trust as their foundation
- Consistency in our behaviour support, understanding and response to emotions and big feelings
- Consistency as a team, one that promotes a togetherness and embeds neurodiversity-affirming approaches and practices.

Consistency in transitions

Transitions can be challenging for many of our children, the change from one thing to another or the stopping of one task to do something else. They may not understand why they need to stop what they are doing for something else; they may not have understood an instruction given, they may not have picked up on the transition cues, or the change to something unfamiliar can create overwhelming anxiety. All of which can be extremely challenging.

What I also observe in many early years settings are busy, noisy and sometimes hectic transitions, where voices are raised and additional sounds added to the space (including the Alexa playing a tidy up song!). We need to make our transitions predictable, planned-for, calm and smooth.

Have a think for a minute about the number of transitions a child may have to contend with over the course of one day.

- Getting out of bed and getting ready for the day
- Getting from their home into the car/beginning the walk to the setting
- Getting from the car and walking to their setting
- Going through the door from outside into the setting
- Starting with free flow and then tidying up for the morning welcome and circle time
- Circle time to free flow
- Tidying up to go into the garden
- Coming in from the garden for snack
- Tidying up after snack for free flow
- Tidying up to prepare for lunch

Count back! That's ten different transitions potentially before 11.45a.m. And for a child who is triggered by transitions, that's ten opportunities for the stress response to kick in and for us to observe their distress signals. How we support children during these transitions is key and consistency in this support is vital for our children.

TIME TO REFLECT

- How many transitions are you asking children to go through each day?
- How are those children responding to them, what distress signals have you observed?
- How are those children currently being supported?
- How consistent are those strategies and support across the team?

Enhanced transitions

The move to another room within the setting, leaving nursery for another school, leaving their childminder to head to school can be big transitions and ones that need careful planning and thought way ahead of time. It's not just the focus on a one-off event but needs to be seen as a bigger project that needs some thoughtful consideration. We need to ensure we are providing as much consistency for the child as possible, so that the unfamiliar, becomes the familiar with minimal impact on their well-being.

This is not a process completed by the early years setting for the child, this is a transition plan that has the child at the centre, with input from parents and any other relevant professionals involved in the child's care. It also needs to be a process that includes the next setting or school that the child is moving to.

Many neurodivergent children need time. Time to understand what will be happening next. Time to feel safe in any new environment. Time to feel connected with those who will be caring for them. Time to understand the flow and new routine. Therefore any enhanced transition needs to be well considered and time must be given to the process.

What do we need to consider?

- Regular touch points between the current setting and the new one
- Sharing of beneficial documents in a timely manner
- Conversations regarding funding currently in place and what may need to be applied for

Visits

- *For the parents*: Taking consideration of who and when they will be attending, how many visits and whether there is time to discuss any concerns or anxieties the parents/carers may have.
- *For the child*: To have an opportunity to feel, smell, visualise and navigate the space. To enable them to have a reference point, to experience the space that can then be reflected on with images and further discussion.
- *The current setting*: Allowing for time to discuss the child's current needs, accommodations in place that are effective in supporting the child. The child's play and communication preferences and how they are being enabled to experience success in the early years setting. This is also an opportunity to ask for permission to take photos. Creating a photo book for the child to show them in picture form:
  - the new door they will be going through
  - the new coat hooks
  - the new classroom layout
  - the new toilets
  - the new teacher and any assistants
  - the new playground
  - an image of the special place or toy they enjoyed when they visited the new setting.

A photo book was vital for my eldest son's school transition, which continued as he moved year groups in school. The six-week summer holiday can be a long time and the photo book allowed me to chat with him and remind him of what was coming up. Having visited the school, he was then able to

match what he saw in the images to how he felt when he was in the space. Really helping us to prepare him for the next move.

A SAFE SPACE

In order to ease the settling in process for both neurotypical and neurodivergent learners, we work towards a safe space! We begin with short visits with a familiar adult. We approach settling sessions as small stepping stones towards connection and trust as the child adapts to our new environment.

With utmost patience we discover the child's likes/dislikes, any comforts or adaptations we can do to make the child feel at ease and secure with their surroundings. To accommodate and reduce anxiety, we use low lighting and calm music, visual support (routine pictures), family picture books to encourage the children to feel like they belong and lots of validation.

(Nikki, childminder and parent)

Spoon theory

This is a great theory to help us to understand how the energy levels of our neurodivergent children, and adults, can impact their ability to regulate. First spoken about by Christina Miserandino, an adult with Lupus, who used the spoons on the table in front of her over dinner with a friend, to explain what it was like living with the condition.

We can use the same theory to identify how regulated a neurodivergent child may be when they arrive at our early years setting each morning, and to check in with them during the day. If their 'spoon drawer' is lacking spoons (energy), we need to know how to identify this in their mannerisms or their behavioural responses and support them to 'fill their drawer'. Each activity or experience a child has can impact the amount of spoons they have, so maybe a small group task, or a demand placed on them, or their special interest toy not being made available, can all impact the amount

of spoons they have. If they are depleted of spoons (energy), they become dysregulated, upset, confused or anxious.

As educators, we need to understand right from the beginning of the day how many spoons our children are arriving with. We then know if they need some time to replace the lacking energy they have or are feeling to support them to experience success that day.

I often hear handovers at the beginning of the session between parent and educator:

> *Educator:* Good morning, how is he today?
>
> *Parent:* Yeah, he's fine.
>
> *Educator:* Anything to tell us?
>
> *Parent:* No, I don't think so.
>
> *Educator:* Great, have a good day.
>
> *Parent:* Thanks, you too.

Sound familiar? Great we have that moment, but we need to be clearer about the information we need from the parent and the parent also needs to know what information it would be beneficial for us to know about.

A SIMPLE TIP

A simple poster on the front door can remind parents to tell us how many spoons their child has when they arrive with us in the morning (Figure 6.1).

Remembering that what happened the evening before, the kind of night they had and the journey to the setting that morning can all impact their level of energy.

It's also really important that we understand spoon theory in relation to our neurodivergent staff too. I've seen some conversations around pebbles for adults rather than spoons, still with the same concept, but having a pebble jar instead (Figure 6.2).

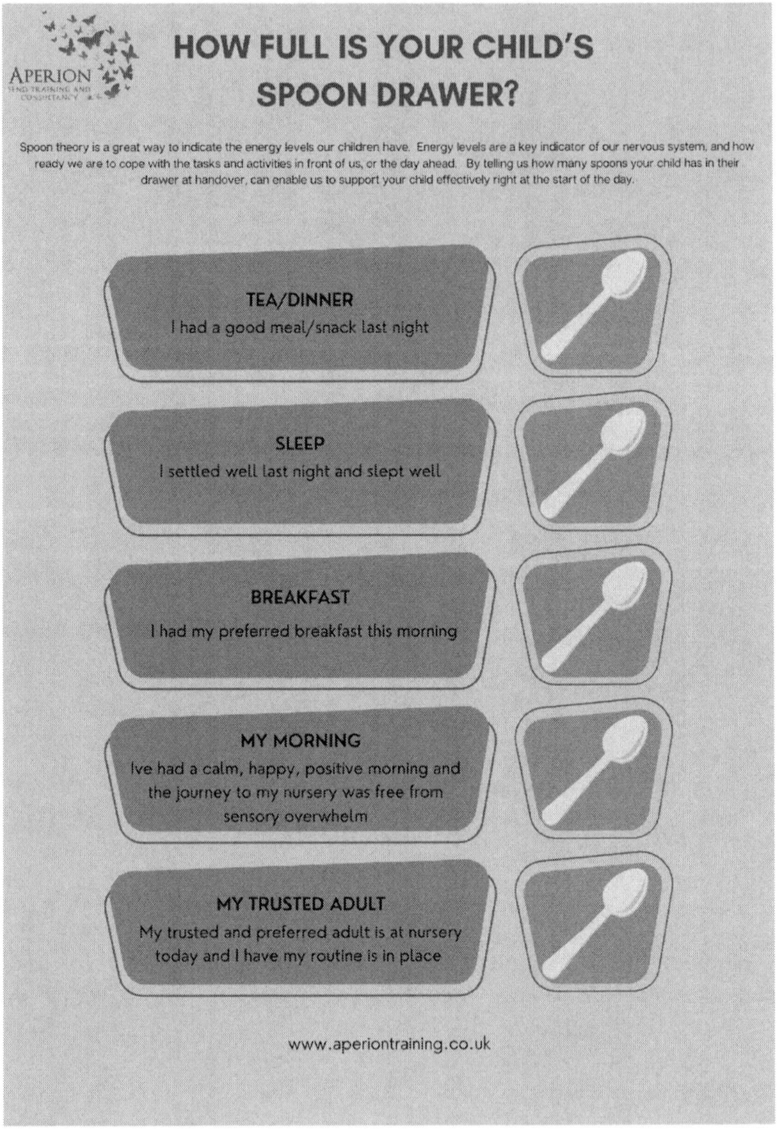

Figure 6.1 Spoon theory

Figure 6.2 A jar of pebbles

A colleague might start the day with five pebbles, but then they are given their first set of instructions, a demand or task placed on them, maybe something that they have to organise. Then they are among the sensory stimulus of a busy toddler or pre-school room, therefore pebbles are used to stay calm and regulated. Then it's break time, which ordinarily would sound great, but that confined space where they may have to interact in small talk with others can cause stress and anxiety. Therefore, removing another pebble. The jar quickly becomes empty, requiring them to refill prior to being able to support themselves for future demands or others in a co-regulatory relationship.

Glimmers

Once we understand what can impact our children's and colleagues' ability to remain regulated, we can help them to understand and seek glimmers. Glimmers are the direct opposite of triggers. I have spoken lots about triggers in this book so far, and we are aware that these transfer the nervous system into a fight, flight, or freeze response to help you remove yourself from a threat of danger. Moving your brain/body into sympathetic nervous system. Glimmers are the cues that provoke the opposite, the parasympathetic nervous system response, or rest and digest. These moments are the safety cue to the survival brain and can be a trauma recovery response.

To fully understand the impact of glimmers, we need to be consistent in our approach to finding them and supporting our children to find them. Glimmers can be those moments, experiences, that bring our children joy and calm, remembering that calm can also be ignited by big movements.

Glimmers can be:

- A walk in the sunshine
- A favourite story being read in their favourite chair
- A favourite song being sung
- A bear hug wrapped in a blanket
- Jumping up and down in the garden popping bubbles

Become a glimmer seeker and teach your children to be glimmer seekers too!

Consistency in routine

When I ask the question, 'What are some of the early indicators of autism?', most educators tell me that they can struggle when things change, when the routine alters even just slightly. Therefore, one of the most effective ways to support many of our neurodivergent children is by providing a consistent, well-structured environment and routine. Reducing the possibility of unpredictability, creating a sense of safety in the familiar.

This is where the use of a visual timetable or a visual routine can support that predictability. If a child knows what's coming next and it's consistently applied, you create that safe space. An environment where everyone is aware of the next steps, children can quickly learn the cues for change – whether that be a song, or a cue card, or a movement prompt, thus ensuring the uncertainty or misunderstanding of cues is removed or reduced.

Visual timetables act out the sequence of the day. By having images of each part of the sequence on a Velcro strip at the child's height, it allows then to take off the image of the part of the routine that has been completed, therefore seeing what's coming next. These visuals can also allow for some small changes to be made where required as they are easy to adapt. They are also used to enable the child to add to the routine if they are feeling the need or desire to.

Therefore, we also need not only: (1) provide that consistent, familiar and predictable routine, but also (2) provide one that can also be flexible when necessary.

We need to ensure the familiar and the predictable, allowing for flexibility in our routine, in our expectations for children are key to meeting their individual needs. Rules, boundaries and expectations form part of our routine, but if these create a barrier for our children to participate in a way that feels safe and enjoyable for them, then we do also need to be offering flexibility and an understanding consistently across the team as to why this is the case.

CASE STUDY: THE LIGHT MONITOR

I remember when my eldest son was in year 1 (prior to identification), they had clear roles that the children could lead on. The door monitor or the white board monitor or the glue monitor. He was given the role of the light monitor. It was his role and his responsibility to make sure that the light switches were turned off as the class left the room. Therefore, he was always at the end of the line, the last to leave and had the important job of saving the electricity bill at school!

One day the teacher called me in at the end of the day to tell me that there had been an incident at school where he had got extremely

upset. I was told about the roles and that he had taken it a bit too seriously, causing upset to another child. He had his job and it was made very clear to him what he had to do. Hence, when another child turned off the light as he went past, my son became extremely distraught. It was his job, not the other child's. It was now Thursday and since Monday morning it had been his responsibility, his consistent routine to turn the light off. This was a sudden change to proceedings, one which he hadn't been warned of, and therefore he became dysregulated, confused and upset.

Routine, consistency and familiarity are important to him, not only that, they are a necessity.

When the predictable needs to be flexible: consideration of need

There are certain rules, boundaries and expectations that need to be in place for all children to keep them safe and to keep them healthy. However, there are some 'rules' that we place on children that are based on our expectations for 'appropriate' behaviour, or compliance and for some of them, just because it's always been a 'rule', but no one can remember why!

Rules and expectations can be a funny thing. Some of my favourites are:

- 'We can't mix the water with the sand, they have to stay separate' (not sure who is able to build a sandcastle or sand shapes with dry sand???)
- 'We need to keep the blocks in the construction area and the animals in the small world area' (not sure how we can then build a zoo or pen for our animals to keep them safe???)
- 'We all need to sit still with our legs crossed and our hands in our laps while I read the story' (Have you ever sat like that? It's the most uncomfortable position ever, and I would be thinking continually about moving to feel more comfortable and not hear a word of the story being read to me!)

We need to offer flexibility in our curriculum, in our environments and with our rules and expectations for our children, removing the barriers that could be preventing them from feeling safe enough to join in.

TIME TO REFLECT

- How many of the rules and expectations that you have in your setting make sense to you? How many of them are there, but you have no idea why?
- Which of your rules or expectations could be made a little more flexible to enable neurodivergent children to take part and experience success?
- What or where are the barriers to you creating more a more flexible environment for the benefit of all?

Let's take consideration of the rules and expectations that could be made more flexible for our neurodivergent children:

1. *Aprons for art*: You know the ones that I am talking about. The hard plastic aprons with the tight sleeves, that are always wet or damp. These feel awful against the skin and can be a barrier for our children to participate in any creative activities like painting or sticking. For some, the rules are to wear these for sensory/messy play and can be an immediate 'no, no' for many. You may think it's the art or messy activity itself that they are struggling to engage with, but have you considered it could actually be the apron rule itself?
   Consider an alternative. Consider no apron at all and the expectation is to ensure children wear old clothes or an old nursery t-shirt. Pop into your local charity shop or second-hand store and grab some old shirts that can be worn over their clothes to protect them.
   Seek a potential alterative to determine if the rule is too rigid and considerations need to be made to remove a barrier.

2. *Shoes and coats on outside*: Of course, when we go outside, we pop our shoes on and in wet or cold weather we wear a jacket or coat. But what about our children who prefer not to wear shoes and can't wear a coat because of the restrictive feel of it? How can we be flexible to ensure they can experience the outdoor space, safely and where their sensory needs are still met?

   Can they just wear their socks or bare feet? Have you had a conversation with the parents, what is their stance on it? Have you completed a risk assessment? Does that risk assessment consider risk versus benefit for the child?

   If they do need to wear shoes, what alternatives can you offer them? Let's have a conversation, using clear and simple language that they can take off their shoes, but that they need to choose what to wear instead. Provide a range of footwear (Figure 6.3) that they can decide from, in sight ,that they can feel and touch to help them make the decision. You are then giving the choice and the control back to them, allowing for autonomy and ensurimg their voice is heard.

Figure 6.3 A selection of children's footwear

3. *Taking a special object for a nappy change or to the meal table*: I've spoken above about transitions being tricky and the use of objects of reference to support them can be of huge benefit. Show them a nappy, if it's time for a nappy change, rather than just using your verbal communication. But we can also support transitions with transitional objects. If a child is playing intently with a special object and it's time for lunch, can we create flexibility in the rules and allow that child to take the object to the table with them?

   The consistency in taking it with them can support regulation and ease the impact of transitions.
4. *Chairs*: For most of the settings I go into, each table activity has at least four chairs around it. Yes, I can hear you say, of course, it has, as a rule, it's for children to sit at the table to complete the activity or task.

   But are you aware that the humble chair can be a barrier for children joining in? Just imagine for a minute that you have are real desire to feel and experience a great provocation that has been set up on a table in your pre-school room. It has some of your favourite things on it and it's pulling you in to touch and engage with it. As you approach the table, the adult invites you to sit down, pulling out the chair and tapping the seat. This is the trigger.

   If you sit down, your legs are trapped under the table, there are other children at the table, who, for you, are unpredictable in their play. So, if there are any sudden noises or movements that may be dysregulating, with your legs trapped, you can't get away quickly. Therefore, you would rather not sit down and complete the task, it feels safer that way. Provide chairs at the table, but maybe just two rather than surrounding it. Enable children to stand up at the table, to join in, in a way that feels safe for them. Where they can escape quickly if need be and also where their movement needs can be met as they rock or push against the table.

Consistency in your approach to behaviour

Behaviour is always so controversial. Our responses to children's behaviour can be traced back to so many factors. Our own upbringing, past traumas, cultural expectations, societal demands and expectations and individual opinions on how children 'should' behave. However, besides all of that,

we have a duty and a responsibility to understand why children' behaviour occurs in the first place and to respond rather than react. But this MUST be a whole setting approach.

We need to shift policy to reflect behaviour that challenges us, to supporting self-regulation, to understanding and supporting children's big feelings, rather than behaviour management.

We need to shift from consequences, rewards and sanctions to an approach which focuses on the relational approach and effective co-regulation, supporting connection and creating a sense of belonging and trust for our children. Only by doing this, do we build an emotionally safe space for our neurodivergent children.

Dr Mine Conkbayir (2023) describes how this approach emphasises the importance of adults gaining the child's trust by building an empathetic and nurturing relationship with them. She built on the work of Dr Stuart Shanker and his theories of effective co-regulation through this approach.

What is behaviour anyway?

- Is it there to act as a wind-up tool from children to parents/carers/educators?
- Is it a response to an unmet need?
- Is it a communicative tool?
- Or is it a safety response from the body or the brain, and the behaviour we see is a consequence of that response and an indicator of what we as the adult can do to offer support and guidance?

We always need to look at the wider picture and not just see what's in front of us, we need to understand the reason, the why. Once we know the why, we respond through connection, through empathy and understanding, rather than react in the heat of the moment, or without considered thought.

Reaction vs response

Reactions are instant, emotional, and can often be based on our experiences and preconceived ideas. Responses are deliberate, more considered,

intentional and made in the moment. The response, rather than the immediate reaction, affords us space to think; it's a more conscious thought process.

So, how do we respond rather than react?

First, we need to understand the child in front of us. We need to understand their triggers. We need to understand what dysregulation looks like for that child. We need to know what impact the environment may have on that child. We need to understand if they are a sensory seeker or a sensory avoider and how this impacts their behavioural responses. We need to understand their stims and their self-soothing behaviours. We need to understand and know what they need for regulation or activation.

Once we know these things, we are then able to respond with conscious thought to the behaviours we see in front of us. And once we know the child, we can then begin to adopt a five-step process to our conscious, considered and consistent approach to behaviour:

1. Awareness
2. Recognise
3. Distance
4. Question
5. Choose

Awareness

Be mindful of what's happening, who is involved, and being aware of the whole situation. Take a moment to really understand. What just happened, what can you see, who can you see, who are the children involved, what happened just prior, what time of day is it, what could have been a contributing factor?

Recognise

Acknowledge what's happening in front of you and your own internal emotions that might be at play. We may have had previous experiences that push us to react in a certain way, we may assume that situations like this always involve one particular child. We might not be in a well-regulated state ourselves and may need to recognise this as a contributing factor to a conscious

response. Also recognise that we may not be the right person in this moment to respond to the child.

Distance

Just take a moment, give yourself a second or two to just think, in order for you not to react. This may mean seeking the support and time required from a colleague and understanding that this is OK. This short pause before a response can make a huge difference to your moment of collaboration with the child at this time.

Question

Could your initial thoughts be the best response, can you respond alone, would the child be better with a response from another member of staff, what is the situation, what were the potential triggers, is the child in any immediate danger? We also need to question ourselves on what we know about the child and what they need from us in this moment of dysregulation. Knowing their sensory needs, their connection needs and their safety needs can really be of benefit here.

Choose

Deliberately and consciously choose a response that aligns with the needs of the child and your neuroaffirming approach, support and connection with the child in your setting.

Remember that our children are not choosing to behave in a way that challenges you. Our children are responding to the stimulus around them in the only way they know how. Their brain and body are triggered into the survival response and they react in the only way they can, to be safe.

We need to consider the use of a tool to aid the detection, to help us understand the reason behind the behaviour. Many educators have used ABC (Antecedent, Behaviour, Consequence) charts as that tool. And for years it has been a form that educators can record what they see, determine a potential pattern or trigger and then note the consequences. Consequence?? What do you think of when you read the word 'consequence'? Historically,

this has always meant, what is the consequence for that child after they have shown us an 'unwanted' behaviour? And it's this terminology that we need to move away from. The language, the narrative, that says that the child is in the wrong and needs to have a sanction placed upon them.

We need to consider that, more often than not, it is in our hands and control as educators. What we do or not do can be the reason behind the behaviour. Controversial? Perhaps. But it's clear that environment, not knowing our children's sensory triggers, the expectations and demands placed on them, by us, as the adult, can impact their behavioural responses. So let's use a tool that enables us to reflect on our offer, on our practice, on our current knowledge that can potentially eliminate the trigger and the subsequent behavioural response.

I've replaced the behaviour identification tool, ABC charts with TRUST forms (Figure 6.4):

T – Trigger – environmental, sensory, level of demands, transitions, trauma, anxiety

R – Response – how did the child respond to the trigger? What does dysregulation look like for them?

U - Understand the need – why did this behaviour occur? What is the unmet need? What information is the behaviour giving us? What are they trying to communicate to us?

S – Support required – what support does the child need from you to regulate at this moment to regulate?

T – Time to reflect – what can you and the team reflect on to remove potential triggers? What support might the child need going forward? What do the team need to know about the child to support them further?

It's the last bit that is crucial to make the difference needed.

APERION
SEND TRAINING AND CONSULTANCY

TRUST FORM

This form is designed to support you in identifying potential triggers for a child's dysregulated behaviour and the strategies that may be required to support a child during this time. The next step is for reflection, and to remove potential stressors going forward. Reflection is the important step to understand what we need to do as educators to better support the child and provide a safe space for them to thrive.

Trigger Consider: environmental, sensory, level of demands, transitions, trauma, anxiety	**Response** How did the child respond to the trigger? What does dysregulation look like for them?	**Understand the Need** Why did this behaviour occur? What is the unmet need? What are they trying to communicate?	**Support Required** What support does the child need from you at this moment to regulate?	**Time to Reflect** What can you and the team reflect on to remove potential triggers? What support might the child need going forward? What do the team need to know about the child to support them further?

If you or your team need any further support, guidance or training around any of these areas, then get in touch.

www.aperiontraining.co.uk Cheryl Warren @aperion_training

Figure 6.4 TRUST form

Applying the TRUST form in practice

CASE STUDY: A CHILD WHO BITES

Charlie is 2 years old, has been biting regularly since before the age of 1. He has good language skills, however, the team have observed differences in his sensory processing. The team are experiencing three+ biting incidents per day and Charlie attends four days a week 8a.m–6p.m. Charlie does have a basket of 'chewy' resources available in the room and wears one around his neck for the most part of the day, he often uses these when he is focused on a specific task. for example, he often has his chewy in his mouth when building towers or painting. His preference is solitary play.

The incident

9.30a.m. Six children present. Charlie was playing alongside another child with silk scarves. The other child cried out and an educator went to comfort the child. Charlie said, 'I bit him on the arm.' He then moved away from the situation, helped himself to a book and sat alone with his book for around 5 minutes before moving on to exploring the sand pit.

The trigger

- Communication – child too close to him, he was communicating his need for space.
- Sensory – he is an oral sensory-seeker.
- Big feelings and emotions – he was over-excited and can find it hard to regulate those big emotions.

Response

Child bit another on the arm causing the other child to cry.

Understand

Was Charlie excited with the activity?

Big feelings and emotions can also be excitement and for many children with sensory differences, even the feelings of happiness and excitement are strong and there is a struggle to understand what to do with the emotion. If a child's arm was close by, it could just have been pure luck that the child's arm was in close proximity.

- What was mentioned in handover?
- How was he the night before?
- How was his journey to nursery?

Sometimes it's about what happened before, so we need to understand the wider picture. Some children with sensory differences need some sensory input at the beginning of the day to help them regulate and settle. But we need to know what energy levels and levels of regulation they have when arriving at nursery. (See spoon theory discussed earlier.)

- Is he in good spirits generally?
- Is he under the weather?
- Could he be unwell?

This will unbalance the nervous system and therefore anything else that dysregulates and adds to the overwhelm, spirals quickly.

- Which children were with him?
- Is there a clash of personalities?
- Have there been incidents of biting towards this child before?

This just is the case sometimes with children. The dynamics are important to understand, this way we are able to deploy staff effectively.

- Is he an oral sensory-seeker?

The chewies can be a great resource, but has he been taught how to use them? If we see him 'go' for another child or put something in his mouth, we need to immediately replace it with the chewy.

Support

The child took himself off to the book area for some quiet-alone time after the incident. He clearly understands his own self-regulation strategies and needs to be supported with this. He needs to be supported in understanding his sensory-seeking behaviours and also taught effective strategies for his big feelings and emotions.

Reflect

- Deploying staff to small group activities he's involved with to help Charlie manage big feelings and emotions.
- Understand Charlie's oral sensory-seeking behaviours and provide a sensory diet to support this.
- Replace his need to bite with immediate access to his chewies.
- Improve handover to determine his energy levels on arrival.
- Use of visuals to link to other activities and strategies to replace the biting for his oral seeking-sensory needs.

TIME TO REFLECT

- Consider situations at your setting, how can you apply the TRUST form to support you?
- What can you have an impact on to provide that safe space that our children need?
- What are your current processes for gathering information that you need about each child?
- Who do you need to find guidance or training from to support you to reflect on your environment and your process?

Consistency in a strength based approach and the language we use

As a parent, I have been acutely aware over the years of the areas of development my children have struggled with and still find challenging today. I know that my children are different, that the world hasn't always been accepting of their differences and that society places a label of 'problem' on my children. All because my children don't fit into a neat little box that always shows compliance, that always shows understanding of a task, that is always able to ,in inverted commas, 'achieve the desired outcome' placed on them by the system.

My eldest son, as you know, is autistic. He is not my son *with* autism. Autism is part of his identity and how he identifies himself. It's not a condition he carries around in a bag. He would introduce himself as X, age 16 and I am autistic. Not hi, I'm X and here is the autism I carry around with me! Keating writes, 'Larger numbers of autistic adults in the United Kingdom (UK) endorsed "autistic" and "autistic person" (i.e., identity-first language) than "person with autism"' (i.e., person-first language; see Kenny et al., 2016). Interestingly these findings are echoed in Australian samples, with autistic participants rating the terms 'autistic', 'person on the spectrum' and 'autistic person' significantly higher than 'person with autism', 'person with ASD', and 'person with Autism Spectrum Condition (ASC)' (Keating et al., 2022).

He is autistic. What he isn't, is slightly or mildly autistic or a little bit autistic. The functioning labels that have been used for many years have now been removed. Our children are autistic rather than high or low functioning or mild or severely autistic. The concern the autistic community place on these functioning labels is that it often reflects on the support they are given. If they are perceived as mildly or a little autistic, it diminishes the impact that their autism can have on them in different situations.

Labelling autism as 'high function' can imply it's less significant in someone's life. It can minimise the challenges many people face internally.

Policy

One of the things I am asked to support schools and nurseries with, is their SEND policy. The team are aware that it's not a true reflection of what they do, nor the language they want to be using, but ask, how do they rephrase it, how do they write an affirming policy?

The baseline of our messaging needs to be a positive one, a strength-based one. A message that doesn't write our children off, that doesn't make people fear our children, that doesn't label our children as a real problem that needs to be fixed.

Policy statement: 'To identify children who are giving cause for concern'

Call emergency services, lockdown, be on guard, there is a concern. No, there is not a concern. Our children are not a concern. There is not a 'problem'. We may be identifying differences in development or behavioural responses but there is no concern.

Just reflect for a moment from a parent's perspective. And I've been that parent. I've had an education setting pull me aside to talk about how my child was doing things differently and they were a little worried, and there were concerns. It's not great! Let's talk about the differences you are observing, not about the concerns you have.

Just that slight alteration and consistency in your wording can have a huge impact on the subsequent conversation and the collaboration between setting and parent. It also shifts the language for your team. It removes the negative connotations. It describes a child as different, yes, but a concern or a problem, no.

Policy statement: 'Behind expected levels'

Can I first ask, what are you referencing? What is your baseline for 'expected levels'? Because most of the frameworks we are using to support our early years delivery have been written for neurotypical children, so, yes, you won't see many of our children reflected in those statements.

- Our children develop differently, full stop.
- Differently is not 'less than expected'.
- Different is not behind.

Know your children and understand the progress they are making. Understand that our children will have a spikey profile, and that's OK. Understand, observe and record all that our children can do and are able to do. I suggest a shift in policy language to 'Where differences in development or behavioural responses have been identified, we will ...'

Here is a poem written by a parent of a neurodivergent child:

Please handle me with care

Please handle me with care
Your approach is unfair

There's many like me
We're neurodivergent, you see
we do not develop typically
navigating our surroundings so differently

We're unable to conform to a world of norms
And easily triggered piloting internal storms

We yearn to fit in and learn as atypicals do
But we need a safe space to thrive like you
You must connect if we are to learn freely
To receive the same education as our peers completely

Comforted not confronted, we crave to feel safe
A responsive relationship is where connections are made

We need tools and strategies to make it all more manageable
Handle us with care, your patience is invaluable

We struggle to regulate,
our nervous system is overwhelming

Our stimming and behaviour need normalising

Let's shift the narrative
Your approach is imperative
If a flower doesn't bloom, you change its surroundings

Advocate for us to be our authentic selves
True inclusion matters more than anything else

(Nikki Walsh, childminder)

Final reflections

Being consistent is so important to truly embed a neurodiversity-affirming approach. It has to be something everyone does. Everyone needs to be upskilled. Everyone needs to be trained. Everyone needs to be supported and, once this is the case, everyone is then invested. Senior teams, management, childminders, all need to lead by example. They are the driver of consistency that can and will make the difference.

Consistency in your environments, routine, expectations and approach to neurodiversity-affirming practice may be tricky to embed at the beginning, it may feel like an uphill struggle. However, once in place, I promise you, it will make your job easier as you and the team will be working smarter! It's not about adding more to your already overwhelming and busy roles within early education, it's ensuring that your practice is effective, supportive and enables the essence of emotional safety for all. This in turn reduces children's heightened anxiety, parents are heard, and staff are supported.

Resources

Instagram

@aperion_training
@jessie_and_the_family
@jodiewarren

@mrgteacher
@neurowild_
@reframingneurodiversity
@ruth_jones_slt
@sensory.slp
@speechdude

Podcasts

Childhood Understood
Eu-Hu podcasts
Not your typical podcast
Reframing neurodiversity
The SEND network
The SENDCast

References

Cambridge English Dictionary. (2024). Consistency. Available at: https://dictionary.cambridge.org/dictionary/english/consistency

Conkbayir, M. (2023). *The Neuroscience of the Developing Child: Self-Regulation for Wellbeing and a Sustainable Future*. New York: Hallmark.

Keating, C. T., Hickman, L., Leung, J., Monk, R., Montgomery, A., Heath, H., and Sowden, S. (2022). Autism-related language preferences of English-speaking individuals across the globe: A mixed methods investigation. *Autism Research*, 16(2), 406–428. https://doi.org/10.1002/aur.2864

Kenny, L. et al. (2016). Which terms should be used to describe autism? Perspectives from the UK autism community. PubMed. Available at: pubmed.ncbi.nlm.nih.gov/26134030

Rubin, G. (n.d.). Getting started: Habits. Available at: gretchenrubin.com/getting-started-habits

7 Collaboration with parents and carers

Not only do we need to create safe spaces for our neurodivergent children, but we also have to provide those same, safe and supportive spaces for their parents and carers. To enable children to experience success, we need to ensure the whole family thrives as a unit. This chapter will explore further the crazy life of being a parent to a neurodivergent child and the support professionals can offer that will truly make a difference. It's full of case studies from settings across the UK which evidence that when we work together, go above and beyond, the impact is huge.

Life is a rollercoaster!

I mentioned in Chapter 1, the first meltdown brought the realisation that my parenting journey was going to be heading down a very different path to the one I had imagined. It's one thing supporting your child, learning new ways of parenting, new strategies, understanding how your child needs you to be a different kind of parent. But it's another when you begin to discover how the wider society sees you. Their sheer disgust and horror at your child's behaviour and your 'obvious poor parenting' and then realise how it can profoundly impact you in the short and long term. But, as Jenn Soehnlin (2018) says, you have to 'Embrace the unique way your child is blooming – even if it's not in the garden you imagined.'

DOI: 10.4324/9781032642994-7

IN THE BOAT

I remember a time when, as a family, we took a trip to Henley-on-Thames for the day and decided to hire a little boat on the river. We chatted this through the whole process with my son, lifejackets, getting safely in and out of the boat, the expectations once in the boat, etc. Once he felt safe and reassured, he wanted to go.

We got him in the lifejacket and into the boat and we set off. Just 5 minutes in and we were approaching a bridge and very quickly my son spiralled into a dysregulated state, a full meltdown. He had a fear of bridges when he was younger, he found it tricky walking over them and now we were discovering he wasn't a fan of going under them either! My son's sympathetic nervous system had taken over and he was in flight mode (not great when you're in the middle of the Thames, on a boat!). Not an ideal situation for him to try and run from, which then fuelled the meltdown further. Screaming, swearing and shouting we took the boat back to shore and just close enough to the jetty, as he jumped off and ran down the towpath.

Now, as a family, we know why he responded this way to the situation, we had seen it before, we knew the triggers and knew what he needed from us, right there in that moment. But the general public around us didn't. But because they see a child shouting, screaming and swearing, and he's not in a wheelchair or in a plaster cast and his disability is not evident, we are judged as bad parents.

I've seen far too many times to remember the looks, the eye rolls, heard the tutting and one adult whispering to another, asking why I can't 'control' my child, or saying 'children these days get away with murder, I would have just given mine a smack'.

There is a mix of wanting to run away and hide from the judgement, then there is also an element of a defensive lioness mode that comes over you. And, boy, do you want to shout and scream at them and fight for your child to be understood to protect them from the world. After a while, this

wears you down and you just stay at home because it's easier. You don't go to events you've been invited to because you just know your child won't cope with it, so then you stop even being invited. You avoid visiting people and places, because it's just easier that way. Add to all of this for many families a child who has a limited diet, struggles to go to sleep, or stay asleep, so you're all so tired, emotionally drained and feel you are on your own and have nowhere to turn.

Then let's look at the impact of education. How does it feel to be told your child is behind, your child isn't 'where they should be', your child is 'not meeting developmental expectations', your child won't be allowed to go on the nursery or school trip because 'we can't accommodate them', or it's too 'risky'? And, trust me, don't even bother with nativity plays or nursery or school graduations.

You're not sure what the future looks like, you're not sure how you will be able to break down the barriers that your child is facing, you don't know where to get help and who to turn to.

Parenting a neurodivergent child

There are such a range of emotions involved in parenting a neurodivergent child. Some of them can be quite emotive and difficult to hear, but it's useful to understand, because once you understand, you can empathise and be a greater support.

Grief: the hardest emotion to hear about

Grief is one that isn't discussed openly enough, but is important for me to be honest with how I felt, as it may be of help to others. Prior to having my first son, I had been in childcare and education for 14 years, I had been taught child development and expected milestones, I had observed hundreds of children as they played, socialised, behaved and engaged with the world around them. I had spoken to many parents about the tricky times of limited sleep, potty training and mealtimes.

Before and during pregnancy, I had played the role of mum, over and over again in my head. How life was going to be as a family with my own children, the things we would do and the experiences we would have.

Learning and discovering your first born is autistic, you quickly realise that the parenting journey you thought you were going to have, isn't going to happen, and that's difficult to initially acknowledge and come to terms with. You do grieve the life you had mapped out in your mind. You must learn to let go of the vision, the dreams and the plans you initially had. You go through the stages of grief, not necessarily in any order and you can go backwards and forwards across them, until you land on acceptance. However, please note, that even once you get to the acceptance phase, you do still head back to anger and depression on occasions.

As Carrie Grant writes:

> I was expecting neurotypical children, I was expecting that I would do x, y and z and I would have been good at that. I'm compliant, I would have done everything I needed to do, but that wasn't going to work for my kids. So, we had to find new ways of getting their magic out and that for me was excavation, finding out, it's exploring who they were meant to be, before the world got to them, and told them who they should be.
>
> (Twenty, 2024)

I was the same as Carrie, it's accepting that this is the new way, this is the way it is for you, so let's make a new plan. And while that sounds very hyped, banner-waving and whoop whoop rally, the reality is that even when you get there, there are still times when you want and need to hide away from the world and cry.

Being the family advocate

I needed my own cheer-leading squad of sorts. I needed my troops, my crew, I needed to be surrounded by those who understood, who were able to hear my cries and my rants, who were able to laugh at the ridiculous, who could support me when times were tough. All without judgement or criticism.

I needed advocates, I needed to be understood as a mother, we needed to be understood as a family. We needed to be heard, we needed to be accepted, we needed to have trust and faith in those closest to us and who were around my son.

It was a mixed bag for us. And it was clear who we could rely on and who we couldn't as much. We needed advocates.

Jodie Warren, a coach and trainer with 20 years' experience in inclusive education, offers some great advice when it comes to supporting our parents and carers:

1. *Meet parents where they are*: Early years educators are likely to find themselves in the position of being among the first to recognise differences in development. To tailor support and collaborate effectively with families, it is crucial to meet parents where they are. When first broaching the subject of possible needs, you might share observations and explore whether anything similar has been noticed at home. Approach initial conversations with an attitude of curiosity and with the intention of learning more and gaining a full and clear picture of possible need rather than reaching an agreement as to next steps.
2. *Parents as partners*: If we are to partner effectively with parents, we need to allow time to actively listen and proactively learn from them. In doing so we send a clear message that, rather than parental involvement being a tick box exercise, families' experiences, observations and understanding are key to identifying and implementing the most effective support for their child. To build on this and to enable parents to contribute meaningfully to meetings, consider the following:
   - How and where are jargon and acronyms used?
   - How could the same concepts be explained and shared so that families not only can understand but also remember what they mean?
   - Do parents know what to expect in meetings?
   - Are parents given the option to bring someone with them?
     How does your setting ensure shared understanding of agreed actions and timelines?
3. *Language matters*: The language used can reflect either a deficit-based or a difference-based model and in doing so it can influence how parents are introduced to the concept of differences.

- What difference could it make to a family if, from when they were first highlighted, their child's needs were viewed through a neuroaffirming lens?
- How differently might they respond if they were supported to recognise when proposed support outcomes were underpinned by the goal of enabling their child to thrive as themselves rather than being driven by the goal of enabling their child to behave more neurotypically?

Where needs ignite dysregulation, the shift to recognising those behaviours as symptomatic of an unmet need or a gap in a child's understanding or skills makes a huge difference. How might conversations differ if discussion focused on understanding and supporting those needs rather than managing the observed behaviour and highlighting limitations or perceived 'problems'?

Early years educators are in the unique position of being able to set the tone for parents' or carers' experience and expectations when collaborating with their child's settings. By adopting a neuroaffirming approach and proactively seeking meaningful parental input, we can support parents to advocate confidently, collaboratively and effectively to improve outcomes not only for the child but also for their family.

TIME TO REFLECT

- What does parent advocacy look like in your setting?
- How do you advocate for the children currently in your care?
- Does everyone in the team understand the importance of advocacy?
- Do you know where to seek local support for advocacy services?

What advocacy looks like in early years settings

The rest of this chapter is filled with the amazing work happening day in and day out in early years settings across the UK. Work that is supporting and advocating for families just like mine. I know it's tough out there, I know that there can be so many tricky days, but to see and hear the impact you have on children and families is so powerful and I'm hoping will give you the push to keep going. (All children's names have been changed.)

CASE STUDY: SUPPORTING SAM

I met Sam at 9 months old when he started in our baby room. His parents had identified that he may have difficulty hearing as he wasn't responding to his name, however, they also mentioned he needs to be in a quiet room so he could sleep.

We quickly observed that Sam has excellent physical skills and also observed that he wasn't responding to his name and wasn't babbling, he would become very distressed when doors opened. He was soon walking and would get engaged in repetitive cycles of going in and out of doorways and round and round the sand pit.

I met with mum and suggested Portage support which was initially rejected. We started a developmental journal and Every Child A Talker assessment and support for Sam, as well as a creating a clear individual learning plan.

As Sam reached 2 years old, we were able to refer to our early years inclusion service, paediatrician and speech and language service. He was assigned to TIER 5 and a specialist outreach teacher. Once we received reports, I asked his parents if they wanted to apply for Disability Living Allowance and I supported them to complete the paperwork.

I would meet with Sam's parents regularly to talk about his progress and discuss life at home. They had a phone call from the health visitor which wasn't very positive as they felt their concerns were not being taken seriously. With permission from the parents, I contacted the health visitor and talked through what we were observing in nursery.

His behaviour was becoming very challenging at home for his parents, and again with the parents' permission, I made a referral to a local service who offered four months of family support.

Sam is in now part of our forest school which he has found it much easier as it supports his sensory needs, he is more regulated and enjoys the freedom and the space. It has made a big difference as he doesn't notice people coming into and out of the space.

The parents had begun discussions with us about observing some differences in his development and mentioned autism. We are unable to identify and confirm but said that we would support them. Another local professional came into nursery and informed me that the parents were not wanting to pursue that identification, which was a surprise. This professional had told the parents the child was not autistic so shouldn't pursue confirmation. I made a complaint to the head of the department and supported mum with a complaint too.

His parents were really struggling with his behaviour at home. I arranged a 1-1 meeting with myself and parents with a trainer who delivers a lot of parent courses for Parent Carers in our area. She explained that Sam doesn't know many emotions and how to express them so although he is laughing after the tricky behaviours, it comes from a place of anxiety and stress. He is very demand-avoidant so she was able to give Sam's parents advice about how to reduce demands and anxiety. Mum was upset but was really appreciative of the advice and support.

We have lots of conversations about how we just parent with what we know and the important thing is when we know more, we do more. They have a much better relationship with Sam now they understand him better. I have lent them books, including, *Your Child Is Not Broken* (Mavir, 2023) to help them understand him.

I have completed the neurodiversity profile tool for Sam as this is the way in now for the neurodiversity pathway. I have shared this with his school he is soon to transition to. He has made such good progress, and we will be very sad when he moves on in September

(Karen, nursery SENCo)

CASE STUDY: COMMUNICATION IS KEY

We began to notice Tim was not coping in the nursery setting and becoming upset by various activities. One of our staff had recently sent out an article on early intervention for neurodiverse children and things we as teachers need to be aware of.

I approached the manager and deputy about the differences I had observed for Tim and they arranged a parent-teacher meeting. His parents were also aware of the challenges he was facing and had also been observing these differences. Up until then I made sure to tell his parents of all the milestones and things Tim was doing well at, as it seemed to me it was quite obvious to the parents that Tim was struggling.

After the parent-teacher meeting the parents were extremely happy for the chance to discuss openly the differences we were seeing in the nursery and home and discussed the strategies that could be put in place.

He is doing so well now and can communicate when he is not wishing to do something. He also tells his friends 'give me space' or 'please, stop, it's too loud for me'. If he needs an extra tight hug, he will come and ask, 'I need to squeeze something' instead of squeezing his friends. He loves the routine in the nursery and we have the relationship with his parents that if he is having someone else pick him up, they can message us and we can prepare him. Without these preparations he would experience a meltdown, or it would take a while to talk it through. It has made a huge difference for Tim and the whole team.

We also adopted a neuroaffirming approach to celebrating with our class. Tim would flap his hands when anything exciting happened – an extra-yummy lunch or when he heard that someone in his class had a baby sibling – the stimming would begin! So, we all joined in flapping and jumping. Tim was so pleased at this affirmation. It made him feel accepted and acknowledged.

A message from Tim's parents:

As a neurodivergent household, we were not surprised to see some of these traits in our son and hear from his teachers that they had noticed he was having trouble coping with the regular activities. The teachers arranged a parent-teacher meeting to discuss, and we have felt very well supported as we work through each specific issue as it comes up.

Tim is sensitive to overstimulation and has trouble dealing with other people's distress or surprise changes in his environment. He has benefitted tremendously from a unified approach between his class and home. When there is something unusual coming in his life, we make sure he and we are prepared. The good communication is essential to this. This has allowed all of us to get a good idea of what he can handle (which is always changing) and stretch his boundaries as much as possible without overwhelming him.

We have never felt like Tim is being pushed to conform to unrealistic behavioural standards – rather, all help we have received has been with an emphasis on what works for him, and we as parents have felt that our opinions and choices were respected, even though he is our first child and we don't have much experience. We are tremendously thankful for this holistic approach and have been happy to see Tim improve greatly since age two in what he can cope with. He trusts the adults in his life and is able to communicate when he is getting overwhelmed.

Communication is key.

(Fran, class teacher)

CASE STUDY: VALUING PARENTAL INPUT

I had worked with the family previously with their eldest daughter but a while later they got back in touch, and mum explained that the youngest daughter did not have confirmation of neurodivergence, but she was noticing similar traits to her older sister. Lots of anxiety around large groups, social expectations and particularly noisy environments and so she was now on the pathway for assessment.

The challenges she was facing in the reception class meant it was becoming harder and harder to get her up and ready and out in the

mornings as she was dysregulated. Within the setting itself, she was frequently overactive (running around and climbing on things) and struggled to follow the routine, expectations and engage in activities. After each day she was having prolonged meltdowns at home.

I began my work with visits to the home, I wanted to get to know they young girl in her safe space, to discover her interests and strengths and her communication style. I wanted to focus on short sessions but regular contact to develop a strong connection. She was initially quiet and wary of me as a new person in the home but each time I just joined alongside whatever she was doing if she was happy with this.

By my fourth session she was very comfortable and engaged more confidently and happily with me, directing my play and suggesting new activities she would like to complete together. While she was verbally communicative, it was clearly important to notice her non-verbal state as this gave a lot of information as to how she was feeling even when she was not necessarily aware.

While those sessions had been intended to build a connection between myself and the young girl, the fact that I valued the family's knowledge of their child and observed carefully the actions taking place meant that we had some crucial, useable knowledge to influence how I might then work with the reception class to improve things there for her:

- The need for connection
- The awareness of her energy levels reflecting her emotions and feelings
- The knowledge of activities that helped her to regulate
- The knowledge of her need for connection and support from a trusted partner working alongside her but not to try to instruct or direct the activities.

I met with the key staff in the setting, the lead teacher, a support assistant assigned to that group and the SENCo and with mum as well. I explained what I had already learnt and highlighted that the information from family had been crucial in my work already. Modelling this respect for mum as a knowledgeable member of the team was really important for me. The setting was receptive to most of this, but they

were concerned about how they could offer the physical space for the regulating activities, and they were wary about the need to be autonomous over some activities.

We arranged six sessions over two weeks for me to come in, initially to come and support the young girl to begin to make stronger connections with the setting staff, then moving on to modelling how some of these aspects could be incorporated into the setting without huge challenges and then a chance to give support as the staff made those adaptations themselves.

I worked with the staff in the moment to highlight when her behaviours became more excitable and physically active and pinpointed that this meant she was likely to be uncertain or worried about something. They found this really useful and were quickly able to identify these moments themselves.

The staff and I worked on developing a plan for those moments and for a member of staff to either be able to work even more closely with her to offer co-regulation through the challenging situation or to be able to offer her a calming activity of bouncing on the setting's mini-trampoline or they also discovered that playing 'row the boat' with a stretchy Lycra sheet around behind the girl for the adult to pull on in time to the song was great for this too (they did not have a swing available). Although the staff had initially worried about working alongside without task direction, when I unpicked their concerns with them, it seemed the biggest issue was their worry about how often this would need to happen. Once I discussed with them that there was not an expectation that this be at all times but that maybe they could pick two or three key activities in a day that they could offer this, their concerns were reduced. They were worried about not placing demands but once I had modelled for them and had focused on my own activity while chatting with the young girl, they were able to see that it wasn't as difficult as they had expected.

What made it over and above? Engaging the family on a level field as one of the professionals on the team, valuing and being receptive to their expertise on the child and involving them in all the decisions and problem solving made the difference.

(Charlotte, specialist autism teacher)

CASE STUDY: MEETING ALL OF TOBY'S NEEDS

Toby came to our setting at 2½ years old. Toby was born prematurely and had a long list of health conditions, including quadriplegia (cerebral palsy affecting all his limbs), severe epilepsy and cystic fibrosis. Toby was also blind, non-verbal and had global developmental delay.

Due to his conditions, all his nutritional needs and his medication were given to him via a feeding tube through his stomach and he needed a suction machine to keep his airways clear so he could breathe. In medical terminology, Toby was a young child with complex medical needs, his conditions were life-limiting and he had a profound and multiply learning disability (PMLD).

However, to his parents, he was their beautiful son who had a smile that made everyone else around him smile. To me, as a SENCo, he was a young child who had a right to attend an early years setting of his parents' choice, which at the time, his parents did not even think that was a choice they had or even an option available to them.

It was through a chance meeting at a community portage stay and play session that I first met Toby and his mum. I was at the stay and play session supporting another child who was starting at our setting in a few weeks' time. Toby's mum approached me and asked some questions about the setting and expressed how she would have loved it if Toby could attend, even for just a few hours a week to give him some 'normality' as her friends' children were already going. She let out a sigh and said because of Toby's health conditions and complex needs, it is something that he would never get to experience. I asked her why she thought that, and with a look of confusion, she explained that she did not think any setting would allow him to go because they would not be able to meet his complex needs. I suggested to Toby's mum to come and visit our setting and talk to me about what his needs were and we could work out a way that we could support him.

We registered Toby at our setting, I just needed to figure out all the practicalities, and this meant that Toby could not start with us straight away. I needed to access training for myself and other practitioners so that we could meet Toby's medical needs in terms of using his feeding

tube, knowing when to use his oxygen and suction machine. We had to learn his feeding, medication and physiotherapy routines. All of this needed to be coordinated between the setting and other professionals, while also navigating the other children in the settings and ensuring child-practitioner ratios were maintained.

My manager worked on 'good faith' in terms of me advocating that the funding for the additional support that Toby needed would come to the setting. I strongly believe and advocate that all children have the right to an education and should be supported in being able to access their entitlement, so I kept pushing for Toby to attend.

A few months after Toby started with us, it was Mother's Day. We helped Toby make his mum a card with his handprint on the front. It was a simple card and by the end of making it, Toby, me and the classroom had more paint on us than his card and we all were laughing! Mum looked at it and burst into tears and hugged me. She said thank you and it was the most amazing thing ever to have a Mother's Day card made for her by her son and it would be something that she would treasure for the rest of her life. It was at that moment that I knew that all the hard work in getting Toby into the setting was worth every second.

Toby continued to attend our setting every week for 6 hours until he left to transition to school. It was not always easy and there were a lot of barriers to overcome. However, Toby was such a joy to work with and really touched the hearts of everyone around him. He had a little cheeky, mischievous side to his personality which just filled us with joy.

For parents of children with SEND, many of them are thrown into a battleground of professionals and services and they are overwhelmed with the challenges that they are facing. As early years practitioners, we become allies and advocate for them and their child. We become an interpreter of the language of other health, education and care professionals for them. We give parents a voice when they cannot find the words to speak, and we sit with them when they feel they do not have any strength left, and we support them in getting up again.

(Hannah, SENCo)

CASE STUDY: PARENT SUPPORT DURING TRANSITIONS

Jess is 3 years old, is neurodivergent, as well as has having an ongoing skin condition, she lives with her mum and four siblings, three of whom are also neurodivergent.

I became aware of the support being offered to Jess and her mum when she was due to transition into my preschool room. Initially I was apprehensive for Jess as to how we would manage such a high level of need, in addition to the other children who already attend with complex needs.

I worked alongside our setting SENCo to ensure the transition was appropriate and mum felt comfortable. Each time I spoke with mum I became more aware of her nervousness and protectiveness of Jess. I worked regularly with our SEND Advisor Team, to ensure consistency between rooms during the transition, as they had been working with Jess to support her learning and development and to enable her to access the environment in the same way as the other children.

As I started to get to know mum more and she became confident in how Jess was settling, she became more open and felt comfortable to share her thoughts and feelings with us more. Mum grew very close to all the members of our SEND team and is happy to talk to anyone when necessary, and often seeks us out to thank us or ask questions about Jess's progress or any additional paperwork that needs completing.

I have worked with my colleagues to ensure that we all have meaningful relationships, not just with Jess but with mum as well, meaning that mum feels comfortable leaving her with us, which has proven successful. Jess has recently increased her nursery sessions, which has helped mum work more to provide for the rest of her family and also attend parenting courses, as advised at the specialist case planning meeting.

We have worked in partnership with mum on completing Jess's Individual Education Plans, as it's important for us to represent the parents' voice and aspirations. We are currently working towards

securing an EHCP and additional funding to support her within the mainstream school environment. I have attended specialist case planning meetings for mum and her family to discuss Jess, and how she is getting on at nursery, which really opened my eyes to how hard family life is for mum and how much we need to continue supporting her and Jess as she progresses through our nursery.

Jess is doing so well and has really begun to show signs of progressed levels of understanding with regards to our daily routine. She has also started to 'allow' team members to sit and play with the same toys she is playing with.

We are also beginning to see her smile a lot more and respond positively to one-to-one play and interaction, even using some vocalisations, and we've recently heard some laughter, which has been an absolute joy to share with mum at the end of her session. We are excited to see how Jess can progress even more over the next year and we are working with mum on finding the most appropriate school for her and will continue to support both of them in this transition.

(Catherine, early years educator)

CASE STUDY: SHARING RESOURCES FROM HOME TO SETTING

Kane is 3 years old. During the settling-in process the parents told us about a possible speech delay and possible autistic traits they had observed and how they had been liaising with health visitors who had recommended our setting. Parents were very on board, and we scheduled in a meeting the week after the Kane had started nursery.

During the meeting we discussed strategies and resources to support both at nursery and at home. We used Wellcomm screening and followed our graduated approach to create smart targets and put support plans in place. We supported the family with resources such as

visuals, core vocabulary grids, now and next boards, ready steady go activities and fidget bags to use in the setting and at home.

When Kane started to show an interest in toilet training, we put together home learning bags with visuals for toilet training and books. We also signposted the parents to a toileting workshop. We ensured that the team working with the child had relevant training which was delivered by our internal SEND team and consisted of Makaton taster sessions, sensory awareness, Wellcomm and IEPs.

We liaised with our area SENCo and attended workshops held by them to ensure we have the knowledge and the support to enable us to help the family. We reached out to his health visitor and his private speech and language therapist and they regularly attend the setting and/or gave us updates.

We initially had concerns about his hearing and when this was raised with the parents, we were informed that a hearing test had been carried out but the results were inconclusive, so we reached out to the Ear Nose and Throat (ENT) clinic, with parents' permission, to have another test.

We had a training session on sensory circuits delivered to the team by the area SENCo and we invited the child's parents to join us, as we had identified that the child responded well to regular sensory circuits throughout the day. Following the session, we had a meeting with mum who told us that she had been doing the sensory circuits at home, particularly before they left the house, and they had noticed a huge difference on how Kane adapted to different social situations. Mum had commented that he was calmer and more regulated and for them, as parents, they found it helpful to understand how the circuits work with his sensory-seeking needs.

We have provided the parents with contact details for the area SEND team and they have been engaging in workshops and clubs held by them, which we all feel has positively helped Kane. We have a strong partnership with his parents and other professionals, and we continue to work together to implement new ideas, strategies and resources which has enabled us to create an environment that the child is thriving in.

The parents have commented that they feel 'a weight has been lifted' and they have recommended us to other parents of children with SEND.

(Kiera, nursery manager)

CASE STUDY: GOING ABOVE AND BEYOND

Leo lives with mum, dad and new baby sister. As there is a family history of autism and dad works in a Specialist Secondary School, Leo's parents were aware of the presenting emerging differences, in conjunction with the setting also sensitively raising their observations of his developmental differences. A meeting was organised with the parents, Leo's key person and the setting SENCo to discuss a strength-based holistic plan to progress forward in line with the Assess, Plan, Do, Review stages of the Graduated Approach.

Parents were provided the opportunity to lead the meeting, any terminology was explained and afterwards parents were offered a leaflet to take away that detailed the processes to come with early action. This meant the parents could digest the information in their own time and provided additional advice and guidance through signposting to support websites, both local to the setting and nationwide, and offered some further jargon busters!

Initially I offered to carry out some setting observations within the four broad areas of difference and assessments, such as a WellComm screening, to identify and establish Leo's strengths, interests and motivators, as well as his current developmental stage to be able to plan and implement targets on an Individual Education Plan that would build on his skills. Three SMART targets were written that were realistic and achievable within an eight-week time frame, due to the wish to celebrate success at the end of the cycle, and parents' aspirations and voice was included front and centre of the Individual Education Plan.

Leo was pre-verbal, but it was important to provide him a voice to express his wants/needs and choices. Once he had started to master the understanding of objects of reference and choosing from real-life objects, I was able to use the setting's visuals to create a plethora of visual supports, such as choice boards and now and next resources.

It was also important for me to advocate for external professional support for Leo, which was implemented through referring to the Speech and Language Team, Occupational Therapy Team and Local Authority SEND Team. This enabled everyone to work collaboratively to implement targets and strategies that were developmentally appropriate for him to progress. At each step of the way, parents were included and involved in reviewing and renewing targets.

Leo demonstrated high levels of anxiety around mealtimes, through struggling to be at the table with his peers and eating a restricted number of food items. I worked in partnership with his parents to understand which foods he ate at home and purchased the exact same foods/brands for the setting as well as asking the setting chef to replicate certain meals that mum made, to ensure we were making reasonable adjustments to reduce his anxiety at mealtimes.

Furthermore, I worked with the team on creating a differentiated mealtime for Leo, which meant he sat down as soon as the food trolley was brought into the room (as this became his object of reference). He ate his individualised foods/meal and when finished, he retreated to the nearby carpet area when he engaged with resources bought especially for his interests. Mealtime was not a drawn-out, anxious experience but he was also close and safe while his peers finished their meal.

Knowing from parents that one of their real difficulties was encouraging Leo to leave the house or go to new places, I worked with the local Autism Community Centre, the A Team Hub, and organised a stay and play session for all our children/families with SEND at the setting. This would be a motivating place for Leo to go, but also create links to community support groups for parents. They were thrilled that Leo had access to a trip that was intended specifically for him, having too often faced adversity or being excluded from forms of societal events.

The parents reported that they felt listened to, understood and knew that Leo was safe, cared for, valued and accessing neuroaffirming practices that held high aspirations for him. This led to him increasing his sessions when mum had his baby sister, which allowed her to have more independent time with her second child, something she greatly appreciated.

(Becky, Lead SEND advisor)

Working with the whole family is integral to our inclusive approach to the children in our settings. To enable the child to thrive, we need to support the whole family to thrive. Have you got the right processes in place in order to know you are asking the right questions, listening to the answers and placing yourself in the role of an effective advocate for the family?

TIME TO REFLECT

- How would you respond to me as a parent seeking your support as their family advocate?
- How will you help me understand my child?
- How will you help me feel able and give me the strength to meet my child's needs?
- How will you ensure my thoughts and feelings are valid?
- How will you help me understand the importance of celebrating the small wins?

Intersectionality

We need to also bear in mind that our families will have different experiences with regards to support, access, opportunity and understanding. Intersectionality explains how a person's identity such as race, gender or

sexuality impact the opportunities they are given. Neurodivergence spans across the world demographic, however, those from ethnically minority communities are marginalised.

Historically, autism was linked to white males, but we need to be very clear in our understanding of intersectional neurodiversity, with it having no barriers or attachment to one race, gender, or sexuality.

Race and ethnicity

While I was attending a nursery recently, a parent informed the SENCo that she didn't want to have the conversation about neurodivergence regarding her son. She explained that she is raising a black son in London, and things are tough enough already for her and her family. She wasn't ready nor felt able to 'add' another factor upon him as she felt this would marginalise him further.

Neurodivergence in girls

We are seeing increased understanding and research with regards to the difference in presentation of many neurotypes in girls. The diagnostic tools used for assessment still heavily weigh on the development of boys, and so many girls are still being missed, or forgotten. Girls are more socially adept, they may have special interests that are more accepted, and they very quickly learn what they need to do to 'fit in', and mask their neurodivergent behaviours.

In our sector, we need to be aware of our biases, work hard to remove them, and ensure that we are providing the same level of support, understanding and acceptance for all our families. Be conscious of the different layers that build someone's identity. Educate yourself on the co-existing factors in order to support all families to the best of your ability and ensure that you play a part in creating a change towards true inclusion.

Final reflections

This chapter has been full of inspirational stories from educators just like you. Those who are supporting children and families day in and day out. Who are breaking down the barriers to ensure our children are supported to thrive in the best way possible. It takes a whole team approach, with effort and dedication from everyone involved. But it can be done.

Our children need you, and, as parents, we need you.

Resources

Further reading and research

Jo Gaunt (2024) *Your Safe Space.*
Sarah Alix (2024) *The SEND Handbook for Parents and Carers.*

Instagram

@aperion_training
@expectingandaccepting
@Heidi Mavir
@jessie_and_the_family
@jodiewarren
@neurowild_
@reframingneurodiversity
@stephstwogirls
@theabilitiesinmefoundation

Podcasts

Childhood Understood
Eu-Hu podcasts
Not your typical podcast

Reframing neurodiversity
The Hidden 20%
The SEND network
The SENDCast

References

Alix, S. (2024). *The SEND Handbook for Parents and Carers*. Abingdon: Routledge.

Gaunt, J. (2024). *Your Safe Space*. Independently published.

Mavir, H. (2023). *Your Child Is Not Broken: Parent Your Neurodivergent Child Without Losing Your Marbles*. London: Pan Macmillan.

Soehnlin, J. (2018). *Embracing This Special Life*. Independently published.

Twenty, H. (2024). E1: Carrie Grant — The Hidden 20%. Available at: https://www.hidden20.org/podcast/episode-1-carrie-grant

8 Conclusion

This chapter brings together the main messages from the book and sets out a plan of future action, now with the information, new skills and a deeper knowledge base. Ultimately, all educators need to ensure that they are neurodiversity-affirming educators, providing a neuroinclusive environment for children in their early years, day in and day out. What it means to be a neurodiversity-affirming educator is explored and also how small changes and altering the narrative can make a huge difference for children and for neurodivergent colleagues. This chapter will explore the journey and the experiences everyone in the early years environment has, to reflect and consider new ways of working that offer that neuroinclusive provision.

So where do we go from here?

We need to as individuals becoming neurodiversity-affirming educators to then as a team deliver on true neuroinclusive practice. But what does being neurodiversity-affirming mean?

Affirming means to declare one's support for. Supporting children to be who they are, to agree with, to give encouragement to, because you want them to succeed. Think of yourself as that football supporter. You cheer, you sing, you give encouragement to the team to score the next goal. You cheer their successes and even when things don't head in the direction you thought they were going to, you are there again the following week, pitch-side, cheering them on and supporting them all the way.

DOI: 10.4324/9781032642994-8

Affirming their play

So, what do we affirm, what do we give our neurodivergent support in?

Not placing our neurotypical play agenda onto them. It's saying the way you play is OK, and I'm going to join you exactly where you are. How you are lining up your cars, how you are sequencing the dinosaurs in height order, how you are repetitive with your schema and continually transferring objects from one place in the nursery to another. Or how you are continually naming the colours of the plastic balls as you place them in the saucepan full of water – then shout loudly across the garden, 'Look at the balls, look at the balls', then carry the heavy pan to another part of the garden, clearly feeding your proprioceptive sensory system, then take the balls out, and do the whole thing over again! Affirm their play, declare your support for them.

Affirming their communication preferences

Is their preference to use gestures, to use simple signs, to lead you where they want to go, to use visuals to show you what they need, to have objects of reference used to support transitions? Do they use echolalia as a way of engaging and learning language, are they a gestalt language processor and learning key chunks of phrases from TV or stories? Affirm their communication preferences, declare your support for them.

Affirming their stage of development

Support them right where they are. Understanding and affirming, validating that our children do show focus, attention and concentration, this just might look a little different. They may find it tricky to sit on the carpet, but it is because the carpet itches, or because other children are sitting too close. Therefore, they need to get up and move, or wriggle, or sit on a bean bag, or stand just to the side. It's not a lack of focus or attention, they are just unable to be on the carpet because of their sensory sensitivities and sensory needs. Understanding that they don't need interventions to be more focused, to aid

social skills, or to be more neurotypical or school-ready! Affirm their stage of development and declare your support for them.

Being an educator in a neuroinclusive early years setting is always viewing the children through the lens of, how can we …? Not 'we can't'. Times are tricky across the early years sector as I write this chapter, we are in the midst of a staffing crisis, a severe lack of funding and a lack of support for settings with regards to special educational needs and disability. Many owners and managers are asking me how they can be more inclusive and want to enable all children to access their provision. But with the lack of funding and increasing demand for places for children with a range of needs, they are finding it difficult to accommodate needs.

We need to always see each child as an individual case and not look at a neuroidentity on an application form. We need to consider how we can provide those accommodations and adaptions, and how we can meet need.

We have a duty and a responsibility to support all children who attend our early years settings in a way that enables them to thrive, to experience success, to feel safe, to feel valued, to feel like they belong.

Key principles for a change in culture to provide a neuroinclusive early years space

- The environment is flexible, predictable, emotionally safe and provides a sense of belonging for all
- The narrative is neurodiversity-affirming, strength-based, positive and accepting of difference
- The team is supportive, accepting, honest, open and trusting
- The culture is nurturing and has a strong understanding of the development of well-being for all
- The vision assumes competence for all children and enables all children to be heard

We also need to consider some key questions for reflection. By using these questions as prompts we can come together as a team to review the experiences of all key stakeholders across the setting. What is the journey and the experiences of all those with a connection to neurodivergence at your setting?

The neurodivergent child's experience

- What is it like for me here?
- Is my voice heard?
- How are my views taken into account?
- Is this space predictable and safe for me?
- Are you accepting of me and my behaviours, just as I am?
- Are you supporting me to develop new skills?
- Are you allowing me to play as I like?
- Are you supporting my holistic well-being?

The family's experience

- Do I feel heard?
- Do you allow us extra time?
- Do you acknowledge our struggles as a parent/carer?
- Do you celebrate the small wins with us?
- Do you provide us with a safe, non-judgemental place to share and talk things through?
- Do you help us with the day-to-day struggles without judgement?
- Do you enable us to access services that will support our family?
- Do you explain process and policy for funding and support with us?
- Do you allow for adjustments that enable our children to be a part of key events?
- Are you supporting our well-being as a family?

The educator's experience

- Do I feel heard?
- Am I given a safe space to share the tough times?
- Am I given support when I am no longer able to co-regulate?
- Are my views taken into account?
- Are you able to provide adequate training for me to effectively support ALL children?

- Do you allow me time to complete the paperwork required?
- Are you providing a safe space for me to be my true authentic self?
- Do you allow me time to regulate when things get overwhelming?
- Are you supporting my emotional and physical well-being?

'What also seems evident is that when the needs of autistic children are addressed in the early years of schooling, they are much more likely to have positive longer-term outcomes' (Wood, 2019). To become that neuroaffirming educator, we do need to go against the grain, we need to ensure we don't shy away from the conversations, we do need to address the wider stance on our children working towards 'compliance-based targets'.

Checking the language we use

Table 8.1 shows how attitudes and what is said can be rephrased in a neuroaffirming way.Chatham (2024) advises:

> Who are our goals for? For example, 'good sitting' might look differently for every child! Some children may be using all of their energy to sit still instead of listening to what the educator is saying. It may be better to focus on 'good learning' as we want the child to access the lesson. For many, that means 'good sitting', 'good looking' and 'good listening' but for some children they may be accessing the learning and paying attention when displaying behaviours many would not consider conducive with learning.

Table 8.1 Checking the language we use

The child needs to change	*The adult has a neuroaffirming lens and questions what they can do to better support the child*
They don't want to do it	Why are they not engaged in this activity?
It just won't work for this child	How can I reduce the barriers they are facing?
They refuse to follow directions	What makes following this direction difficult?
They will never be able to do that independently	What support do they need to experience success?

Table 8.2 Neurodiversity-affirming language vs deficit model language

Deficit model	Neurodiversity-affirming model
George is showing some red flags	George is displaying some emerging traits of a neurodivergent profile
Emily is obsessed with letters	Emily is passionate and has a special interest in letters
Jake is so rigid and inflexible	Jake thrives in predictable situations and finds safety in the familiar
Valentina has poor eye contact and is difficult to engage	Valentina engages best with others during child-led play and low-pressure interactions

Table 8.2 presents some examples of difference in neuroaffirming language and deficit model language.

Neurodiversity-affirming goals and targets

While we can create that inclusive space with a team who are committed to a strength-based neuroaffirming environment, if the goals and targets we set for children are not in line with this, then it's counter-productive. So how do we make our goals and targets supportive and neuroaffirming?

The goals and the targets we create SHOULD NOT:

- Aim to make children appear less neurodivergent
- Aim to make the child fit a model of 'normal' and act like their neuro-typical peers

They SHOULD:

- Support the whole child
- Support development in authentic ways
- Support emotional development and regulation

Advocate for the need for goals that support a neurodivergent child's regulation, connection, and overall well-being. Goals should not only seek to change the skills of a child, but we should have goals that aim to change the world around the child. This includes addressing other people's knowledge, perspectives, and skills in supporting and accepting each child, as well as their physical environment.

Communication goals should not just focus on verbal speech, they should also include all forms of communication, whatever is preferred by the child in that moment. Our priority is connection. We do not push or pressure children to communicate using only speech, if that is not within their abilities.

Social interaction goals should not be based on forcing a child to appear more neurotypical, pushing eye contact, for example. Affirming social goals can exist, if they are aligned with what a child wants. When setting social skills or communication and interaction targets for children, focus on the child learning skills to help them to be able to communicate their wants and needs in a way which works for them.

We want to support children to increase their self-awareness of their own preferences and their own needs. We need to support them to self-advocate. Focus your goals and targes on learning all about emotions, feelings, supporting self-regulation and alternative strategies for their big feelings and emotions.

REPLACEMENT WORDING FOR GOALS AND TARGETS

✗ Child will engage in functional pretend play and will interact appropriately with others.

✓ When given full access to all forms of communication, the child will advocate their preferences and will show readiness to play with the people they are comfortable with.

✗ Child will make eye contact for 3 seconds.

✓ We shouldn't have any goals for eye contact. This is not comfortable, not affirming and can put individuals into a heightened state of stress and anxiety.

× Child will express a desire for food or other items using PECS/ signs or words.

✓ Using a total communication approach, including spoken, AAC devices, signs, gestures, behaviour and educator modelling, the child will increase expressive communication and self-advocacy to request, protest, comment, direct, ask questions, share needs and give opinions.

× Given a verbal instruction, the child will look at the person and say 'okay' and do it right away in four out of five incidents.

✓ Child will communicate personal academic and sensory needs, accommodations and support, to which they are entitled, in their preferred communication style.

Supporting the whole team

To be truly neurodiversity-affirming, we also need to provide those safe spaces for our whole team. Please remember that neurodivergent children grow up to be neurodivergent adults. Now I'm hoping that this doesn't come as a complete bombshell to you, I'm hoping that this was blindingly obvious!

Autism, ADHD, PDA, dyslexia and all other neuro identities are lifelong. They are not going anywhere, it's part of the individuals' profile, their make-up, it's their neurotype. It always makes me laugh when people ask me if my son has been cured or if he has grown out of his autism! They tell me that the things that were tricky for him when he was 3 don't seem tricky any more, or he doesn't act like he did when he was 5. My response, after a bit of a giggle, mixed with a little disbelief, is always, well, I'm sure you don't act and behave like you did when you were 5 either!

He has grown, developed, progressed, and learnt strategies that now enable him to manage in mainstream society, however, his autism hasn't disappeared. The difference is that I now have a 6ft teenager in overwhelm and meltdown, rather than a 3ft toddler. He still has them, he still finds some aspects of life a challenge, his neurotype still impacts his energy levels and regulation abilities, but this looks different as he self-manages them more.

What are the accommodations and adaptions that can support our neurodivergent team?

Here are a few strategies that you can try to accommodate neurodivergent colleagues in the early years setting.

Turn the lights off when they are not needed

Harsh LED lights that are flickering in the background not only can be a distraction, but also add to the surrounding visual stimulus that is already in abundance in an early years setting. They can be so hard on the eyes, they can cause headaches and for the most part, it is unnecessary to have them on. Now, I'm not silly … I live in the UK, for 6 months of the year it can be dark by 5p.m, so, of course, lights are needed. However, when they are not, turn them off … or you could consider using softer lights, fairy lights, lamps or dimmers – just to remove the harshness.

A study by Nair et al. (2022) reported that children have various colour preferences and respond differently to different shades. Different colours and shades have varying effects on autistic children, with many neutral tones and mellow shades proven to be autistic-friendly with their calming and soothing effect, while bright, bold, and intense colours are refreshing and stimulating, but that can be overstimulation. And they concluded that the stimulus of bright-lighting causes behavioural changes in autistic children prone to light sensitivity.

And while I always advocate for natural light being the preferred light source, therefore ensure that blinds are always down and curtains drawn, as the bright sunlight can be just as impactful. So, consider the materials that can just soften the harshness, maybe voile or muslin draped from the windows when needed.

First lunch break

Imagine a small room, with no natural light and maybe even without a window – ring any bells for a staff room?!! I've held many a meeting over the

years in spaces just like this. Now imagine four or five people in there, in a cramped space with a fridge, kettle and microwave. Now imagine it's 2.15p.m. and you are the last to go for your lunch break.

You walk in the room that has two other people in it and the whole team before you have made a cup of coffee, have poured water onto their pot noodle or have re-heated last night's Chinese. Then you open the fridge to get out your lunch and there is some milk that's been in there for a little longer than it should. You then really need to sit in the comfy chair with your headphones on to watch the next episode on your Netflix series, as this is a good way for you to decompress and unwind, but someone starts chatting to you. Previously you've been told that you can come across as rude because all you want to do is sit and be still and breathe for a bit.

Now imagine you are autistic and you've managed to keep it together all morning, it's been tough because it's been noisy, loud and unpredictable and you need some quiet, calm down time to get ready for the afternoon. But the smells, the sounds, the continuation of false lighting just raise your nervous system even more. You then realise the afternoon is going to be spent on high alert and you're on the edge of a meltdown.

Just having their lunch break first could make all the difference, no matter what shift they are on, the accommodation put in place for them, by management is that they go first. This results in your neurodivergent team member having a quieter room with fewer people, they can walk into the space that doesn't smell of everyone else's lunch, and where they can have their lunch in peace, with the option to decompress with their headphones on, fill up their emotional regulation cup, ready to start the afternoon.

Regular short breaks

Early years spaces are noisy, busy and unpredictable, that's just how they are, full of excitement, awe, wonder and expectation. But for many neurodivergent adults working in those spaces, as much as we might love it, they can also be the spaces that send us spiralling into overwhelm. A simple accommodation is to offer more time for short regular breaks.

Now I am very aware of the staffing challenges in early years at the moment in the UK, I'm very aware of the demands on time and workload, so you may just laugh at this one! But, just bear with me for a moment.

If you were offering regular short breaks to those who require them for regulation purposes, you will reduce burnout. You will improve mental health, you will reduce time off for sickness, and you will increase your potential for staff retention. If you are an early years setting that is known for the adaptions you put in place to ensure the support is effective for your neurodivergent staff, then you will retain and attract more staff.

The breaks can be planned into the routine, they can be scheduled for, and they are there if the staff member needs them. It may not always be feasible, trips out, for example, this could be tricky, but for the most part they are there, they are available as an option to provide equity in the work place.

Examples of expectations

If you are asking staff to complete reports, written documentation, be a scribe for note-taking at a staff meeting or parents meeting, if you are setting targets on an action plan, do you provide clear examples of expectations? Do you provide time to dive deeper into what it is you ACTUALLY need, for the member of staff who may have executive function challenges as part of their neurotype? Do you offer more time for questions and clarification?

Sometimes the expected task outcome for a manager, or senior lead, could be different from that of the member of staff asked to complete it. Don't make assumptions that they will be able to read between the lines, that their version of completed work is the same as yours. Check in with the timescales you have given them, do they work for them, or do they need more time? Do they need any additional resources to support them in completing the task?

Just a little understanding and awareness of potential support needs can make a massive difference.

Regular check-ins

We may have supervision once a term or once a quarter, but that can be too far apart for some. How regularly do you check in with the team? We have a daily – twice daily handover with our parents about the children, would

a hand-over or huddle with a neurodivergent staff member be beneficial at the start of each week?

- How's your weekend?
- What's your week looking like?
- Who is in this week to support you in the room?
- Are you OK with the timings for the staff meeting on Wednesday?
- Do you need me to print anything out prepare anything in advance for you this week?
- Just to let you know I'm on leave on Friday, so Amanda from head office is coming down to cover. Oh, and we have Nick, the maintenance guy, in on Wednesday in your room to fix the leak you have under your sink, so we will need to plan together a slight change of routine that afternoon.

Just a 10-minute conversation can go a long way to remove anxiety, allay unpredictable, new situations that may cause overwhelm and panic or fear that can manifest ahead of a new meeting – again, it's about expectations.

Let's create a workplace that really delivers on inclusion, a workplace that has the interests of the team super high on the agenda. A workplace that says, you belong and are welcome here and we will provide what you need so that you are able to do your job to the best of your ability.

My final message

✓ Be brave in your knowledge of great child-centred neurodiversity affirming practice.
✓ Share the need to make it better.
✓ Be the advocate parents need you to be.
✓ Start to plan to make the change.
✓ Start knocking down all the barriers that stand in the way of our neurodivergent children.
✓ *Become advocates for neuroinclusion.*
✓ *Be the change you want to see.*

Resources

Instagram

@aperion_training
@childhoodunderstood
@Heidi Mavir
@jessie_and_the_family
@jodiewarren
@mrgteacher
@neurowild_
@reframingneurodiversity
@ruth_jones_slt
@sensory.slp
@shauntheteacher
@simoninclusionteacher
@spdtuitionandcoaching
@speechdude
@stephstwogirls@StoriesaboutAutism
@therapeeze

Podcasts

Childhood Understood
Eu-Hu podcasts
Not your typical podcast
Reframing neurodiversity
The hidden 20%
The SEND network
The SENDCast

References

Chatham, C. (2024). Neuro-affirming practice: How can we better support and empower neurodiverse individuals? One Education, 4 July. Available at: https://www.oneeducation.co.uk/neuro-affirming-practice-how-can-we-better-support-and-empower-neurodiverse-individuals/

Nair, A.S., Priya, R.S., Rajagopal, P., Pradeepa, C., Senthil, R., Dhanalakshmi, S., Lai, K.W., Wu, X., and Zuo, X. (2022). A case study on the effect of light and colors in the built environment on autistic children's behavior. *Frontiers in Psychiatry*, 13. https://doi.org/10.3389/fpsyt.2022.1042641

UK Government (2020). Reasonable adjustments: A legal duty. 15 September. Available at: https://www.gov.uk/government/publications/reasonable-adjustments-a-legal-duty

Wood, R. (2019). *Inclusive Education for Autistic Children: Helping Children and Young People to Learn and Flourish in the Classroom*. London: Jessica Kingsley Publishers.

Index

Bold page numbers indicate tables, *italic* numbers indicate figures.

9781032637303